MENTAL HEALTH
WORK REIMA

Ian Cummins

P

First published in Great Britain in 2019 by

Policy Press
University of Bristol
1-9 Old Park Hill
Bristol
BS2 8BB
UK
t: +44 (0)117 954 5940
pp-info@bristol.ac.uk
www.policypress.co.uk

North America office:
Policy Press
c/o The University of Chicago Press
1427 East 60th Street
Chicago, IL 60637, USA
t: +1 773 702 7700
f: +1 773 702 9756
sales@press.uchicago.edu
www.press.uchicago.edu

British Library Cataloguing in Publication Data
A catalogue record for this book is available from the British Library

Library of Congress Cataloging-in-Publication Data
A catalog record for this book has been requested

ISBN 978-1-4473-3561-0 paperback
ISBN 978-1-4473-3559-7 hardcover
ISBN 978-1-4473-3562-7 ePub
ISBN 978-1-4473-3563-4 Mobi
ISBN 978-1-4473-3560-3 ePdf

Cover design by Hayes Design
Front cover image: istock
Printed and bound in Great Britain by CMP, Poole
Policy Press uses environmentally responsible print partners

For

Marilyn

Elliot

Nelson and Eilidh

with love

All that we don't know is astonishing. Even more
astonishing is what passes for knowing.
Philip Roth

Contents

List of acronyms   vi
About the author   vii
Acknowledgements   viii
Introduction   ix

one   Madness and society   1
two   Deinstitutionalisation and the development of   27
          community care
three   Citizenship and mental health   51
four   Contemporary mental health services   79
five   Contemporary mental health social work   111
six   Mental health social work reimagined   137

Postscript: Review of the Mental Health Act 1983   149
References   159
Index   181

List of acronyms

ACD	advance choice document
AMCP	approved mental capacity professional
AMHP	approved mental health professional
ASW	approved social worker
BAME	black, Asian and minority ethnic
CAMHS	child and adolescent mental health services
CBT	cognitive behavioural therapy
CJS	criminal justice system
CMHT	community mental health teams
CPA	care programme approach
CPS	Crown Prosecution Service
CTO	community treatment order
CTP	care and treatment plan
DoLS	Deprivation of Liberty Safeguards
DWP	Department for Work and Pensions
ECHR	European Court of Human Rights
HRA	Human Rights Act
IAPT	Improving Access to Psychological Therapies
IFSW	International Federation of Social Workers
MAPPA	multi agency public protection arrangements
MCA	Mental Capacity Act
MHA	Mental Health Act
MHRT	mental health review tribunal
MMHA	Maternal Mental Health Alliance
NICE	National Institute for Health and Care Excellence
NPSA	National Patient Safety Agency
NP	nominated person
NR	nearest relative
NRLS	National Reporting and Learning System
NSF	National Schizophrenia Fellowship
PTSD	post-traumatic stress disorder
RC	responsible clinician
RCP	Royal College of Psychiatrists
SCP	statutory care plan
SOAD	second opinion appointed doctor
TIA	trauma-informed approach
WCA	work capability assessment

About the author

Ian Cummins qualified as a probation officer and subsequently worked as a mental health social worker. His research interests in the criminal justice system and the history of mental health services reflect his practice experience. He published *Poverty, inequality and social work: The impact of neo-liberalism and austerity politics on welfare provision* with Policy Press in 2018.

Acknowledgements

My late mother worked incredibly hard to enable me to continue my education and take advantage of the opportunities that it offered. She passed on her love of books to me. I hope that she would have enjoyed this one. I owe a huge debt to my brother and my sisters for their love and support. I would like to thank all the staff at Policy Press: Isobel Bainton, Helen Davies, Shannon Kneis and Ruth Wallace have been unfailing supportive of this project. I am very grateful to the anonymous reviewers of the initial proposal and drafts of the book for their time and constructive suggestions. I am, of course, responsible for any failings, admissions or errors in the final version. I am very grateful to Merinda Epstein for permission to use her cartoon of the mental state examination. More of her work can be found at www.takver.com/epstein/cartoons.htm

Academic life is a strange world. I regard myself as extremely lucky to have had the wonderful support and encouragement of colleagues and friends: Janet Chapman, Elizabeth Collier, David Edmondson, Akwugo Emejulu, Paul Michael Garrett, Maria Grant, Marian Foley, Jameel Hadi, Stephen Jones, Gavin Kendall, Martin King, Jane Lucas, Bernard Melling, Jo Milner, Lisa Morriss, Emma Palmer, Kate Parkinson, Donna Peach, David Platten, Nick Platten, Sarah Pollock, Barry Schilling, Jonathan Simon, Imogen Tyler, Joanne Warner, Stephen Webb and Joanne Westwood.

I have also enjoyed virtual support from @asifamhp, @SchrebersSister @Mental_Elf and @Hannah_Bows

Most importantly of all, I would not have been able to complete this work without my wife, Marilyn, and my sons Nelson and Elliot.

Introduction

The aim of this work is to provide a critical analysis of what, I argue is, an ongoing crisis in mental health services. It argues that the roots of this crisis can be traced back to the failings of community care in the late 1980s and early 1990s. From the Spokes inquiry (DHSS, 1988) onwards, the response of successive governments was to focus on procedural approaches, risk and risk management. I argue that the original progressive ideas that were part of the underpinning of community care policies need to be rediscovered, updated and reinvigorated. This process can provide the basis for mental health social work that is based on fundamental notions of dignity, respect and mutuality.

This work seeks to contribute to the debate about the role of social work in mental health services. It is based on the fundamental premise that mental health social work has lost its way. Core social work values have been marginalised. The original aims and values of community care – properly resourced community based resources to support citizens in acute distress – have been lost in a world of managerialist doublespeak and risk assessment. Risk assessment has replaced the ethic of care as the main focus of service user contact. I feel that there is a danger of a kind of therapeutic pessimism dominating debates. There is a need to take a critical but also realistic and ultimately optimistic and positive approach to tackling the challenges that mental health social work faces in a climate of austerity. There have always been practitioners who are very skilled at carving out a creative space in which to work alongside service users and their families. Social workers have traditionally placed tremendous value and importance on this as a way of maintaining professional integrity and identity. This book will argue that the current crisis in mental health services requires a fundamental reshaping of service provision. The focus needs to shift from risk and risk assessment to models of service provision that are securely based on notions of dignity, inclusion and citizenship. These are at the core of social work values but also were at the heart of the original challenges to institutionalised psychiatry. The book will argue that the social work role has been marginalised within mental health service provision. This has been partly due to social work professional identity being subsumed within multi-disciplinary community mental health teams (CMHTs). These developments should be understood in a much broader social and political context. The failure to develop adequate community based mental health services should be seen as an aspect of neoliberalism's attack on the social state. Neoliberalism is a long-term economic, social and philosophical project. Its worst impacts have been deeply entrenched in the UK since the imposition of austerity economic policies in 2010. These policies have been directly targeted at those living in poverty. This group includes people with long-term mental health problems. Responses to austerity can lead to a change in service provision and a rekindling of values. This should take the form of a return to social work that has at its core personal relationships and an emotional connection between workers and those experiencing distress. An understanding of the rise and fall of the asylums, the radical challenge to psychiatry and the subsequent failings of community care can be the start of this rebuilding process. It will allow us to see that the progressive values that influenced the development of community care continue to be relevant. In fact, in a world of austerity and the retrenchment of the welfare state, they are more vital than ever.

The book is broadly divided into two sections. In the first three chapters, I examine the background to the current landscape of mental health service provision. This includes a discussion of historical responses to madness, an outline of the processes of deinstitutionalisation and the development of community care followed by an analysis of the way that individuals have been denied full citizenship as a result of institutional responses to mental distress. I should note here that terminology in the field of mental health is a problematic area. The book uses a range of terms for mental illness and the mentally ill. These reflect the values and usage of the various periods discussed. I accept that some of these terms might be seen as offensive. It also reflects my view that all of these terms are ultimately inadequate. They have become part of a labelling process, which denies or diminishes the humanity of those who experience mental distress. I apologies in advance for any offence caused. The second half of the book examines contemporary issues in mental health and services. The final chapters examine mental health social work, concluding with an outline of suggestions of how a refocusing of practice on relational approaches can be the starting point for new models of social work.

ONE

Madness and society

Historical perspectives

Scull (2015) notes that madness, its description, analysis and impact have been a source of fascination for artists, writers, film makers as well as academics and professionals from a range of disciplines. His magnificent work chronicles the way that madness and the treatment of the 'mad' has seemingly ebbed and flowed between periods of progress and others where treatments have lost any sense of human dignity. Scull shows that there seems to be no limit to the range of abuse that societies have been prepared to inflict on fellow citizens in the name of treatment of mental illness. Attitudes and understanding change over time. There is a danger that a focus on the present day assumes that these changes produce a linear progression. Outdated forms of management of the mentally ill are assumed to have been replaced by better systems based on recognition of the humanity of those who are suffering. This is problematic in two ways. It assumes we can easily make comparisons between approaches and historical epoch – for example asylum versus community care. This is a very reductionist approach that overlooks the complexity of the comparisons. It almost inevitably assumes that progress has been made. This is done without ever delineating what progress might actually mean or look like. It assumes that all moves are forward and we abandon oppressive attitudes, behaviours and forms of treatment as we go. Finally, such ahistorical approaches mean that we do not look at the failings within current systems in any real depth. One of the most important aspects of Foucault's (2006, 2008) work is that he forces us to rethink what we mean by progress or whether we can actually make comparisons at all. Is community care better than the asylum regime? If so, in what sense and how were these changes brought about? These are fundamental questions that are at the core of this work.

Language is, of course, vitally important and reflects the underlying views that societies have of those in particular groups. Mad, mentally ill, psychotic, schizophrenic, person living with dementia, service user, people with mental health problems: all these terms have been used and appear at some point in this book. This is not just sloppy on my part, it reflects that these terms are in common usage but also that they are all unsatisfactory. I have come to the conclusion that they are all ultimately demeaning and de-humanising. To use a personal example, my late mother was, in the last years of her life, was not a *person living with dementia* – she was my mother, a sister, a grandmother, former work colleague and a neighbour. It was only in her contact outside of these family and community circles – in contact with local agencies – that she would have been regarded as a 'person living with dementia' or a 'service user'.

The aim of this section is to demonstrate that decisions about what constitutes mental illness and societal responses to those who are deemed 'mad' reflect broader social and cultural values. The development of mental health services is a messy, complex and often contradictory process. Scull (2015) demonstrates this across a range of cultures and societies. He also argues that the period of deinstitutionalisation and community care is somewhat unusual in that the main focus and loci of treatment of the mentally ill has moved away from institutionalised forms of 'care'. The idea that mental illness does not require or justify some form of institutional care is thus a relatively modern idea.

The Poor Law (1601) established that each parish had a responsibility for the old and the sick. This included 'idiots and lunatics'. The system of outdoor relief meant that those unable to work were sent to the workhouse. Scull (1977, 1986) argues that societal responses to mental illness have to be seen in a much broader context of the emergence of the technologies of the management of deviance within modern, capitalist societies. The features of this new phenomena of technocratic management involve:

- the increased involvement in the state at a local and national level
- the development of a rationalised and centrally administered system for the identification and management of deviant populations
- institutionalisation
- the segregation of deviant groups
- the differentiation of deviant groups into subgroups – offender/ lunatic/juvenile delinquent
- the emergence of professional groups, whose expertise is claimed to lie in the identification and subsequent management of individuals within these deviant populations.

These developments are relatively modern social phenomena. As Scull (1977: 338) argues:

Prior to the eighteenth century, and in many places as late as the early nineteenth century, the control of deviants of all sorts had been an essentially communal and family affair. The amorphous class of the morally disreputable, the indigent and the powerless-including such elements as vagrants, minor criminals, the insane, and the physically handicapped-was managed in essentially similar ways.

In his 1975 paper, 'On being sane in insane places', the psychologist David Rosenhan reports his famous pseudopatient experiment. At the beginning of the paper, he poses the question *If sanity and insanity exist, how shall we know them?* His experiment set out to test the validity and reliability of psychiatric diagnosis. Rosenhan and seven colleagues presented themselves at the admissions offices of psychiatric units. They stated that they were hearing voices – which were saying one of three words: empty, hollow and thud. They stated the voice was the same sex as the pseudopatient. Rosenhan chose these symptoms as he felt that they were examples of what he termed 'existential symptoms' (Cummins,2017a). The patients were admitted, prescribed anti-psychotic medication before being discharged as they were 'in remission'. Rosenhan's work contains a powerful critique of the dehumanising aspects of institutionalised psychiatry. It also demonstrates the power of diagnosis. It becomes a prism through which the behaviour of that person is viewed. It also conveys a set of assumptions about the individual. Psychiatry is a branch of medicine where the patient becomes the diagnosis and vice versa. Phrases like 'he is a schizophrenic' or 'she is a manic depressive' have fallen out of fashion among mental professionals but they remain in use in common usage. Mental illness and the potential stigma of diagnosis is a matter of identity. As with all oppressive identities, it is one that individuals challenge.

The emergence of psychiatry in its modern form as a distinct branch of medicine is linked to the development of the asylum as a discrete institution. Scull (1977, 1986) argues that the asylum is new form of social control. Its creation was the result of the capitalist system's new set of social relations. The dynamism of capitalism undermined and ultimately removed traditional patterns of social order and relations. He notes that the development of the new industrial economy led to increased demands on the parishes for temporary or poor relief. This increase was resisted by the newly emerging bourgeoisie and industrial capitalist class. This group became convinced that the overgenerous system of poor relief created poverty rather than served to end it. This position was given ideological support by the writings of Malthus (1798). This period marks the emergence of the modern ideological position that sees poverty as the result of individual failings. Poverty is thus seen as a moral rather than a structural issue. The arguments about whether the causes of poverty are structural or individual have continued until this day (Welshman, 2013; Garrett, 2015, Cummins, 2018).

In the area of what we would now term mental illness, treatment and management have been largely been coercive and based in institutions. Many would argue that this remains the case. The period of community care is a rupture or departure from this overall approach. In England in the 18th century, there was a proliferation of the number of madhouses – private institutions (Porter, 1987). Concerns about these institutions led to the passing in 1774 of the Act for Regulating Private Madhouses. This introduced medical certification for insanity. It is from this period on that it is possible to see the expansion of the role of the alienist – doctors specialising in the diagnosis and treatment of those suffering from mental illness. Scull (2015) argues that these developments can be viewed as much about arguments and disputes in the medical profession as scientific ones. For example, the opening of the York Retreat was viewed suspiciously by the medical profession. This was partly due to scepticism towards moral management but more importantly it was run by lay people.

In the first half of the 19th century, a system of county asylums emerged. The opening of these institutions was often subject to local debate about the costs to the local ratepayer but also whether these institutions should establish harsher or more punitive regimes. Cox and Marland (2015) provide an excellent account of these debates and how local politics and politicians had a key role in shaping these huge institutions which were to become such a feature of the social and cultural life of modern urban communities. In this period, there was a swathe of parliamentary inquiries and select committees that examined the conditions in asylums and the treatment of pauper lunatics. In an echo of modern concerns about the privatisation of health care, one of the recurring features of these debates was the role of private madhouses. The Poor Law Amendment Act 1834 made it explicit that indoor relief and the conditions in the workhouse were to be such that they would act as a deterrent to admission. Pauper lunatics were to be removed to asylums. The Lunatics Asylums Act 1845 meant that each borough and county had to establish an asylum at public expense. These changes were partly based on the optimistic belief in medical progress was being made in the treatment of mental illness. The 1845

Act also meant that responsibility for the management of the asylums was moved from lay administrators to medical practitioners. This marks the point where madness was widely regarded as an illness and thus should only be identified and managed by medical professionals. The result of these changes was the growth in the numbers of those certified. By the turn of the 20th century, the asylum had become the custodial institution that was still easily recognisable in the mid-1950s.

York Retreat

The York Retreat was established in 1796. There remains a psychiatric unit on the site to this day. Tuke, who established the Retreat, was a Quaker and the system of moral treatment reflected his religious beliefs but was also an attempt to provide a more humane response to mental distress. Like many developments in the history of madness, it was a response to a scandal (Cummins, 2017b). In 1790, Hannah Mills, a local Quaker, died as the result of appalling neglect in the local lunatic asylum. The Quaker community raised funds to build an alternative institution. The Retreat was not only a new physical space, it was based on a different ethos. The use of physical restraint, which on reflection is a somewhat weak term for the reality of people being chained and manacled, ceased. Moral treatment placed an emphasis on the benefits of fresh air, country walks and the development of personal relationships. The core beliefs here have echoes in some elements of the modern recovery model and trauma-informed approaches (TIAs). It would be wrong to overemphasise these or attempt to make some ahistorical link. It is rather that there are important themes or traces in modern challenges to the institutions of psychiatry that appear in previous developments. The link is that there is a need for that any response to be built on the basis of the recognition of the fundamental dignity of those in distress.

Michel Foucault

Foucault is one of the most influential and widely cited writers in the humanities and social sciences. He died in 1984 but, if anything, his work has grown in its influence and application since his early passing. *Madness and civilisation* originally published in France in 1960. *Discipline and punishment* was published in 1975. Together they provided an original, complex and at times contradictory explanation and analysis of the emergence of modern governmentality and two of the most important modern systems for the management of deviance

– the asylum and the prison. These two institutions are inextricably entwined and have been since their emergence in their modern recognisable forms (Seddon, 2007). Foucault's analysis argues that claims to universality for models that 'explain' madness or criminality need to be viewed as functions of the social, cultural and economics of the society that produces these claims.

Foucault's work is based on, at that time, an unconventional approach. He identifies what he termed an *episteme* – the underlying set of attitudes that underpins cultural attitudes in any historical period. He outlined the concept of the *episteme* thus, 'In any given culture and at any given moment, there is always one episteme that defines the conditions of possibility of all knowledge, whether expressed in a theory or silently invested in a practice' (Foucault, 2005: 18). The notion of the *episteme* is a key element in understanding Foucault's approach. His alternative history of the development of the asylum regime can be read as an attempt using a range of sources including literature and political tracts to reconstruct the episteme in the Classical Age via an analysis of the attitudes towards and treatment of the 'mad'.

Foucault identifies four historical *epistemes* (Merquior, 1991):

• pre-classical – the late Middle Ages and Renaissance up to the mid–17th century
• classical period – the mid–17th to the 18th centuries
• modern period – 19th century to the mid-1950s
• contemporary – from the 1950s onwards. This is a period that Foucault identifies as one that saw the development of new techniques in the management of populations and citizens.

It is possible to see the developments that took place in mental health services after Foucault's death in 1984 as marking a new episteme – the neoliberal epoch and community care.

The main thesis that Foucault puts forward in *Madness and civilisation* is that from the mid-17th century onwards the deserted lepropsaria – the leper colonies – became asylums. This represents and is a result of the cultural shifts in attitudes to madness – part of the changing episteme. Foucault argues that, prior to this, the 'mad' were seen as either possessed of a special form of reason – the wisdom of folly tolerated and or ignored. They were not subject to identification, regulation and control in the way that the modern asylum regimes demand. The asylum is one of the modern institutions, such as prisons, schools and factories, that requires the management of individuals by classification or category. Foucault's work is a complex delineation of these shifts in cultural attitudes and practices. They result in the fact that in the early modern period madness becomes classified as a disease – and all that entails for the social status of those involved. The asylums are thus part of the development of a new technology of power for the management of those deemed deviant. Foucault sees the regimes that were established by Philippe Pinel in Paris and William Tuke in York not as developments or progress. They should be viewed as new ways to exercise control – some aspects might be more effective than the older previously well-established technologies of power.

Criticisms of Foucault

There is no doubting the influence of Foucault's work. It has been subject to significant and ongoing criticism. The first criticisms of Foucault relate to his use of sources and the historical accuracy of his claims. These are made most forcefully by Scull (1986) and Sedgwick (1982). Scull argues that Foucault used a very limited range of sources to build his case that these cultural shifts occurred. It is also suggested that Foucault had a rather naive or romantic view of the nature of mental illness and societal attitudes that existed before what he termed 'The Great Confinement'. Sedgwick (1982) demonstrates that the custodial methods and restraint – in Foucault's argument part of a new technology for treatment of the mentally ill – had been used in the periods prior to the development of the asylum regime. Sedgwick is particularly critical of the link between the closure of leprosaria and the establishment of asylums. Foucault denied making this claim (Stone, 1984). It is, however, generally presented as one of the key elements of his argument.

The second theme in the criticism of Foucault is the fact that he does not appear to accept that any of the actors in these new asylum regimes were or could ever be motivated by humanitarian concerns. The nihilism at the heart of much Foucault's writing is most evident here. This, ironically, given the complexity of his work, results in a position where he does not incorporate any other motivations apart from social control into his explanation of the rise of the asylums. Finally, there are those who seek to lay the blame for the well documented failings of community care at Foucault's door (Cummins, 2017b). Weissman (1982) is an early example of this. It was a key theme in the argument between Foucault and the historian Lawrence Stone (Stone, 1984). This is an unfair criticism. Foucault's work was clearly a factor in the intellectual climate that rightly challenged the abusive nature of much of the asylum regime. He did not do this alone. He certainly cannot be held accountable for the failure to provide adequate community mental health services that led to the homelessness experienced by the woman that Weissman (1982) examined. Such an approach overestimates the power and influence of his work but also is a simplistic analysis of the web of factors that ultimately produced deinstitutionalisation. It is clear that Foucault was not arguing that individuals experiencing distress should be abandoned by the state. His work is a historical exploration; it would be for others to draw their own conclusions about what insights it provided about the mental health systems of the 1960s and 1970s when Foucault was carrying out his research. Foucault is not putting forward an alternative form of mental health provision in this area of his work.

Big pharma

Webb (2006) notes that in Western societies significant proportions of the population are living longer, have more and there is more material prosperity. Despite this technological progress, modern society seems obsessed with risk and risk management. Jones (2008) outlines what he terms a modern affliction – 'affluenza' – a depressive middle class sickness brought on by social and material envy. The number of prescriptions issued for anti-depressants has doubled in the past decade. In 2015, the total was 31.6m more than in 2005 – and also an increase of 3.9m, or 6.8% on 2014 (Meikle, 2016). Thus Western societies are consuming larger and larger quantities of these drugs. In addition, in that charming phrase that mental health professionals use, many people 'self-medicate' – take street drugs or alcohol instead of, or in addition to, officially prescribed treatments.

Moncrieff (2004) summarises a series of concerns about the relationship between drug manufacturers and psychiatric medicine thus,

> Drugs are central to modern psychiatric practice and to much psychiatric thought about the nature and causation of mental disorders. Psychiatry has therefore become an important target for the large and powerful pharmaceutical industry. Drug companies direct lavish advertising and hospitality towards psychiatrists and provide funding for much medical education and some mental health service initiatives.

The argument is that the drug industry continues to reinforce – for its own economic interest – a narrow biomedical approach to the causation of mental illness. To put it rather crudely, drug companies need to develop new demands and markets for their products. This can only be done by the continued medicalisation of essentially social or behavioural issues. This is the real driver behind the increase in the size and detailed outlining of more and more complex and bizarre syndromes in Diagnostic and Statistical Manual of Mental Disorders (DSM-5). These moves are often the butt of satire – shyness becomes *social anxiety disorder*. However, there is a real danger here of ignoring or mocking the real impact that, for example, social anxiety has on the people who experience it. Being critical of the medicalisation of distress need not involve this. It is simply a statement that the solution to such problems is not necessarily going to be found in expensive medication that creates significant profits for the pharmaceutical industry. Psychiatry is an important area for the pharmaceutical industry because it seems possible to both create new syndromes and offer the cure to them at the same time. Moncrieff (2004) makes the very important point that medication offers a simple, complete and technical solution to a range of complex social and personal problems. In so doing, it marginalises the real causes of these issues, such as the impact of interpersonal violence or the long-term effect of living in poverty.

Drug treatments are a relatively recent introduction into psychiatric medicine. Since the 1950s, they have played an increasingly important and central role in the response to mental distress. The early psychiatric drugs have been seen as acting more as forms of restraint – the 'chemical cosh' (Braslow, 1997). The earliest anti-psychotics had a series of potentially damaging side effects such as tardive dyskensia. The drug companies, through huge and sophisticated marketing campaigns including inducements to doctors, played a key role in the increased dominance of bio-psychiatry. This was very much the case in the US, where psychiatry in the post war period was very heavily influenced by psycho dynamic, particularly Freudian, perspectives. Luhrmann (2000) outlines what she describes as the *two tribes* within the American psychiatric profession to capture this. One of the leading figures in the bio-psychiatry divide of this debate was Robert Spitzer. Spitzer (1975) wrote a critical response to Rosenhan's (1975) pseudopatient experiment. He then went on to chair the taskforce that led the production of DSM-III in 1980. Spitzer and Wilson (1975) created not just a new, broader more detailed form of psychiatric diagnosis and classification; they argued that diagnosis should be seen as a form of technical, professional discourse rather than a stigmatising label. This does not take account of the social context of diagnosis, which has social, moral, ethical, political and cultural implications (Sontag, 1978).

Moncrieff (2004) outlines the way that certain drugs, Prozac being an example, have been so widely prescribed that they are well known and have become part of the cultural landscape. Elizabeth Wurtzel's (1994) memoir *Prozac Nation* became a best seller distilling a certain kind of fashionable existentialist angst. This was satirised or attacked at the time for being the musings or, depending on one's point of view, whining of a privileged white middle class woman. The memoir highlighted the pain and suffering that the author experienced and the social pressures that created these.

One of the most fundamental criticisms of the increase in the use of drug treatments is the use of medication in cases involving children and young people. For example, there has been a huge increase in prescriptions for Ritalin – a treatment for Attention Deficit Hyper Activity Disorder (ADHD). In 2010, 661,000 were dispensed compared with 359,100 in 2004 (Boffey, 2015). It is important to remember that these are prescriptions given to children. This is in itself a concern. In addition, many would see this as an example of the much broader trend of the medicalisation of social or behavioural problems.

Moncrieff (2004) concludes that:

> This increase in use of prescribed drugs has been achieved firstly by extending the boundaries of well recognised conditions like depression and psychosis. Secondly, lesser known disorders such as panic disorder and social phobia have been publicised, and thirdly, drug treatment has started to colonise areas where it was previously thought to be unhelpful such as substance misuse and personality disorder.

Stigma

It is almost impossible to consider questions related to mental illness without examining stigma. Goffman (1963) published *Stigma: Notes on a spoiled identity* after his work on asylums. However, the two can be read as two halves of the same argument. The work on stigma forms a backdrop to the way that total institutions function in the creation and maintenance of the social ostracism of the mentally ill. In Ancient Greece, stigma were the marks that were cut or burned into the body of those who had transgressed the laws and morals of the time. In Hawthorne's (1850) classic *The scarlet letter*, Hester Prynne is forced to wear a scarlet 'A' on her dress to shame her as she has a young child that the local community assume is from an adulterous relationship. Stigma is clearly in the modern world socially constructed. We do not force the mentally ill to wear a scarlet letter 'M'. However, people with mental health problems face a series of negative and discriminatory attitudes. It should be emphasised that it is not only a question of what might be termed social attitudes. People with mental health problems face ongoing discrimination in areas such as employment and housing. There are many other examples. In the field of social work practice, mental health status may be a factor in a number of areas of assessment. For example, the issue of a mother's mental health status may be used in disputes over custody to bring her parenting skills into question. This is not to say that these issues should not be considered. It is to underline the importance of the need for a proper examination of all the factors. It also highlights the dangers in using a reductionist approach that makes some sort of simple positivist link between mental ill health and parenting capacity.

Goffman highlighted the powerful and ongoing social force that is stigma. He argues that we are often complicit in the maintenance of stigmatised status of individuals and groups. It is impossible for us to escape this as we are part of a normative order. There are two potential stages to the normative process of stigmatisation – the *discreditable* and the *discredited*. The attribute that is seen as stigmatising is not necessarily apparent or visible. Individuals are aware that there is a potential reaction from others if they reveal or the stigmatising attribute is disclosed. Mental illness is a clear example. It is, therefore, possible that an individual might keep this hidden. Goffman termed this 'passing'. 'Passing' carries with it the possibility that the individual will be unintentionally or deliberately outed. The impact of stigma can be seen on the individual and those around him or her. Despite a great deal of progress, there a deeply engrained stigma remains attached to mental illness.

Models of mental health and illness

There are a number of approaches to models of mental illness. There has traditionally been a divide between medical (or disease) and social models. Critical psychiatry approaches (Cummins, 2017b) question the power of the psychiatric profession and the supposed scientific neutrality of diagnosis. I will briefly consider the main models here. I would argue that there is an increasing recognition that the social/medical model division is reductive and redundant. There is a complex interplay between a range of factors – including social and biological ones.

The disease model and its critics

The disease model of mental illness is based on the premise that mental health problems can be identified and classified. The symptoms of mental illness be they hallucinatory experiences or low mood and suicidal thoughts, can be traced to a physical cause – for example, lesions in the brain or a chemical imbalance. As in other areas of medicine, this leads to a system of classification. The specialised training of psychiatrists enables them to make diagnosis. The diagnosis not only indicates the likely prognosis but also the best course of treatment. This approach clearly follows a traditional model recognisable in other areas of the medical profession. For example, there will always be differences between practitioners in any discipline but this model indicates that there will be a consistency of diagnosis. The model puts psychiatrists in a powerful position as they have the knowledge and expertise required to make these decisions. In addition, it establishes a paternalistic relationship between the doctors and patients. As Ignatieff (1985) notes, one of the responses by psychiatry to the criticisms of Foucault and others was a sense of shock that they could be seen as anything other than humanitarians concerned with the relief of suffering.

The supporters of the disease model highlight the extent of progress that has been made in research into specific mental health problems. For example, 1990–99 was designated by President George Bush Senior the *Decade of the Brain* as part of a wider effort to increase public understanding of the impact of brain research. This, alongside other developments such as the Human Genome Project, which mapped every gene in the human body, the claim or hope is that there will be a medical breakthrough that will unlock the ongoing mystery of mental illness.

The criticisms of a purely medical model or an extremely biological determined approach to psychiatric illness are explored throughout this book so will not be examined in depth here. Bentall (2004) argues that this approach should be challenged in a number of areas. The first is the scientific validity of diagnoses such as schizophrenia and bipolar disorder. It is argued that there is much more of an overlap between symptoms than has previously been seen as the case. At the heart of this critique is a fundamental challenge to the notion that diagnosis is destiny. This is the sense that the negative connotations of a psychiatric diagnosis are seen as an end to the possibility of living a life as a full and active citizen. As Bentall (2004) and others highlight, large numbers of people are able to live productive lives and make a positive contribution to society despite experiencing symptoms of severe psychiatric disorders at some point. For example, there is an international network of people who hear voices but approach this is in a completely different way to seeing it as a symptom of illness.[1] The network supports people to manage their lives, including the experience of hearing voices, without any input from psychiatric services.

The disease model remains incredibly powerful. The rise and expansion of the DSM is one sign of this. The increased dominance of bio-psychiatry was in part due to the success of the radical critics of psychiatry, such as Foucault, Fanon and Laing (Cummins, 2017). More recent research has indicated that there are a range of social, cultural and environmental factors that have a role in or increase the likelihood of the development of mental health problems. These include such factors as migration, growing up in poverty, being a member of a minority ethnic group, or being subjected to sexual and physical abuse. Varese et al's (2012) meta-analysis indicates that these childhood adversities increase the risk of psychosis by a factor of three. Those who experienced multiple traumatic events were at greater risk. There is a relationship between these factors. For example, growing up in poverty was one of the factors identified, and the risks are higher for some groups of children – for example children from BME backgrounds are more likely to be brought up in poverty. This is an example of the need for an intersectional approach that looks at a wide range of factors including historical, sociological and economic ones.

Bentall (2016) argues that the impact of the focus on a biomedical approach creates and helps to sustain a binary notion of well/ill. This is the root of Goffman's notion of stigma. We need to be able to place individuals in some form of 'lower' or 'discredited' category for stigma to operate. Bentall (2016) states that:

> To make matters worse, research shows that an exclusively biological approach tends to increase the stigma associated with mental illness. The more that ordinary people think of mental illness as a genetically determined brain disease, and the less they recognise it to be a reaction to unfortunate circumstances, the more they shun psychiatric patients. An exclusively biological approach makes it all too easy to believe that human beings fall into two subspecies: the mentally well and the mentally ill.

---

[1]   www.intervoiceonline.org/

Bentall (2016) concludes that one of the most profound impacts of a model that is constructed in very narrow biomedical terms is it individualises all problems. Thus the solutions are presented as individual ones. This ignores structural inequalities. In addition, there is a danger that this becomes a form of victim blaming. The social factors that have an impact on mental health require social welfare and policy interventions. Reduced inequality, better public housing and other social amenities, challenges to discrimination and action on homophobia are the sorts of areas that we are discussing here. This is not a definitive list. However, there are issues that call for an active form of social citizenship – something that has been under attack from the recent retrenchment in social and public services.

The mental state examination

Social workers working in the mental health field clearly do so alongside a range of other professionals. It is important that social workers recognise the ways that their colleagues will approach these issues. This is not a matter of abstract debate about the epistemological underpinnings of different disciplines. Working in a CMHT or any other multi-professional setting, it is important that social workers are aware of the way that other disciplines process or assess the importance of information. The mental state examination (MSE) is the standard psychiatric assessment process.

A psychiatrist is advised to consider:

- appearance
- mood – subjective and objective assessment
- thoughts
- speech
- behaviour
- drug/alcohol use
- forensic history
- family history.

One thing that immediately strikes the reader is the potentially subjective nature of the assessment. How do we assess someone's appearance and what are the implications of this? Psychiatry is an overwhelming white middle class profession. Doctors who are not originally from these backgrounds develop a set of knowledge, skills and attitudes – in Bourdieu's (1989,1998) terms a 'habitus' – as part of their professional training. This creates a prism through which they see the world and their patients. This is not, of course, limited to psychiatrists: it is true of all professions and groups. The importance here is that it also creates a yardstick for the assessment. In addition, there is an inbuilt danger of cultural misunderstanding or confusion as the result of class, race and gender differences. The potential for misunderstanding is captured in Merinda Epstein's marvellous cartoon.

Cartoon: Mental state examination

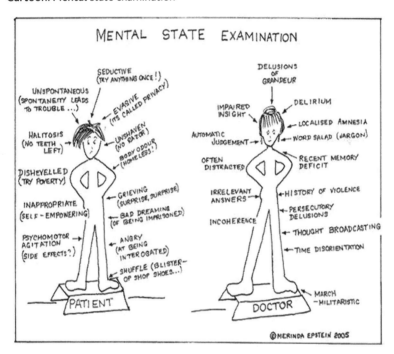

Behavioural models

Skinner's (2002, 2012) work in developing behaviourism is, perhaps, not as influential as it once was. In contrast to psychodynamic approaches that focus on underlying causes of behaviours, this approach focuses on symptoms and behaviours. Skinner believed that behaviour was learnt or 'conditioned'. In the majority of cases, through either punishment or reward, we learn behaviour that enables us to successfully adapt to society. We pick up clues and know the sanctions for inappropriate behaviour. In this model, mental illness is seen as maladaptive behaviour. These maladaptive behaviours may reinforce original symptoms. For example, if you experience a fear of certain social situations you will avoid them. However, by avoiding them there is a danger that your anxiety about being drawn into them will increase. Behaviourism has been critical of the doctor/patient relationship, which is seen to encourage dependency. From this perspective, the consultation rewards the patient with attention for maintaining their position in the sick role.

Behaviourist ideas are at the root of patient contracts – rules about behaviour during periods of admission or when they can access services. Behaviourism has been used as a means of inducing conformity. In the 1960s and 70s, wards introduced a 'token economy' whereby tokens were issued for 'good behaviour'. Good behaviour was usually interpreted as behaviour that did not inconvenience the ward staff. In addition, the tokens were usually cigarettes. Apart from this dubious aspect of the token economy, one of the problems was the difficulty in ensuring that all staff followed any regime consistently.(Nolan, 2000)

Behaviourism is at the root of some of the more shameful abuses that scar psychiatry – aversion therapy to 'cure' gay men being a clear example (Dickinson, 2014). Skinner actually concluded that reward is a better way of modifying behaviour than punishment. This message seems to have been lost in translation. For example, individuals who self-harm have been banned from A&E departments or complain that they are treated as time wasters – regarded as not worthy of treatment and compassion.

War and psychiatry

The experiences and responses to the catastrophic trauma of war have had a huge influence on the development of social policy and institutions of the welfare states, professions and public institutions. Psychiatry is one such area. This is apparent after both World Wars and the Vietnam War. Prior to World War I, degeneration and eugenics were popular theories and widely held across the political spectrum (Carey, 2012). Degeneration was a set of theories based on notions of social Darwinism that captured middle class concerns about the threat to social order that was posed by the development of the modern urban poor. This was epitomised by concerns with spread of disease but also crime (Stedman-Jones, 2014; Welshman, 2013). Booth's poverty maps of London make an explicit link between economic and moral status (Cummins, 2018). In his *L'uomo delinquente* (1876), Lombroso outlined what he saw as the physical attributes of the criminally insane. These included a low, sloping forehead, and hard and shifty eyes. Alongside these alleged psychical attributes, there existed a series of other qualities that included the lack of a moral sense and a tendency to impulsiveness. These physical and psychological qualities combined to produce the archetype of the urban working/criminal classes. There were concerns that the growth in the population of these groups would lead to economic and social disaster.

The national trauma of World War I presented a challenge to the discourse of degeneracy – the heroic figure of the soldier was at odds with the previous image of the working class male. Putkowski and Sykes (1990) show that many young working class men who suffered psychological trauma received swift and brutal punishment as deserters. However, officers also experienced trauma – what came to be known as *shell shock*. Barker (2013) in the *Regeneration* trilogy explores this contradiction through the characters of the two famous war poets Siegfried Sassoon and Wilfred Owen. They actually met at Craiglockhart Hospital near Edinburgh where both had been sent for treatment. Sassoon had been educated at Marlborough and Clare College, Cambridge, so was clearly a quintessential member of the English upper middle classes. He joined up at the outbreak of war and was decorated with the Military Cross. Sassoon had written an open letter criticising the conduct of the war. His anger and the trauma he experienced could not be portrayed as signs of degeneracy. One of the other key figures in the novel is William Rivers, an anthropologist who trained as a psychiatrist, who is overseeing the treatment of the men. The wider impact of the *shell shock* was that it gave impetus to moves towards psychodynamic explanations. For example, the Tavistock Clinic was opened in 1920 and the influence of the asylum doctor faded. The impact of the response to shell shock faded in the post-World War I period. The Mental Treatment Act 1930, for example, was more focused on compulsory detention.

Post-traumatic stress disorder

The experiences of war and its impact, including the symptoms of what is now termed *post-traumatic stress disorder* (PTSD), have been described in many forms from many wars. These symptoms include flashbacks, upsetting memories, and anxiety following a traumatic event. PTSD is now recognised as a potential reaction to a range of traumatic events including being subject to sexual violence. The term was first officially recognised as a mental health condition in 1980, only five years after the end of the Vietnam War. The key elements in a diagnosis of PTSD is that the person has experienced a trauma – an event that is outside the range of normal human experience; and the traumatic event is then re-experienced or revisited. This could take the form of recurrent and intrusive thoughts or nightmares. Flashbacks or dissociative episodes are not uncommon. Those who experience PTSD often have difficulty sleeping alongside a range of other symptoms such as poor concentration or hyper vigilance.

The key phrase in terms of the definition of trauma is an event that is outside the range of usual human experience and that would be markedly distressing to almost anyone. Thus trauma begins in the experience of war but then moves to a much broader recognition. It is also an inherently psychodynamic model. There is an element of the stress/vulnerability model as clearly not all those are who exposed to these traumatic events go onto to experience the symptoms of PTSD. Rechtman (2004: 914) noted 'there is probably no other psychiatric diagnosis that has so closely met lay people's and professionals' expectations'. This reflects the shifting politics that resulted in the recognition of the disorder in the first place. Andreasen (1995) argues that PTSD is a diagnosis that is very unusual within psychiatry as it is one that does not have stigmatising connotations. This is partly because of its roots in the recognition of the potentially damaging impact of conflict. In addition, the trauma is the result of being victimisation or subject to interpersonal violence. Therefore, it is argued that this produces a more sympathetic and understanding response. The notion of PTSD is now deeply embedded and, it seems to me, largely accepted within popular culture. This seems particularly in the case of the responses to the experiences of war veterans.

One of the key themes of this chapter and the book more widely is that it is not possible to examine definitions of and responses to mental disorder without examining the social, political and cultural contexts in which they are developed. PTSD is a case in point. The Vietnam War (Sheehan,2009), Burns et al,(2017) as well as inflicting untold suffering on the people of Vietnam remains a fault line in US society. US soldiers returning from Vietnam were faced with a society divided on the fighting of that war. In this dislocated social context, the fight for the recognition of PTSD as a disorder was also part of a wider social struggle to claim legitimacy for the experiences of those drafted into the chaos.

In 2001, a British psychiatrist, Derek Summerfield published an article exploring what he termed 'invention of post-traumatic stress disorder'. Summerfield had worked for various non-governmental organisations (NGOs) and had clinical experience in war zones and refugee camps across the world. This is very important as Summerfield was not suggesting that individuals did not suffer psychological trauma.

He saw PTSD as essentially a Western (US) construct that was then exported to the wider world. He also questioned the ways that PTSD was being used to medicalise the experiences of war and exile. He examined what he saw as the financial implications – the development of monetary compensation for trauma – but also the expansion of what might be termed the trauma industry. Tabloid stories, such as a train driver awarded £35,000 after hitting a goat that strayed onto the line (Toolis, 2009), have become the staple of much tabloid reporting. The trigger event, in this narrative, is represented in more and more trivial terms. It thus becomes further removed from the origins of the diagnosis. There is a clear discourse here. There is an assumption here that all such claims are bogus and that those involved are seeking to defraud the system and motivated by the prospect of financial reward.

As noted above, PTSD is now deeply embedded within popular culture. The wartime hero struggling to cope with a return to civilian society has become almost a stock figure within films, novels and drama. From its roots in a particular experience of war and conflict, it has become a much more broadly used term.

Cognitive models

The cognitive approach sees disordered thinking as the cause of mental ill health. The model starts from the premise that our thoughts shape the way that we see the world, we respond to situations, events and people through a filter that, in a sense, we have created for ourselves. This cognitive bias means that we focus on information that supports our pre-existing view of the world. For example, it would suggest that a depressed person would focus on more negative information. The cognitive model therefore identifies patterns of thinking that are seen as maladaptive and then sets about working with patients to alter these. The model was developed from Beck's (1979) treatment of depression. The growth in the use of cognitive behavioural therapy (CBT) in mental health settings is the clearest evidence of the influence of these approaches. The elements of faulty logic or thinking that are identified can be summarised as follows:

- *Arbitrary thinking:* Reaching a conclusion without evidence to support it or when the evidence contradicts the conclusion.
- *Selective abstraction:* Focusing on one detail taken out of context, ignoring other relevant features of the situation, reaching a conclusion for the whole experience on the basis of this one aspect.

- *Overgeneralization:* Drawing a general rule or conclusion based on one or more isolated incidents and then applying the concept to other related or even unrelated situations
- *Evaluation:* Errors in evaluating the significance or importance of an event.
- *Personalisation:* Relating external events to oneself when there is no basis for making such a connection.
- *Absolute and binary thinking:* Viewing all experiences in one of two opposite categories; and then placing yourself in the most extreme negative category.

CBT as noted above has its roots in the treatment of depressive illness. However, its use as a treatment has been extended to other disorders including substance abuse, bipolar disorder, personality disorders, and anorexia nervosa (Beck,1997). It has also been used alongside medication in the treatment of psychotic illnesses (Butler et al, 2006). There is a growing trend towards the delivery of CBT online. The National Institute for Health and Care Excellence (NICE) has approved the use of online CBT for the treatment of depression, anxiety and panic disorder. It has clear advantages from the organisational point of view in that it is cheap and easy to deliver – the responsibility lies with the individual. There are also no waiting times. The NHS website[2] very much presents this as an opportunity to take back control of your own health. There are clearly positive aspects to this but there is also a danger that this amounts to another way in which social and structural issues are essentially individualised. 'Faulty' models of thinking might actually reflect the relative powerlessness and marginalisation of individuals and groups.

Improving Access to Psychological Therapies

The Improving Access to Psychological Therapies (IAPT) programmes began in 2008. The aim of the programme is to shift the focus for the treatment for depression and anxiety from approaches based on the prescription of medication to psychological approaches. Nearly a million people in the UK access IAPT services each year and there are plans in *The five year forward view for mental health* (Independent Mental Health Taskforce, 2016) to extend these services. The priorities for development are:

---

[2]   www.nhs.uk/conditions/online-mental-health-services/Pages/introduction.aspx

- Expanding services so that at least 1.5m adults access care each year by 2020/21. This means that IAPT services nationally will move from seeing around 15% of all people with anxiety and depression each year to 25%, and all areas will have more IAPT services.
- Focusing on people with long-term conditions. Two thirds of people with a common mental health problem also have a long-term physical health problem, greatly increasing the cost of their care by an average of 45% more than those without a mental health problem. By integrating IAPT services with physical health services the NHS can provide better support to this group of people and achieve better outcomes.
- Supporting people to find or stay in work. Good work contributes to good mental health, and IAPT services can better contribute to improved employment outcomes.
- Improving quality and people's experience of services. Improving the numbers of people who recover, reducing geographic variation between services, and reducing inequalities in access and outcomes for particular population groups are all important aspects of the development of IAPT services.[3]

The IAPT programme is an explicit recognition that a 'pill for every ill' approach will not ultimately succeed.

Trauma-informed approaches

One of the consistent elements of social or vulnerability models of mental illness is that they recognise the potential impact of trauma. In addition, Sweeney et al (2016) note in their review of TIAs that mental health systems can be sites of initial trauma or further trauma. There are broad definitions of trauma but Sweeney et al quote the SAMHSA (Substance Abuse and Mental Health Services Administration – US) definition of trauma:

> trauma refers to events or circumstances that are experienced as harmful or life-threatening and that have lasting impacts on mental, physical, emotional and/or social well-being.

Thus trauma can be a single event or a series of events. The definition is broad enough to include experiences of interpersonal violence, for example sexual abuse, physical assault and social trauma, such as

---

[3]   www.england.nhs.uk/mental-health/adults/iapt/

inequality and marginalisation. Over the last decade, research evidence has increasingly supported the notion that trauma is linked to adult psychosis and a wide range of other forms of mental distress (for example, Bentall et al, 2014 ; Fisher et al, 2010; and Kessler et al,1997). Individuals may experience personal trauma while at the same time being caught up in community traumas. For example, individuals fleeing a war zone may be subjected to forms of interpersonal violence alongside the trauma of being a member of a persecuted group in society. These traumas can be compounded by the reaction of authorities or public services to the individuals and family. The treatment and demonisation of asylum seekers in the UK, where the official systems increasingly involve a series of degradations, suffer a denial of fundamental humanity and dignity (Tyler, 2014; Backwith, 2015). Such events have the potential to retraumatise individuals who have experienced the arbitrary abuse of state power.

Retraumatisation

Retraumatisation occurs when a person experiences an event that triggers memories of a past traumatic event. This event then triggers similar emotional responses – fear, anxiety, depersonalisation – to those of the original event. Bloom and Farragher (2010) argue that current mental health systems with their inbuilt focus on coercion and control have the potential to retraumatise survivors. This may occur via the use of physical restraint and seclusion but also by more subtle pressures – for example cooperating with a community treatment order (CTO) or taking medication (Sweeney et al 2016). In addition, psychiatry has a history that has seen it be part of the processes that create gender, racial and other stereotypes as well as recasting reactions to these social injustices as individual pathology that can be 'cured'. In discussing the use of control, one has to confront the fact that the Mental Health Act (MHA) 1983 gives professionals the legal powers to detain people.

On being detained

The impact on individuals who have been detained under the MHA needs to be examined in a much more open and honest fashion. I think that this also applies to the professionals involved. These issues are secondary to the impact on those detained. DrEm_79 outlines the potentially devastating consequences of compulsory detention for an individual. She highlights the profound impact of the loss of autonomy and the need for professionals to be open and honest about why they have chosen this option.[4]

The pressures on services and the poor conditions on wards create a tension between the professional ethics and those mental health professionals working in them. Bloom and Farragher (2010) argue that staff are required to work in 'trauma-organised systems'. Social workers and mental health professional enter these systems with the aim of relieving suffering rather than inflicting it. The long-term impact on staff is the development of therapeutic pessimism or a loss of a sense of why they entered the profession in the first place. This is superbly illustrated in Filer's (2013) novel *The shock of the fall* where the staff are unable to communicate with a young patient Matthew so do not understand the extent of his mental distress.

Paterson (2014) defines TIA as 'a system development model that is grounded in and directed by a complete understanding of how trauma exposure affects service user's neurological, biological, psychological and social development'; services need to organised and delivered in ways that recognise that service users have potentially been exposed to various forms of trauma. The service needs to thus ensure that users are ethically informed and safe. TIA mental health services are thus strengths based approaches. They seek to recognise that complex behaviours have a function in both helping survivors manage and respond to situational triggers. Spandler's (2001) and Spandler and Warner's (2007) work on self-harm is an example of this approach. It puts forward an approach that, rather than seeing self-harm as a behaviour that needs to be managed, views it as a behaviour that has intrinsic meaning for the individual. This leads to a fundamental shift in thinking. TIAs are thus described as a move from 'what is wrong with you' to 'what happened to you' (Harris and Fallot, 2001). Sweeney et al (2016) conclude that TIAs lead to a service ethos where 'Survivors in crisis are not viewed as manipulative, attention-seeking or destructive, but as trying to cope in the present moment using any available resource.'

There are a limited number of examples of TIAs in the UK. Sweeney et al (2016) note that the acknowledgement of the potential impact of trauma presents real difficulties for psychiatry. In the past, it has been seen as unhelpful 'family blaming' – for example, in the work of Laing (1967). However, there is a perhaps a more fundamental reason. Acknowledgement of the impact of trauma entails a confrontation with the realisation that humans are capable of such acts of interpersonal

---

[4]   ww.bmj.com/content/358/bmj.j3546

violence and that the impact of such events is potentially lifelong. For mental health services, it requires a shift in the thinking that underpins services; as Sweeney et al (2016: 183) note, 'mental distress is understood as a scientific, medical and pharmacological problem, rather than a human, familial or social issue'. Moves to see these issues in social terms are continuing but there is much to do.

TIA models should appeal to social workers in mental health settings – as well as other areas, for example work with children and families. They chime with many of the issues that the profession seeks to engage with. They are also ecological in that look at the individual as well as the social, cultural and political context. TIAs specifically require a rethink of the use of coercion in mental health practice. TIAs have at their heart a relational model of practice but also call for a working and organisational culture that recognises the potential for harm that can be inflicted on service users and professionals in systems that are not firmly grounded in the values of compassion, dignity and reciprocity.

Social models of mental illness

This approach has two main elements. It examines the social factors that contribute to the development of mental health problems. These include poverty, unemployment, poor housing and social isolation. Such approaches then go to explore the way that individual responses to these social factors are medicalised. An example would be Brown and Harris's (1978) classic study of the social origins of depression in a group of working women in London. It found that women who experienced what they termed 'vulnerability factors' – early maternal loss, lack of a confiding relationship, more than three children under the age of 14 at home and unemployment – were at increased risk of depression. They also identified a range of protective factors which included a strong sense of community or a close bond with a family member – so greater levels of social support. Hammen and Goodman-Brown (1990) carried out a longitudinal study which concluded that growing up in a dysfunctional or chaotic family with high levels of stress increased the likelihood that children developed depressive illness as adults. Such social studies emphasise that the focus on a medical response cannot address the wider causes that are at the root of these issues.

Conclusion

Zubin et al (1992) suggest that everyone has a different level of vulnerability to the development of mental health problems. Vulnerability may be the result of both biological factors and psychological factors. One of the mistakes that is often made is to assume that social workers all have the same views and will parrot them in any given situation or area of practice. This is far from the case. Mental health is an area where this appears to be particularly the case. I well remember being quite shocked by the hostile (not personal) attitudes to the approved social worker (ASW)/approved mental health professional (AMHP) role when I moved from practice to academic posts. I had, of course, thought that I was one of the good guys in practice, standing up for the rights of the marginalised. It was a shock to see that some colleagues viewed the role as a cog in the wheel of institutionalised oppression funded by 'big pharma'. Social work approaches are obviously influenced by the social model of illness. It is for individual practitioners to reach their own conclusions about where they stand on other issues about the validity of psychiatry as a discipline. These decisions will have an impact on the work and roles that social workers choose to take. A radical rejection of psychiatry influenced by, for example, Szasz (1963, 1971) should logically exclude one from statutory services or acting as an AMHP. In fact, a true follower of Szasz would be fundamentally opposed to social work and anything other than a residual welfare state (Cummins, 2018). I suspect that the overwhelming majority of social workers would place themselves somewhere in the centre of a continuum that had bio-psychiatry at one end and radical anti-psychiatry at the other. This allows for a model of practice that incorporates criticisms of mental health services, a commitment to working alongside service users to challenge discrimination and injustice, while recognising the impact that mental distress can have on individuals, families and communities.

TWO

Deinstitutionalisation and the development of community care

'Community care' is a term that has become a short hand for a range of policies. These policies have been introduced in a range of areas – adult and older people's services and services for people with learning disabilities. The term is most closely associated with the mental health field. It came to be a pejorative one that was most closely associated with the failings in mental health services in the late 1980s and early 1990s (Cummins, 2013). One of the key themes of this book is that any analysis of the current crisis in mental health services has to take account of the events of that period and the policy responses to it. Community care and its history is a key factor in the current position of mental health services. In tracing the history of community care, this chapter will explore the ways in which the progressive idealism that challenged coercive institutionalised forms of psychiatry has been replaced by a more bureaucratic dominated mode of mental health service. The original critics of institutional psychiatry, such as Laing, Foucault and Goffman, are a diverse group of thinkers. What they share is a concern with the way that psychiatry was a form of social control and an exercise in power. The chapter will argue that the impact of the failure of community care to live up to its original ideals is part of the reason for the continued focus on risk and risk management that are key elements of modern mental health practice.

The case for community care

On one level, it seems rather odd to have to make out the case for community based mental health services. Surely, the asylum regime has become so discredited. However, it is important to remember that the asylums were not always the institutions that they became or have become in the popular imagination. In addition, making the case or exploring the roots of community care can act as a counter to a backlash which has seen some argue for the return of the asylum. I have argued that community care is a progressive notion that was poorly implemented (Cummins, 2017b). It would be a mistake to assume that progressive values were the only factor. Financial factors cannot be ignored. The core values of community care – commitment to human dignity and respect for individuals are in danger of disappearing in a world of managerialist doublespeak. Turner and Columbo (2008) have argued that risk and risk management have replace a concern for the welfare of service users as the main focus of contact between service users and professionals. This constitutes a very clear indictment of the culture and structure of mental health services.

The air of therapeutic pessimism that pervades services and those working in them and using them is superbly produced in Nathan Filer's (2013) Costa award winning novel *The shock of the fall*. In the novel, the narrator, Matthew, is a young man who has been diagnosed with schizophrenia. He writes the novel at a day centre which, illustrating the financial pressures that mental health services face, is about to close down. He documents his own frustration with a system that seems to have lost sight of the humanitarian impulse which should form its base. He recounts the way that every cup, sticky note and pen on the ward has been provided by drug representatives. He cannot, therefore, escape the names of the drugs that he is being forced to take and that make him feel lethargic and worthless. Matthew attempts to share the causes of his distress and his understanding of it with staff. The nursing staff responsible for Matthew's care seem incapable of or unwilling to understand his growing frustration, pain and anxiety. They talk a form of officialese that reduces his emotional state to a series of meaningless managerial platitudes instead of a TIA that addresses these issues. This might be termed a trauma blindness approach. One of the great successes of the novel is the way that Matthew recognises that the staff are, in many ways, as unhappy and frustrated within this system as he is.

Asylums in crisis

Community care is a policy that is most closely associated with the late 1980s and early 1990s. However, the rates of admission to asylums had been declining since the 1930s. In 1954, there were 154,000 patients in British mental hospitals, in 2002/03 there were 33,000.[5] There have always been criticisms of the asylum regimes. The modern criticisms of the asylum can be traced back to the 1950s. The critical analysis of the asylum as an institution began in that decade and gathered momentum supported by a range of perspectives. Barton (1959) identified 'institutional neurosis' – a term that he used to identify the impact of the asylum regime on patients. He compared

[5]   https://publications.parliament.uk/pa/jt200405/jtselect/jtment/79/7908.htm

the impacts to those that they had been observed among concentration camp survivors. Wing (1962) outlined the ways in which the regime contributed to social withdrawal, meaning patients would struggle to manage independently outside of the hospital setting. There was a series of scandals in hospitals – for example, in Ely Hospital (Howe, 1969). Scott (1973) saw the asylum regime as one that made individuals passive and socially withdrawn. These studies highlight that the asylums were physically, culturally and socially isolated and isolating institutions cut off from reforming mainstream health and social developments.

Goffman: madness, stigma and the asylum as a total institution

Goffman's work on asylums has had a profound impact, not solely in the area of mental health. His work is an ethnographic study of a large psychiatric hospital. As noted above, Goffman (1963) published his work on stigma – *Stigma: Notes on a spoiled identity* – after *Asylums* (1961). However, the two can be taken together. In his sociological analysis of the impact of mental illness, Goffman (1961) saw it as a form of a challenge to the social normals. It is an example of what he termed 'havoc'. In a state of *havoc*, individuals cannot be 'self-governing'. The management of havoc is one of the key functions of society. This management has two major forms: the removal of the individual from the society; or the discrediting of the individual or the group. In the case of mental illness, both functions occur. Goffman outlined a process that he termed 'gathering', whereby family, friends and agencies of the state – such as social work and the police – combine to isolate individuals and mark the mentally ill as deviant.

In *Asylums* (1961), Goffman provides an analysis of daily life in the institution. As he notes in the total institution, the three areas of modern life – sleep, work and play – all take place within the same physical space. The term 'total institution' – coined by Everett Hughes, who taught Goffman as a post-graduate – covered institutions such as prisons, barracks and psychiatric units, where these barriers were broken down. In a total institution, all aspects of the inmates' daily lives are controlled by the staff group. In his work, Goffman argued that in these institutions staff developed a culture of hostility towards patients. The aim of the regime is to control the 'havoc' that led to the admission of the patient to the institution. This is done by series of formal but also informal rules that amount to an attempt to control totally all aspects of the individuals' lives. Any transgression is seen as evidence that confirms the original admission to the institution was justified.

In this schema, the institution functions as a means of social control. Goffman does not recognise the asylum as a therapeutic environment. More than this, he discounts the possibility of it ever becoming one.

In *Asylums*, Goffman outlined what he calls the 'moral career of the mental patient'. Career here means the process of professional involvement in the individual's life and ultimately the experiences of institutionalisation and social exclusion. He describes a process whereby 'pre-patients' – those who had not yet been admitted to the asylum – are surrounded by what he terms a 'circuit of agents': family, social workers and police. These combine to assess the behaviour of the individual and deem it unacceptable, requiring institutionalisation. Goffman describes the development of these concerns as a 'betrayal funnel'. Admission to the asylum is a form of *civil death* – the stripping away of individual dignity and the loss of identity. These processes involve the imposition of the institutional regime – one becomes or is made into a patient. From that point of admission onwards, daily life is run on a timetable and a set of regulations over which you have no real control. Total institutions operate on behaviourist lines with rewards – cigarettes, access to TV and other privileges. For Goffman, the institution is a powerful dehumanising machine. There is a paradox in its operation. The asylum regime seeks to deny individuality but by so doing patients are driven to maintain their own identity.

Goffman's analysis is based on his ethnographic study of the daily life at the institution where he was working. Despite this, the patients and their voices are strangely absent. The portrait of the regime is one that is fundamentally abusive. There appears to be little therapeutic input. There is also an air of paranoia in his description of the relationship between families, staff, other agencies and the patients. For example, the *betrayal funnel* can be seen as the increasing concerns of those trying to respond to the changed or worrying behaviour of their loved ones. This analysis sees all responses to mental illness as a form of social control. The major gap in this analysis is that it does not allow for any other motivation than a desire to exercise power and control.

Critical psychiatry and the challenge to asylums

Anti-psychiatry is a term that has come to cover a range of psychiatrists, sociologists and historians who, in the 1960s and 1970s, challenged the power of institutionalised psychiatry. Thinkers such as Laing, Szasz, Foucault, Goffman and Fanon presented a radical critique of the scientific basis and institutions of modern psychiatry (Cummins, 2017b). Laing, Szasz and Fanon were all psychiatrists but, aside from that, had little in common intellectually or politically. Szasz came from an anti-statist libertarian intellectual tradition. Laing was an apostle of the 1960s radical counterculture seeing psychiatry as part of the mechanisms of social control of late capitalism. Fanon was a radical critical political theorist. Scull (2011) argues that anti-psychiatry was a confused and often contradictory movement, demonstrated by such a diverse range of thinkers. In many senses, it was not a movement in the political sense. It is more accurately viewed as a loose grouping of critical perspectives on psychiatry. Psychiatry was a site of the radical debates about the nature of modern society.

Two of the most popular novels of post war American fiction *The Bell Jar* (Plath, 2005) and *One flew over the cuckoo's nest* (Kesey, 2005) explore the experiences of psychiatric patients. Kesey uses the psychiatric ward as a metaphor for the exploitative nature of modern capitalism. *The Bell Jar* examines the impact of social pressures on modern women. The position of psychiatry as a site of particular interest for the social sciences is demonstrated by the fact that major figures such as Foucault and Goffman produced work in this field. Major social theorists of today – for example, Wacquant and Garland – have focused on prisons rather than psychiatric hospitals to produce a contemporary analysis of social control mechanisms. The influence of Foucault and others is continuing and profound. Their analysis of psychiatry became the basis for a broader critique of society. In addition, critical psychiatry presents these issues in terms of civil rights. These concerns are based on the symbolic violence that is opposed on a marginalised group but also the conditions in asylums and the use of compulsory treatment.

In the huge range of work produced by these radical thinkers and critics, it is possible to identify key themes that form the basis of the challenge to institutionalised psychiatry. I would sum these up as follows:

- Psychiatry cannot be viewed as scientific.
- Psychiatric diagnosis is not a neutral act.
- Psychiatry is overly reliant on compulsory treatment.
- Institutionalised psychiatry is dehumanising and abusive.

These concerns continue to remain central to critical perspectives on the nature, role and structure of mental health service provision. One of the dangers is that the current crisis leads to the development of a somewhat nostalgic view of the asylum regime. This call for a return to the asylum overlooks the fact that these institutions were not able to consistently provide a therapeutic environment that treated patients with dignity and respect. The question is whether institutions in this form would ever be able to do so. For the radical tradition, the answer is an emphatic no.

The psychiatrists, novelists and sociologists who were grouped together under the label of anti or critical psychiatry had a profound influence on societal responses and attitudes to mental illness. Many more people will have read Plath or watched Forman's film of *One flew over the cuckoo's nest* than would have had direct personal experience of mental health services, particularly inpatient services. The critiques of institutionalised psychiatry discussed here and which helped to drive the development of community care remain relevant today. Mental health services are very different – perhaps not as different as we would like to think – but some of the key issues raised in that period are, largely, unresolved. Psychiatry remains overdependent on coercive institutionalised care, we continue to underfund mental health services, and the dominant psychiatric discourses still do not fully take account of the social, cultural and economic factors that impact on mental illness. Since the period of the late 1960s, the growth of bio-psychiatry, as symbolised by the growth of the DSM over the course of five editions, is evidence of this.

The asylum developed into a Gothic institution. Asylums were seen as austere, forbidding places cut off from the wider society. The mere name of the local asylum carried with it a series of messages not only about the institution but also the patients. Isolated geographically and psychologically from wider society, the asylum has come to represent a broader set of responses to mental illness. The reality is more complex than this image suggests. The motivations for the establishment of these institutions and the regimes that they produced are more complex than some narratives of institutionalisation allow. I should be clear here: I am not denying that the asylum regime was abusive but we need to recognise that they also represented some form of progress.

Scull (1977) argues that the development of the asylum has to be understood as part of a wider Victorian response to the problems of urban poverty. It is one of the modern institutions of social control that developed during the early Victorian period – schools, prisons and factories were other examples. These institutions are seen as producing capable workers and citizens but also punishing or disciplining miscreants. In Scull's analysis, the 'mad' present a difficulty in that they are not deemed to be productive members of capitalist society. The solution is therefore to isolate or remove such individuals. It is important to note that Scull here is focusing on the urban poor. There has always been separate provision for the rich and wealthy – a fact of mental health services that continues to this day. As well as being part of the process that confirmed psychiatry's status as a distinct branch of medicine and all that entailed in terms of professional status, the asylum acted as a warning of the potential dangers of not conforming to societal norms and expectations.

The development of community care was influenced by critiques of the asylum regime. It might seem somewhat bizarre that one of the most influential of these is, in fact, not an analysis of the institutionalised psychiatry of the 1960s and 1970s when writers such as Laing and Szasz were working. It is rather a historical study. Foucault (2001) *Madness and civilization: A history of insanity in the age of reason* is an iconic and ground breaking analysis of the development of asylums in France. Despite the fact that it is concerned with a specific period in French intellectual history, this work has become one of the most influential in any discussion of the role of psychiatry. More generally, Foucault's work is concerned with the exercise of power both by individuals and the state. He examined the development of the institutions of the prison and the asylum but also attitudes to sexuality. In *Discipline and punish* (1991), Foucault argued that we live in a disciplinary society where power is exercised through a series of institutions. For Foucault, power and knowledge are inextricably linked. Power is a function of knowledge. Foucault argued that power is everywhere. It is not simply exercised by individuals or institutions when there is a transgression. Power/knowledge can also open up new ways of thinking about ourselves as the exercise of power also means resistance. Foucault (1982) argued that a series of what he termed 'dividing practices' have developed whereby subjects become objectified as 'mad', 'sick' and so on. These practices are the application of a branch of knowledge from, for example, medicine that justifies the institutionalisation of the subject. This process of the development and application of knowledge is clearly an example of the exercise of power. It also leads to the creation of new categories of subject or cases or, as he puts it, 'specifications of individuals'. Thus the modern 'mental health patient' is the creation of the production and application of psychiatric knowledge. These specifications or classes and categories of individual/patient become increasingly more detailed and complex. This is the result of the processes of production and application of knowledge becoming more detailed and complex.

Scull (1977) argued that there was an underinvestment in the asylum regime, which reflected the view that the individual patients were regarded as unproductive. Foucault presented a somewhat contradictory position suggesting that the level of investment that did take place is indicative of the symbolic role that the asylums played in society. As noted previously, the geographical isolation of the asylums was a key factor in their development as institutions. Foucault examined the architectural design of both asylums and prisons. His analysis of the two institutions has many overlaps. For Foucault, the panopticon proposed by Bentham was not simply an architectural design: it was the physical representation of a new disciplinary society. The core of this society was the surveillance of the individual or communities deemed to be potentially deviant. The new institutions of modern society and new forms of knowledge about populations allowed for the production of what he termed a 'carceral archipelago' for the management of society. Both prisons and asylums consistently failed in their alleged aims to produce model citizens/workers. However, for Foucault, this is a misunderstanding of the ultimate role of such institutions, which is the management – not the treatment, reform or rehabilitation – of deviant populations. The modern disciplinary society involves a shift from the management of the body to the management of the psyche.

The accounts that Foucault and Scull provide are counterpoints to a Whig interpretation of the history of the asylum. This perspective argues that the asylum as an institution was an improvement on the previous approaches. These amounted to the societal abandonment of the 'mad'. Such a view would regard reformers, such as Tuke at York, as motivated by the basic humanitarian impulse that it is the driving force of medicine. Critical theory challenged the notion of the neutrality of the medical profession seeing it linked to social control. Ignatieff (1985) argues that the liberal notion of the asylum as progressive is based on a series of key notions. The first is that mental illness is an illness. This fundamental notion has been challenged by all those thinkers seen as part of the anti-psychiatry movement (Cummins, 2017b). Mental illness is seen to constitute a core part of the human condition. Finally, the dominant position of the medical profession in the assessment and treatment of mental illness is seen as appropriate. In this model, which sees the development of the asylum as part of a progressive response, the development of psychiatry as a profession involves the application of a new rational technocratic body of knowledge to the treatment of mental illness. This is naturally a top down process. Patients are subjects. This status is an exclusionary one, entailing or justifying the removal of civic and social rights. This analysis sees the motor of change for reform as individuals who expose the failings of the old regime.

Martin (1985) highlighted the failings in the asylum regime. He argued that abuses were inherent within the asylum regime. It was not a question of abusive individuals but systemic faults. These included, for example, the fact that the institutions were isolated but also there were small numbers of staff with overall responsibility for large numbers of patients. The physical layout of the wards – dormitory accommodation and so on – meant that abuse or the potential for abuse was at the core of the regime. Martin found that those patients who were most isolated, those with fewer visitors or had no family members were at greater risk of abuse. He identified a lack of leadership from senior staff and consultants. The lack of a therapeutic environment, the lack of contact with mainstream services and isolation, alongside poor staff attitudes and practice are very redolent of Rosenhan (1975) . The picture Martin (1985) painted is a very bleak one – crowded and dysfunctional institutions with poorly paid and poorly trained staff with a lack of commitment to an ethic of care. The scandals that Martin outlined were part of the impulse and drive to community care. Regrettably, the features of abusive institutions that Martin outlined have appeared and continue to be present in a number of scandals in this field. For example, the abuse that was exposed at Winterbourne View – a facility for people with learning disabilities (Flynn and Citarella, 2013) – showed that there is potential even in smaller, community based facilities for abusive cultures to develop.

The portrayal of the asylum has focused on the dehumanising aspects that have been explored above. There have been limited attempts to examine the asylum as a complex institution. One exception is the Gittins (1998) history of the Severalls Hospital in Essex. It is important to emphasise that this is not a study that overlooks the abusive aspects of asylum regimes. It does, however, recognise that the asylums were communities – with a range of facilities and social facilities. This is not a naive view that attempts to gloss over the abuses that occurred. It is rather an acknowledgement that there were some positive elements in these settings. These institutions were, after all, 'home' to the patients for long periods. Generations of staff often worked in the same hospital – a potential for a secretive and abusive culture – but also a potential strength. Gittins argued that for some groups the asylum was an alternative to life outside. For example, she outlines the way that working class women who were patients often faced a life that was dominated by poverty, pregnancy and abuse. However, ultimately, the asylum was unable to prevent the development of institutional abusive cultures. This is not to suggest that there were not humane and decent staff working in these institutions. It is a recognition of the fundamentally exclusionary nature of a regime that subjected individuals to inhumane and degrading treatment and denied them full citizenship.

Perspectives on deinstitutionalisation

Enoch Powell's (1961) Water Tower speech (1961) can be regarded as the start of the policy of community care in England and Wales. One of the ironies of the community care a policy is that, on the whole, it is associated with progressive values and claims, but in the UK, its introduction was largely overseen by Conservatives committed to a reduction in the welfare state. The liberal interpretation of the rise and fall of the asylum focuses on the humanitarian impulse of reformers. In this narrative, the development of new major tranquillisers is seen as a key factor and moment in the policy history. Pilgrim and Rogers (2013) note that this is problematic as it does not explain how community care came to be an umbrella policy adopted across a number of settings. This was made most explicit by the introduction of the NHS and Community Care Act 1990. By the 1980s, the pressures on the asylum regimes meant that they were no longer sustainable. Community care was a policy that was adapted across a range of areas. However, it came to be most closely associated with mental health policy and the failure to develop properly funded and resourced mental health services.

The drive towards community care was heavily influenced by the challenge to the conditions in the institutions. There are many strands of thought within this movement which succeeded in making the treatment of mental illness in its coercive institutionalised form an issue of human rights. Radical theorists, such as Basaglia (Foot, 2015) in Italy, used their critique of mental health services as part of a wider attack on capitalism. In these schemas, the treatment of mental health patients came to be representative of the broader inequities of the system. Basaglia was able to oversee the dismantling of a hospital based system of psychiatric care. Laing established short-lived attempts at therapeutic communities. These radical alternatives are the exception in that community care was based on an assumption that some form of institutional care would remain in place. Those institutions would be very different from the asylums of the 1950s – there would be places based on core values of dignity. The division between institution and community care is essentially false – there will be a need for both. Inspired by the work of Goffman (1963), it was argued that prolonged periods in hospital are damaging to individuals. Therefore, services need to be able to intervene at an early stage to provide support. This is an essentially public health model of provision involving tiers of service. Asylums had resulted in an imbalance as most of the funds were concentrated in this sector. There is a similar imbalance within modern mental health service. Budgets are still dominated by the provision of services related to acute inpatient care.

Basaglia: Law 180, radical politics and mental health reform.

The Italian psychiatrist Franco Basaglia and the work that he undertook in the reform of the Italian mental health system came to be seen as a potential model for community based services in the UK. His work in the late 1970s and early 1980s was seen as ground breaking. In Ingleby's (1980) influential text *Critical psychiatry: The politics of mental health*, the reforms that Basaglia had a key role in enacting are given particular prominence. Basaglia's work needs to be understood in the context of a much broader political tradition (Foot, 2015). Influenced by the work of the Marxist political theoretician, Antonio Gramsci (1891–1937), Basaglia regarded the treatment of the mentally ill as a case study in the marginalisation of a group and the systematic of denial of civil and political rights.

Basaglia was born in Venice in 1924. In 1944, he was imprisoned because of his opposition to Italian fascism. This was, not surprisingly, a seminal moment in the development of Basaglia's political ideas and had a profound influence on his career as a psychiatrist (Cummins, 2016a). He was an outstanding student who appeared to be destined for a glittering academic career. However, he fell foul of the bitter world of academic politics. He was moved in 1961 to a post of Director of the Asylum at Gorizia. This was clearly seen as a punishment (Foot, 2015). Gorizia is a small time in northern Italy on the border with modern day Slovenia: a geographical outpost and psychiatry was an outpost within medicine. This physical and professional isolation meant that Basaglia was in a position to put his radical ideas into practice. Basaglia frequently compared the conditions in the asylum in Gorizia, where he later was appointed as medical director, to those that he had experienced as a prisoner. He was influenced by Goffman's (1963) notion of a total institution.

When he arrived in Gorizia, Basaglia was shocked by the physical conditions that greeted him. The wards were dirty and patients lived in insanitary conditions. In addition, there was a culture where patients were routinely subject to violence and restraint. Basaglia made an explicit comparison between these conditions and concentration camps (Cummins, 2016a). Basaglia was profoundly influenced by the work of the Italian Holocaust survivor, Primo Levi. Levi himself rejected this comparison between the two total institutions. Basaglia held the, possibly over romanticised, view that psychiatric patients should be seen as a class of political refugee from the conformity of capitalist society. The asylum regime thus acts to punish this departure from social norms. This may appear jarring in the modern context but it was a theme in radical critiques of psychiatry and the asylum regime. It is present in *One flew over the cuckoo's nest* (Kesey, 2005) and in Marcuse's (1964) *One-dimensional man.*

Basaglia was a charismatic radical. He did not think that the asylum could be reformed. He set about dismantling the institution. The team that surrounded at him at Gorizia represented a revolutionary cadre. The new regime that he established represented a complete shift from the previous one. The coercive abusive regime with its emphasis on physical restraint was abolished. A new working culture was developed. As far as possible, the divide between staff and patients, a key feature of Goffman's total institution, would be abolished. The most important symbol of the ancien regime was the use of electroconvulsive therapy (ECT). The symbolism of abandoning its use cannot be overestimated. Daily life at Gorizia was dominated by a series of open daily meetings where staff and patients came together to make major decisions. Thus Gorizia was very much in keeping with the anti-authoritarian spirit of the 1968 protests.

Law 180

The Italian Mental Health Act 1978 came to be known as Basaglia's Law or Law 180. It can be seen as the culmination of the work that he began at Gorizia. His aim was to end the possibility of indefinite detention which previous legislation allowed. Law 180 established that dangerousness was no longer grounds for detention. Compulsory admission had to be to a psychiatric unit attached to a general hospital. The asylum was effectively abolished, replaced by a series of out-patient clinics and wards in general hospitals. This model was often held up as one that community care in England and Wales should follow.

Critical perspectives on Basaglia

Basaglia's work faced a similar range of criticisms to Foucault in that he was seen to have made the position of patients worse. This perspective argues that the asylum might have been abolished but what actually replaced it? For many, the answer was not a great deal, certainly not an integrated, fully funded system of community based mental health services (Cummins, 2016a). There are clear overlaps with the experience of community care in the UK. For example, Basaglia's reforms lost significant support following a murder committed by a former patient. Giovanni Miklus attacked his wife with a hammer. Basaglia and one of his colleagues were charged but cleared of manslaughter (Foot, 2015). There is a second more theoretical critical perspective on Basaglia. Papeschi (1985) argued that while Basaglia does not seek to deny the existence of mental illness, he sees the causes as only social. In Basaglia's schema, mental illness became an essentially social problem, thus the solutions to it were to be found in changing social attitudes alongside a new range of welfare and political policies. Basaglia's radical politics led him to classify the asylum alongside other 'institutions of violence' which generate and reproduce the conditions of social exclusion. Thus Basaglia is seen, from this perspective, as a radical utopian who is ultimately committed to a revolutionary transformative politics. Papeschi (1985) argues that in this argument, the real damaging impact of mental illness is not fully recognised – another criticism of radicals such as Laing.

One of the great achievements of Basaglia and other radical critics of psychiatry and the asylum as an institution was that they were able to bring the totally unacceptable and abusive practices of the asylum to the attention of a national and international public. This did this by successfully and properly recasting the issue of institutionalised psychiatric care as one of human rights. If we strip away some of the excesses of Basaglia's argument, at its core is a claim for the recognition of the dignity and thus the human rights of those who were abandoned in the Gorizia asylum and similar institutions.

Fanon, race and psychiatry

Frantz Fanon was a radical political theorist and activist. Born in Martinique, which was under French colonial rule, in 1924, he served with the Free French forces in World War II. After the war, he studied medicine and then qualified as a psychiatrist. He moved to Algeria and was a member in the Algerian Font de Liberation (FLN) that fought against French colonial rule. He was deported to the US and died of leukaemia in 1961. Fanon's work is discussed here as it is part of the radical critique of psychiatry. In particular, he examined the relationship between psychiatry and the colonial processes of 'Othering' that are outlined in Said's (1978) *Orientalism*. The influence of Fanon has been to recognise that these Othering processes continue in the post-colonial world.

Said and Othering

Said identified three interrelated aspects of the process of Othering:

- *Homogenisation:* the cultures of a region are stripped of their diversity and complexity and become one.
- *Binary representation:* there is a divide between East/West with the colonised becoming an inferior or subaltern culture.
- *Essentialism:* the complexity of individuals and cultures is abandoned in a favour of series cultural characteristics that are regarded as innate and unchanging.

Said's work has been used as the basis for a series of insights from critical theory into the development of social attitudes to minorities. It is important to emphasise that these dominant narratives are never accepted in a simplistic fashion. They are always the site of challenge and debate.

Black Skin, White Masks

This is Fanon's most famous and widely read work. It is now, rightly, regarded as a classic of anti-colonial literature. It was first published in 1952 and is a version of his rejected doctoral thesis. Fanon's work seeks to examine the psychological impact of colonialism. The economic and social impacts were readily apparent in the exploitation of the natural resources and peoples of colonised lands. Alongside this, there existed a society where settlers controlled a society and power was exercised along clear racial lines. Fanon argued that the distorting nature of these societies produces trauma. Colonialism rules by violence, fear and segregation. The native culture is trivialised and robbed of significance and value. For Fanon, decolonisation is required to have two important aspects. The first is clearly the removal of the colonial power. The second is to overcome the alienation and dehumanisation that results from a position as a subaltern population (Macey, 2001).

Racism and mental health services

At first sight, it would appear that Fanon's work is perhaps more relevant to revolutionary politics than debates about mental health services. Fanon was a psychiatrist but much of his writing is not in this area. The starting point has to be an acknowledgement that the legacies of colonialism and racism remain. In 2002, Keating et al, in *Breaking the circles of fear*, outline the discrimination black men experience with regards to mental health services. The overall view is that this still remains, in too many areas, a coercive rather than therapeutic experience as *Breaking the circles of fear* and *Delivering race equality* (Britain,2005) highlight. Prospero and Kim (2009) explore the ways in which this historical legacy and current practice combine to deter black people from seeking help at an early stage. This continues to be a fundamental problem that mental health services, despite a range of policy initiatives, have failed to tackle. The focus on the experiences of young black men should not give the impression that there are not similar or overlapping ones for women. *Delivering race equality* (Britain, 2005) was established following the inquiry into the death of David Bennett (Blofeld et al, 2003). This five-year action plan was an attempt to tackle these deep seated issues, producing services that were more sensitive to community needs including a target of the recruitment of 500 community development workers. In 2010, *Delivering race equality* came to an end having failed to reach this target. The discussion of race has been marginalised by an adoption of a much broader 'equalities' agenda. Omonira-Oyekanmi (2014) emphasises that it is still the case that young black men are still more likely to be detained under the MHA, restrained or be highly medicated. These personal experiences are supported by wider evidence from the CQC's reports *Count Me In* (2011) and the annual review of the MHA in 2015. In outlining the case for reform of the MHA, Theresa May highlighted the over-representation of young black men in mental health services and the use of compulsory powers to detain them as evidence that the act was failing (Savage, 2017).

Singh and Burns (2006) have strongly argued that the charge that psychiatry and mental health services are institutionally racist does not hold. They suggest that rates of mental illness are higher across the world for all migrant groups – for example, rates of schizophrenia are higher among Finns who emigrate to Sweden and Britons who move to Australia. It is the dislocating experience of emigration that links these groups. It could be countered that this does not mean that these groups are not experiencing forms of discrimination. Singh and Burns (2006) are, surely, correct in their assertion that the problems of racism or over-representation of black, Asian and minority ethnic (BAME) communities within mental health services cannot solely be laid at the door of psychiatry. However, this is not quite the same as suggesting that there are no issues related to race within mental health services when there clearly are. The radical nature of Fanon's work is that he shows that psychiatry had a clear role in the delineation of a series of stereotypes based on racism (Macey, 2001). His work has been the basis for calls for a truly transcultural model of mental health. This would involve a recognition and understanding of the complex political, social, historical and economic factors that create the environments and social space in which mental health professionals and service users exist and interact.

Community care, inquiries and the media reporting of mental health issues

As noted above, community care as a policy has been tainted by an association with the failures that took place in the late 1980s and early 1990s. In exploring the roots of this failure it is possible to track a path back to the fundamentals of community care services based on dignity and respect for individuals. At the core of such services there needs to be a strong set of values. In mental health and other services, there has been too great a focus on organisational structures. The response to the failings of community care was to produce a more bureaucratic system, losing the elements of radical social justice approaches that were part of the initial spark for its introduction.

The process of deinstitutionalisation was meant to replace the discredited asylums with a range of community based services. This would ensure that the civil death that Goffman outlined would no longer occur. The asylum was a closed and hidden institution; the majority of the population had little, if any, knowledge or contact with them (Philo, 1987; Scull, 1989). This is probably as true of mental health units as it was of the asylums. One of the key aims of community care was to ensure that the secretive culture of mental health provision would be if not removed then challenged. However, community care was never able to establish inclusive services. Moon (2000) notes that the physical separation of the asylum continued into the community. The paradox at the heart of the community care is that it has failed to overcome many of the barriers to social citizenship that it sought to end. For many reasons – economic, social and political – the promise of well-resourced community mental health services never materialised. These processes whereby those with the most complex needs were often living in the poorest neighbourhoods, poor quality supported housing, or on the streets or in the prison system (Moon, 2000; Wolff, 2005; Singleton et al, 1998) have been termed 'transinstitutionalisation'.

In 1998, when he introduced the document *Modernising mental health services* (DH, 1998), Frank Dobson announced that 'community care has failed'. The document argued that services were underfunded and suffered from organisational issues – for example health and social care team boundaries were not coterminous. The document also argued that there was too great an emphasis on the rights of individuals at the expense of the concerns of their friends and families. The policy document also suggested that the legal framework was outdated – this was the first shot in the process of the reform of the MHA and the introduction of CTOs. The New Labour policy document has many of the themes that were evident in a series of inquiries into failure in community care services (Ritchie, 1994; Blom-Cooper et al 1995). The focus of these inquiries was on individual cases and the failings of particular agencies. They also examined the legislative and policy framework, seeking solutions in proposing new legislation or forms of service audit. The result was the creation of an audit culture with a focus on risk management. In addition, risk averse organisational cultures developed where practitioners were very concerned that they might be caught up in an inquiry. There are clear parallels with developments in child protection social work where the response to failings in the system has been a shift in the emphasis in policy and practice. The early 1990s saw *The Care Programme Approach* (CPA), *Supervised discharge* and *supervision registers* introduced. *Supervised discharge* and *supervision registers* have been abandoned. *Supervised discharge* was a short-lived forerunner of the current *community treatment order* legislation.

The media portrayal of community care was a consistent factor in the undermining of attempts to create a popular base for support of the policy. In the early 1990s, the media focused on a series of violent offences, particularly homicides, committed by individuals in contact with mental health services. Cohen's (1972) notion of a 'moral panic' is concerned with the ways that the media, particularly the press and later TV, produce a representation of events. Crime is a constant feature of news media and many moral panics are related to these issues, or youth movements or subcultures. Cohen also noted that moral panics develop as a reflection of wider social anxieties and unease. It should be emphasised that in Cohen's schema a moral panic does not appear out of thin air. There is some basis for the concerns raised; the panic is used to identify the reaction and over-reaction of the authorities, media and other commentators. This is particularly important in this area as there is a danger that the moral panic analysis is sometimes used to argue that there are no grounds for concern.

One of the key features of the moral panic is the creation of the figure of the modern folk devil. Modern folk devils have included teddy boys, mods, punk rockers, muggers and paedophiles. These are figures who are 'discovered' or created by media outlets and seen as posing some sort of existential threat to society. Cummins (2012) has shown that in the history of the community care, the folk devil was the 'schizophrenic'. There was an intersection between race and class here as the media portrayals of community care focused on a series of cases involving young working class black men – usually convicted of a violent crime. Cummins (2010) uses the highest profile inquiry of the period – the *Ritchie Inquiry into the care and treatment of Christopher Clunis* (Ritchie, 1994) – to illustrate this point. Cross (2010) notes that the continuing representations of the mad emphasise physicality – size, uncontrollable hair – as a signifier of irrationality but also as a way to underline the imagined threat that the mentally ill pose to the wider community. In the case of Christopher Clunis, these representations of the mad overlap deeply engrained racist stereotypes of young black men. The Clunis case became a cipher for the wider failings of the system and was a constant reference point in the reporting of the issues. The image of Clunis, heavily medicated and staring blankly out from a prison van as he is driven away from court following his sentencing for manslaughter, was reproduced on numerous occasions in discussions of community care (Cummins, 2010).

Hall et al's (2013) analysis of moral panics highlights the way that an event triggers 'public disquiet'. The response to this disquiet includes not only public authorities but the media, which has an important mediation role between the state and the formation of public opinion. Media is plural so it is important to remember that within it there are competing ideas and themes – this is a combination of political and economic factors. In the case of mental health policy in the early and mid-1990s, key figures or 'moral entrepreneurs' – as Cohen termed these public figures – included Jayne Zito who, following the murder of her husband Jonathan, founded the Zito Trust and Marjorie Wallace, a very well-connected journalist and founder of SANE (Schizophrenia A National Emergency). Both were seen as being experts and appeared in the media frequently and were able to influence debates and the development of policy. Both came from a position that saw community care as failing but also that the so-called rights agenda had become too powerful. The Zito Trust closed when the reform of the MHA was complete and CTOs introduced. Wallace continues to appear regularly in the popular press and on TV putting forward the argument that mental health laws are too liberal and there is a need for a return of an asylum style system.

The media reporting of the failures of community care can be analysed via the lens of Cohen's moral panic thesis (Butler and Drakeford, 2005). By highlighting violent crimes committed by people with severe mental health problems, the media helped to create the impression that the 'mad' had been released from asylums and now posed a threat to the local populace. The dynamic of the panic creates a call 'for something to be done'. The asylums could not be rebuilt but new forms of surveillance emerged culminating in the introduction of CTOs. The introduction of CTOs can be seen as a legal and symbolic confirmation that the hopes of community care had been abandoned.

Policy responses to the crisis in community care

The circular HC (90)23/LASSL (90)11 established the CPA. The initial aim of the CPA was to develop a system of case management to ensure that services were provided to those in most need because of their mental health problems. It was a response to the failings of services highlighted by, for example, the Spokes inquiry (DHSS, 1988) into the murder of social worker Isabel Schwarz, as well as wider concerns about the rise in homelessness. Simpson et al (2003) argue the aim of the CPA was initially to improve services. However, in its implementation, it shared a number of the wider characteristics of New Public Management such as audit and regulation (Pollitt and Bouckaert, 2003). The establishment of the CPA brought with it added layers of bureaucracy and audit which did not seem to enhance the effective provision of mental health services. Each service user who was registered on the CPA was meant to have a care plan, key worker and regular reviews. The system became more focused on audit than the provision of care. Simpson et al (2003) argue there were few agreed procedures for risk assessments, care plans were often found to be ineffective and some areas had difficulty keeping up regular reviews. Service users and carers were more likely to be invited to reviews but often found them formal and intimidating and arranged at the convenience of medical staff (Simpson et al 2003: 493).

The introduction of the CPA was followed in 1993 by *Guidance on the Introduction of Supervision Registers*. People considered to be 'at risk of harming themselves or other people' could be placed on a supervision register, with the aim of ensuring that they remain in contact with mental health services. The argument here is not that these particular individuals did not need support from community based mental health services. It is rather questioning not only the effectiveness of such measures as a means of enhancing the delivery of that support but also noting the role that such developments play in the construction of the 'mad' stereotype.

If the difficulties in community care were structural and organisational, then the responses were focused on legislation and policy. A number of inquiries, including the Ritchie Inquiry (1994), suggested that there should be reforms to legislation including consideration of some form of CTO. It also recommended that the establishment of specialist teams to work with those patients who were seen as 'difficult to engage'. The changes in policy and reform of legislation ultimately led to the reform of the MHA. This was a complex and certainly not a linear process. The reform was eventually completed in 2007 but the process was a prolonged one. The failings of community care cast a long shadow and were one of the key drivers in this process.

Modernising mental health services (DH, 1998) New Labour's vision for mental health services provided a very clear analysis of what the new administration saw as the failings of community care. These criticisms included poorly funded and organised services, and a lack of support for families and carers. The document also described the legal framework as 'outdated'. This is a phrase open to interpretation but the review argued that the MHA was based on an institutionalised model of care. The legal and policy framework was not flexible enough to meet the new environment of community care. New Labour was committed to introducing the Human Rights Act 1998 and it was felt that mental health legislation needed to be reformed to be compatible with it. These moves can also be seen as part of the New Labour reforming and modernising project. Some of the key features of the New Labour project and its view of citizenship can be seen in these moves to overhaul mental health policy. Gostin (2007) argues that the reform of the 1959 MHA and the introduction of the 1983 MHA was part of a shift from a paternalist to a rights' based module. The 2007 reform is a significant move to a 'responsibility agenda'.

CTOs exist in a number of jurisdictions across North America, New Zealand and Australia. The CTO that was introduced in England and Wales was heavily influenced by mental health legislation that exists in New Zealand and Australia. CTOs essentially allow for conditions to be placed on the discharge of patients who are detained under Section 3 of the MHA. Conditions might include taking medication, keeping appointments or living at an approved address. Supervised discharge allowed for similar conditions to be imposed. However, there is a fundamental difference − the power of recall. Patients subject to the provisions of a CTO are subject to recall to hospital if they fail to comply with the conditions or there are concerns about their mental health. The introduction of the power of recall was designed to ensure that mental health professionals could intervene at an earlier stage if they had concerns about an individual. The power of recall means that there is no requirement for a further MHA assessment. The period of recall is for a period of up to 72 hours. Compulsion and coercion have been features of institutionalised care for as long as it has existed. This is an extension of that theme. There is a strong narrative in the Ritchie Inquiry and similar inquiry reports that a form of CTO would have ensured that vulnerable patients remained in contact with services. One factor is the assumption that this would have ensured that the patients continued to take prescribed medication. The logic here is that these interventions, particularly medication, would have prevented the awful violent events that precipitated the inquiry. This is obviously unknowable but is surely too great a claim to make. No configuration of mental health services, legislation and resources could possibly guarantee that no such event would occur. CTOs are thus presented as a protective, paternalistic measure that will prevent the repeated admission of individuals to hospital.

When they were introduced, the government assured concerned service user groups and mental health professionals that CTOs would be used in very few cases. This was either disingenuous or naive or a combination of the two. Once such legislation was introduced, mental health professionals would be almost bound to consider it whenever a patient detained on Section 3 was being discharged. In a professional culture that is dominated by the ever present fear of 'appearing at an inquiry or in the Coroner's court' then it was inevitable that the use of CTOs soon became an established feature of the mental health practice. Warden (1998) saw the publication of *Modernising mental health services* as marking the end of community care. This might be overstating the case. However, the introduction of CTOs clearly marks a shift. Progressive idealism has been replaced a bureaucratic functionalism. In this process, the rights of severely mentally ill were restricted. The only group subject to recall by the state are convicted offenders who breach parole conditions. It is important to emphasise that being mentally ill is not a crime. The fact is that recall to hospital without any requirement for a further formal mental health assessment represents a significant shift in the balance between individuals and the state.

Conclusion

One of the key themes of this book is that the development of mental health policy since 1983 can be understood as a reaction to the failings of community care. Societal responses to mental illness have always involved taking into account the rights and autonomy of individuals and balancing these against a wider paternalism (Eastman and Starling, 2006). The development of mental health policy has many echoes of that of penal policy in this period (Cummins, 2010). The response to the crisis was an increasingly coercive legal framework – one which was largely accepted across the party political spectrum. It is perhaps indicative of the reduced status or importance given to mental health issues and patients that such a fundamental shift in the relationship between a group of individuals and the state could be introduced with relatively little political opposition.

Policy development is not linear; it is messy, complex and at times contradictory. In looking at the history of community care since 1983, one is forced to confront a paradox that lies at its heart. In many ways, the rights of the mentally ill are on a much stronger footing, particularly when contrasted with the period of institutionalisation. Those who experience discrimination on the basis of mental illness in the workplace can challenge this. There is wider discussion and acknowledgement of the impact of mental illness. These moves take place alongside campaigns to challenge the stigma and fear that is still far too readily attached to these issues. Mental health professionals have a greater range of approaches to tackling the impact of mental illness. There is a long way to go but there is a much greater recognition that service users need to be at the core of decision making. However, these developments are not consistent. As this consideration of the development of community care shows, the policies and legislation that have the impact on those with the most complex needs have not reflected these progressive themes and ideals. The 1983 MHA – passed by the first Thatcher government – established under Section 117 a right to aftercare for those detained under Section 3. The failure to provide this legal entitlement to one of the most vulnerable groups was recast via the tabloid media and a series of recommendation in inquiries as fundamentally an issue of law and order.

The development of mental health policy cannot be divorced from the broader issues of risk, social work and the development of an audit culture (Beck, 1992; Webb, 2006). These trends are visible across social work as a profession (Warner, 2015). Bauman (2007) argues that the state claims legitimacy by its ability to protect its citizens. In modern society, there is an increasing range of internal and external threats. States and political elites face the danger of losing legitimacy if they are unable to deal with such threats. These threats are seen to include the 'madman' of tabloid legend. In the early 1990s, the UK government of John Major faced a crisis of legitimacy and credibility in a number of areas. Mental health policy became one of these. The response to the crisis in mental health was ultimately framed by the terms of reference provided by the tabloid media. There was little if any attempt to challenge to the key and fundamental premise of much of this reporting – for example, the implicit assumption that the mentally ill are violent – or to acknowledge the complexities of the issues or the potential limits of mental health services. It is simply not possible for any mental health service – however comprehensive – to be able to say that a homicide will not occur. The response was one that sought new forms of surveillance and control – the ultimate being the CTO. The optimism of the initial phases of de-institutionalisation was replaced by the key features of the audit culture that spread across public services from the late 1980s onwards – registration, review and inspection.

THREE

Citizenship and mental health

Introduction

This chapter examines broader notions of citizenship, placing the impact of discrimination against people with mental health problems within this context. It argues that the discrimination that people with mental health problems face amounts to an ongoing denial of the full rights that citizenship should bestow. It then goes on to examine the impact of neoliberal social policy and austerity. These policies in the UK have increased inequality and poverty, which have broader impacts on mental health. In addition, the reforms of the welfare system have targeted people with mental health problems who are in receipt of benefits.

Two important recent works – Scull's (2015) *Madness in civilisation: A cultural history of insanity* and Foot's (2015) *The man who closed the asylums* – highlight the barriers that had to be overcome in the struggle to humanise mental health provision. Scull (2015) shows the way that all cultures, in myriad ways, engage with the experiences of what we can loosely term mental distress. His work also illustrates that societal responses have often involved processes of exclusion, seclusion and abuse. Foot's (2015) study of Franco Basaglia makes very clear the essential political nature of the structure and delivery of mental health care. There is an implicit danger that, in examining the current crisis in community mental health services, the failures and abuses of the past are assigned to history. The assumption being that such progress has been made that these issues are now resolved. The impacts of major mental illness are clearly social as they affect people's opportunities to work, relationships with loved ones and other areas of life. There is a loop here as this social marginalisation, by its nature, has potentially damaging impacts on an individual's mental health and sense of wellbeing.

Mental health is a political as well as personal issue as it intersects a number of areas – social, cultural and economic. In addition, one needs to examine a range of other issues including the power of psychiatry and other mental health professionals. A mental health diagnosis can have ramifications in a number of areas – one's own personal sense of identity but also in areas such as employment and the legal system.

Decisions about the structure and nature of mental health provision are complex manifestations of underlying societal attitudes but also the state of professional knowledge and political values. In this chapter, I will examine attitudes to the welfare state broadly but link these to the resultant configuration of mental health services. In the final section of this chapter, I will consider the work of the American feminist legal scholar Martha Finemann. She argues that the dominant narratives of individualism are based on misleading notions of autonomy.

Neoliberalism

The dominance of neoliberal ideas or governments influenced by its key premises – the need for an economic sphere that is free from state inference and the importance of low levels of personal taxation – is one of the most significant developments in politics and broader culture since the mid-1970s. The political and electoral success of Thatcher in the UK in 1979 followed by Reagan in 1980 in the US ushered in a new political era. The neoliberal doctrines of the Chicago School had been imposed on Chile following General Pinochet's military coup and the murder of the democratically elected Marxist socialist President Allende (Brown, 2015). Pinochet's appearance on the cover of David Harvey's (2005) Marxist analysis of neoliberalism – alongside Thatcher and Reagan – is indicative of the importance of Chile in the ideology's history. The electoral triumphs of Thatcher and Reagan followed by the aping of some of their policies by nominally progressive governments such as Clinton and Blair administrations have been used by some commentators to support a thesis that these triumphs were, in some way, inevitable (Sandbrook, 2013; Moore, 2014). Stedman-Jones (2012) notes that this ignores the contingencies of history. For example, in the case of Mrs Thatcher what might have happened if the Argentinian dictatorship of General Galtieri had not invaded the Falkland Islands in the early summer of 1982 when her government's popularity was at its lowest point is a matter of conjecture.

Key themes in neoliberal thought

In an attempt to depoliticise its core aims, neoliberalism is often presented or attempts to present itself as a technical rational economic exercise. However, it has to be seen as a political project (Wacquant, 2009a). Brown (2015) provides an analysis of the contemporary forms of neoliberalism. At its core, is what Brown terms (2015: 70) the 'financialization of everything'. This excludes other more pro-social concepts such as community, the social good or mutuality. Neoliberalism has resulted in the outsourcing of key functions of the state. Brown notes that neoliberalism requires not only the introduction of market mechanisms to state function but the transformation of state agencies into firms. In the crash of 2008, the banks were described as 'too big to fail'. As Brown argues, the corollary of this is that some are 'too small to protect'. In his analysis of neoliberalism, Foucault (2008) concludes that everyone is imaged as human capital.

Neoliberalism is not simply a reaction to the difficulties that welfare states experienced in the mid- and late 1970s. There were always those who were opposed to the development of the post war Keynesian social democratic welfare state. Hayek's *Road to Serfdom* is a key text in the history of neoliberalism (Stedman-Jones, 2012). It has taken on an almost mythic status. Originally published in 1944, Hayek's work ran completely counter to the dominant themes in post war European economic and social thought. The demands of wartime had meant an expansion of the role of the state. Hayek was fundamentally concerned that this expansion would not be rolled back in peacetime. The two key beliefs in neoliberalism are the supremacy of the market and a belief in liberty – this being defined as freedom from state interference. The role of the state is thus to ensure that there is an environment in which the market can operate effectively. From this perspective, it is not the role of the state to intervene in markets.

Individualism and a concern for the protection of all individuals against over-powerful institutions – either state ones or private corporations – is a key element of all forms of liberalism. It is to be found in its most passionate form in neoliberalism. There are several elements to this. The first is a form of anti-statism which does not accept that there are any areas that of legitimate concern for the state apart from law and order, and defence. These are two areas of the state that have expanded dramatically under neoliberal regimes. The second is a zealous commitment to an absolutist notion of free speech that appears to pride itself on challenging the shibboleths of modern progressive thought. One of the most important aspects of the neoliberal project has been its proponents' recognition of the need to influence and control cultural debates. Wacquant (2009b) highlights the way that the *doxa* of neoliberalism has become the currency of debate. *Doxa* are terms that restrict or construct the areas of debate. There is a political and cultural paradox here. Despite the fact that neoliberalism has been in the ascendancy since 1979, its supporters claim that society and the institutions of civil society – law, media, education and professions – are dominated by liberal elites. In political terms, this allows political figures such as Trump or Farage to pose, despite their own personal wealth and privilege, as political outsiders. Wacquant (2009b) shows that the spread of neoliberal ideas has been carefully managed via a nexus of think tanks, media and news outlets, and politicians. In the UK of the 1970s, the libertarian Institute of Economic Affairs, alongside sympathetic newspapers such as the *Daily Telegraph*, played a key role in moving neoliberal ideas into the mainstream of political thought.

Neoliberalism starts from a premise that markets are the most effective mechanisms for the distribution of resources. It then goes on to expand the areas of life where markets operate. This includes areas of social and welfare provision. Garland (2014) notes that all modern states are welfare states in that there are arrangements and systems to meet the welfare needs of individual citizens and communities. Welfare is one aspect of the modern state. It is the opponents of welfare regimes that characterise states in this way as 'welfare states'. This allows for certain areas of the welfare state to disappear from discussions of its efficacy. Welfare becomes a stigmatising term that is applied to the system of benefits paid to those who are not in employment (Garrett, 2015). This excludes hugely significant areas of provision – pensions being a clear example. Modern welfare states arose, in part, because of the failures of the market. However, the opponents of the welfare state view intervention as a threat to free markets.

Nozick (1974) provided a philosophical underpinning for developments of neoliberalism and the objections to the expansion of the state in the provision of services. The first objection is that the state should be limited in its intervention in individual lives. The second argument is that state providers become monopolies or dominated by bureaucracies, provider interests and public sector unions. Therefore, it is argued, public assets should be sold along aside the introduction of competition and the discipline of the market. As noted previously, a form of hyper individualism is one of the constituent parts of neoliberalism. This is accompanied by the mantra of choice. According to this schema, choice can and should be extended across all sectors. The neoliberal model of low personal taxation, the selling of state assets and restrictions on the power of organised labour can be seen across a number of economies. It was a model that was accepted and exported by leading global institutions including the International Monetary Fund and the World Bank. In order to receive financial support and assistance from these institutions, governments had to accept these key tenets and implement policies based upon them (Stedman-Jones,

2012). In the Global South, neoliberalism was imposed in return for support from key institutions such as the World Bank and the IMF.

Neoliberalism and the state

Neoliberalism is inherently suspicious of the state and state agencies. Friedman (1962) makes the economic argument for the reduction of the state to a series of core functions. Higgs (1987) argues that state expands its power and interests – particularly at a time of crisis or national emergency. Those powers are never relinquished once the crisis has been resolved. Nozick's (1974) *Anarchy, state and utopia* is a philosophical treatise that provides a defence of what is termed 'the nightwatchman state'. The role of the state, it is argued, should be limited to the position of maintaining the rule of law and the defence of the realm. Hayek's work clearly has to be read, on one level, as a response to the Communist and fascist totalitarian regimes of the period when he was writing. However, his work is also a warning against the emerging social democratic regimes of the post war world. These regimes, according to Hayek, also had the potential to over-rule free choice and the market. Such systems carry with them – from their supporters' view that is their main aim – the potential to create a social state. Hayek and his followers argue that the free market may not be perfect but it can reflect individual choice. Government bureaucracies are incapable of doing so. State agencies will reflect the needs of providers rather than consumers. Those subject or reliant on state bureaucracies cannot be seen as consumers in the pure sense of the term. They have no choice. In addition, their decisions have no impact on the behaviour of bureaucrats. The state monopoly means that the regulating impact of competition is absent. Individuals have nowhere else to go, unlike a market where if I am not happy with shop A I can go to shop B. Hayek argued that the post war social democratic state had the potential to limit individual very severely. It had within it the seeds of a much more interventionist model. If its emergence could not be prevented then the future aim of neoliberal policy should be to create an anti-statist intellectual climate as a precursor to rolling back the state.

Neoliberalism's anti-statism is most apparent in its attack on the social state. I am using the term social state here to mean the provision of education, welfare and health services alongside the social protections, for example, enforceable legal rights for workers and social legislation that combats discrimination on grounds of race, gender or sexual orientation. The opposition is a combination of economic, moral and social. The social state will distort the functioning of the market in two ways. The first is that it will inevitably seek to impose regulations and restrictions – in the right's terms – 'burdens on business'. These would include employment and anti-discrimination legislation. In addition, the state can only be funded from taxation on either individuals and companies. Taxation is regarded, certainly by Nozick (1974), as a form of theft. In this schema, taxation removes choice, therefore it is a restriction on liberty. Neoliberalism does not rule out charity or philanthropy. It is up to individuals to spend money how they wish. If it becomes a state run activity then it becomes a form of state bureaucracy.

The moral and social opposition to the welfare state is that it creates form of dependency and rewards anti-social behaviour. In this area, the arguments are most closely associated with work of the American academic Charles Murray (1990). He argued that the modern welfare state had created a new class – the 'underclass'. This group is, for Murray, socially, psychologically and physically separated from wider society. In some senses, Murray's work is a recasting of arguments that have existed in different forms throughout modern capitalism (Welshman, 2013).

Neoliberalism as an ideology did not simply appear in the mid-1970s as a response to the crisis of legitimacy that social democracy faced at that time. Its roots are much deeper than that. The economic and social problems of the mid-1970s provided the conditions for its political and electoral triumph. The relationship between neoliberalism and the state is more complex than a simply a rejection of all forms of state intervention. Chang (2011, 2014) notes that modern capitalism is heavily dependent on the state while at the same time denying this and being largely critical of state institutions. Skelcher (2000) identifies three models of the state: the overloaded state of the late 1960s and early 1970s; the hollowed-out state of the 1980s; and the congested state of the 1990s. The wave of privatisations and sale of state assets that the Thatcher government began in the early 1980s was the key factor in the 'hollowing out' of the state. As well as this process, Skelcher outlines the way that new forms of governance were developed for the public sector. One of the ironies of the era of neoliberalism is that far from reducing regulation and audit, the culture of risk has seen such systems increase dramatically (Beck, 1992; Webb, 2006). The establishment of OFSTED, a government agency that began to inspect schools but now also covers children and families social work, is a clear example of this phenomenon. 'New Public Management' (NPM; Pollitt and Bouckaert, 2003) established a purchaser/provider split. These changes have been particularly felt in social work and social care generally.

However, the key themes can be seen across a number of professions and settings – increased audit, complex and demanding bureaucratic systems, demanding inspection regimes, a reduction in professional autonomy and a resultant professional frustration.

Austerity

In 2008, the banking crisis led to Gordon Brown's Labour government spending huge sums of money to bail out financial institutions. The banks were seen as 'too big to fail'. As well as bailing out the banks, the Brown administration followed standard Keynesian economics by attempting to stimulate demand in the economy. These measures included a reduction in VAT and increased capital spending. The formation of the coalition government in 2010 ended this approach. The coalition presented itself as a government formed in response to a national emergency though, it should be noted, not representative of all major parties as is usually the case in such circumstances. The emergency was the position of the government finances but the cause of that position was presented as Labour's profligacy. Brown (2015) notes that calls to individual sacrifice are an integral part of the discourse of the fiscal crisis as national emergency. In the UK context, Chancellor George Osborne's famous phrase that 'we are all in this together' captures this.

Austerity was presented as a response to a national emergency. It was, as Krugman (2015) concludes, a deeply political project. The aim was to reduce the extent and range of welfare provision across a number of areas. This reduction was not to be temporary – it would be a permanent recasting of the role of welfare and the relationship between the individual and the state. The welfare state does not simply exist to offer protections to the most vulnerable (Hills, 2015). However, in the period of austerity – that is the retrenchment of services – it is those who are in most of need of services who suffer most. Policies such as the Bedroom Tax and work capability assessments have led to an increase in poverty among the poorest and most vulnerable in communities. This group includes people with severe mental health problems who are in receipt of out of work benefits.

Rebuilding a social state

Somers and citizenship

In this final section, I will examine some responses to the challenges of neoliberalism. In particular, I will examine the work of two feminist scholars – Somers and Fineman. Their work on citizenship and notions of vulnerability can be the base for a revised model of citizenship. This revised model of citizenship would be based on ideals of reciprocity and mutuality. Inherent within these notions, there is a rejection of the hyper individualism of an atomising neoliberalism. Giroux (2017) sums the impact of neoliberalism thus:

> In the midst of a massive global attack on the welfare state and social provisions fuelled by neoliberal policies, the social contract central to liberal democracies has been shredded and with it any viable notion of solidarity, economic justice and the common good.

In building a response to these attacks on the core notions of economic and social justice, there is a need to restate core pro-social values. Social work can have a key role to play here. This will include the profession being part of national and international campaigns but also at the level of individual worker.

Neoliberalism's economic and social policies place huge emphasis on individualism. Choice is seen as key. Brown (2015: 132) outlines the way that the devolution of responsibility means that large scale problems – unemployment, environmental problems – are ' sent down the pipeline to small and weak units unable to cope with them technically, politically or financially'. She concludes that this devolution process results in a situation where these smaller units are given the decision making authority but lack the resources to enact the policies. These structures soak up resources. In addition, while paying lip service to progressive notions they create barriers to genuine service user involvement in decision making. This is an analytical lens that can be applied to the development of mental health policy in England and Wales over the period of community care (Cummins, 2012).

Rebuilding a social state

Somers' (2008) analysis of the nature of citizenship, in the context of neoliberalism, can be used as a basis for exploring responses to mental distress. Somers (2008) produces a 'triadic' model of society – the three elements being *state*, *market* and *civil society*. Her analysis describes neoliberalism as a form of 'market fundamentalism'. The application or attempted application of market mechanisms across all areas of society, for Somers, leads to a series of outcomes that harm the economic and social interests of the majority. These would include an increase in inequality, economic instability and volatility, an increase in financial speculation and environmental damage. These are a result of the undoubtedly dynamic nature of the neoliberal project. They also reflect the fact that neoliberalism has entailed and requires a shredding of the social state. As Wacquant (2008, 2009a, 2009b) has detailed, the neoliberal project is not simply an economic one – it is also fundamentally a political one. As well as attacks on the social state, the institutions of the civil society have also come under tremendous pressure. In a triadic model of society, the institutions of the civil society – trade unions, social movements and community groups and so on – act as a counterbalance to both the market and the state. Market fundamentalism sees the civil society as a potential barrier to the implementation and functioning of market mechanisms.

Somers (2008) argues that neoliberalism has a deeply corrosive impact on citizenship. Citizenship is not simply a matter of formal legal rights, it is dependent on processes that combine to ensure that citizens are members of social and political communities. If such processes do not exist or are weak, then there is a gap between a formal declaration of rights and translating them into meaningful substantive rights in practice. For Somers, the way that the state abandoned poor African Americans in the wake of Hurricane Katrina is a prime example of the logical outcome of these processes whereby not all citizens are regarded as moral equals. She argues that the victims of Hurricane Katrina were, in effect, internally stateless persons – possessing only Agamben's (2003) 'bare life'. Somers (2008: 118) concludes that market fundamentalism has led to increasing numbers of people losing any meaningful membership of civil society. Citizenship has become contractualised and commodified.

Giroux (2011) identifies part of the power of the market as the way that it drives out competing ideas. Somers (2008) suggests that the market has distorted the meaning of citizenship. Bauman (2007) describes people living in poverty or marginalised in some way as 'failed consumers'. They are unable to access the material advantages of modern capitalism. As a result, they are also excluded from the realm of the civil society or not even considered by the institutions of government. Somers (2008) notes that the global exclusionary processes are mirrored by internal processes at a national and local level. The Grenfell Tower block fire and its awful aftermath is a clear demonstration of the processes that Somers is discussing. The fire exposed the ultimate impact of the shredding of the social state. The aftermath of the fire has also highlighted the dangers of underestimating the strength of the informal civil society – the most effective action in response to the tragedy was dominated by local community and grassroots action.

Somers' (2008) model requires a balance between the state, market and civil society for individuals to be regarded as socially included citizens. In this model of a balance of powers between the three elements, civil society can act as a bulwark to protect individuals against excesses of both the state and the market. Wright (2015) argues that this spatial representation is in danger of ignoring or simplifying the way that, in modern capitalist societies, the market, state and civil society are connected and enmeshed in many complex ways. Neoliberalism far from seeing the roll back of the state has actually seen its retooling (Peck and Theodore, 2010). The social state, or what Bourdieu termed the 'left hand of the state', may have been reduced. Bourdieu's 'right hand of the state' has grown significantly (1998). Somers concludes that market fundamentalism deepens the divisions of race and class that existed before the neoliberal project.

Somers (2008), in her discussion of modern citizenship, uses the term borrowed from Arendt (1973) – the 'right to rights'. The existence of de jure rights does not mean that citizens can de facto enjoy them. This requires the membership of a polity – as Somers notes, the African-American citizens abandoned by the failures of the Federal Emergency Management Agency (FEMA) did not lose any legal rights but these rights became meaningless. The urban poor of New Orleans, a largely African-American community, were effectively abandoned by the state. The scale of the disaster that Hurricane Katrina created meant that only the state could organise an effective response. Full membership of the civil and political community would have produced a different institutional and governmental response – including taking much greater action to prevent the disaster occurring in the first place. These trends are part of the politics of 'disposability' (Tyler, 2014). The proclaimed universalism of market fundamentalism has created a political culture where particular groups – the working poor, asylum seekers, refugees and the so-called *underclass* – are denied effective political, civil and social rights. This process is bi-directional – economic status allows for the exercise of citizenship rights but it also confers them. All three elements of the triadic model have to function for the creation of a socially inclusive political citizenship. The importance here is that a civil society without a robust functioning social state results in a form of conservative communitarianism – David Cameron's *Big Society* being a prime example – that is unable to create full citizenship. Civil society does not, in and of itself, have the resources and power to challenge the market. There is a fundamental role for the state and its institutions in curbing the role of powerful elements or players in the market and civil society.

Vulnerability

One way that the key neoliberal trope of individualism manifests itself is in the modern development of celebrity culture, self-help manuals and reality TV programmes. It is also a fundamental assumption that is at the heart of a new form of consumerism. This trope is reflected in the way that citizens are recast as consumers in health and other services. The notion that choice can be exercised in all settings, be it buying goods and services or making decisions about treatment options, is now deeply engrained. I should, perhaps, make it clear here that I am in no way arguing for a return to top down paternalism. Quite the reverse, I am arguing for a more genuine form of involvement in decision making. These issues will be explored in more depth in the final chapter. There are two problems with this consumerist approach: it can entrench existing health inequalities; and, in some areas, the notion of real choice may be somewhat illusory, particularly if a level of technical knowledge or expertise is required to analyse the options available.

Fineman (2004) argues that cherished societal notions of autonomy are, in fact, based on a myth. We have all needed care to reach adulthood. We all potentially will require care at some point in our adult lives. The risks that we will require this vary because of a range of cultural, social and economic factors. There are a number of contingencies that we simply can foresee. For example, we may experience a life changing health condition. However, the cult of individualism does not take account of this. Autonomy and capacity are given priority, hence the 'the autonomy myth'. Fineman (2004) argues that a more egalitarian and socially responsive state can be built on the foundations of challenging the autonomy myth and a wider recognition of vulnerability. Vulnerability here is not a paternalistic term. In Fineman's work the recognition of the potential vulnerability of all citizens is the basis for new forms of mutual understanding and reciprocity. The focus on individualism requires us to set aside the basic conditions of recognition and mutuality on which more inclusive social systems are based. Vulnerability is the result of a complex set of personal, social, economic and institutional relationships. In denying the universal nature of our vulnerability, we obscure the ways in which power and privilege operate. Neoliberalism's defence of individualism thus becomes a cover for inequality. It has produced what Fineman terms a 'restrained state', where the defence of the private or family realm serves as a significant barrier to the provision of more egalitarian forms of care.

Peck and Tickell (2002) conclude that neoliberalism has become a universal ideological approach that is difficult if not impossible to escape. In the context of the UK, all politics since her departure in 1990 are a response to Mrs Thatcher. Even her most strident opponents would surely have to acknowledge this aspect of her legacy. Giroux (2011) notes the power of neoliberal ideology in pushing out countervailing arguments or points of view. The economic impact of neoliberalism and austerity has been an increase in inequality alongside a stigmatising of those living in poverty and the marginalised. The attack on the welfare state has been increased by austerity. The political and cultural success of neoliberalism is self-evident. It is a social as well as an economic phenomenon.

Citizenship and mental health

Those that argued for the closure of the asylum regime did so from a range of motivations (Cummins, 2017b). However, one of the key arguments stemmed from a notion of social citizenship. The asylum was seen as an abusive and damaging regime not simply because of the physical conditions – though they were an important factor. The asylum denied patients fundamental rights as citizens. One of the aims of community care was to recast these relationships. The treatment of mental health was thus acknowledged as an explicitly political process. One of the tragedies of deinstitutionalisation is that the fiscal concerns became the dominant engine of reform. These pushed other values to the side. There was an inherent appeal to anti-statist conservatives in an argument that these expensive state institutions should be closed. This was never made explicit – progressive supporters of deinstitutionalisation, perhaps naively, assumed that the money would follow the patients into the community. This happened at the beginning of the policy but was not able to withstand the barrage of public sector retrenchment in the early 1980s (Cummins, 2013). The small state can rapidly become no state. In the same way, individual choice and strengths based approaches can be used to give a pseudo intellectual gloss to service retrenchment.

Mental health problems do not exist in a vacuum. The diagnosis of illness and the configuration and delivery of any form of health care but perhaps particularly mental health care are fundamentally political exercises. It is impossible to divorce these issues from broader political developments. This is one of the key themes of this book. The Social Exclusion Unit (ODPM 2004) produced a report into social exclusion that highlighted the barriers people with mental health problems must overcome to gain employment. Despite the fact that discrimination on the basis of mental health status is illegal, the report highlighted that such practices continue. Recent changes to the benefit system, in particular the work capability assessment (WCA) system, produced further pressures. The 'invisibility' and fluctuating nature of mental health problems can also make it very difficult for individuals and carers to document adequately – that is, to the satisfaction of the assessors – the impact mental illness has on their day-to-day lives. This produces a situation where an individual is assessed as 'fit for work' but faces huge barriers in finding employment because of discrimination and stereotypical attitudes. The whole process of reassessment and possible financial implications is, of course, inherently stressful for the individuals involved. None of this in any way implies that the assessment process is fair or equitable.

This book argues that there needs to be a fundamental shift in the basis on which mental health services are delivered. The moves towards deinstitutionalisation and the resulting failures of community care have been the subject of much debate (Cummins, 2017a) Knowles, 2000; Moon, 2000; Wolff, 2005). Scull (2015) argues that this has distorted our view of mental health provision, which has always been centred around institutionalised forms of care. Recent community mental policies, from this perspective, are a break in this approach. The focus on the failings or gaps in community mental health services has, in some senses, masked the fact that institutional forms of care continue to have a central role in mental health services.

Recent reports in the UK have highlighted the limited availability of psychiatric beds. These are very important issues. However, there is a much broader debate about the nature of mental health services that needs to take place. A rediscovery of the progressive values of community care, alongside the reinvigoration of a social state inspired by the work of Somers, Fineman and others who challenge the domination of neoliberalism, can be the start of this process.

Poverty, austerity and mental health

The Marmot Review (2010) identifies a clear link between poverty, inequality and poor mental health. The issues of causality are complex and examined in more depth later in this chapter. Wilkinson and Pickett (2009) use the prevalence of mental illness as one of their measures of the impact of inequality. More equal societies have better mental health outcomes for their citizens. It is now widely accepted that one needs to examine a range of social, economic, political and cultural factors when examining mental health outcomes (Murray, 2017). These approaches are moving towards a more socially focused approach. Within this, there is a concern about and a challenge to not only the discrimination that people with mental health problems face, but also the way that mental health services are constructed and delivered.

The impact of the 2008 banking crisis continues to be felt across the public and welfare sectors. The bail out of the banks – an act of government intervention to rescue the loudest supporters of the free market – required the injection of huge sums of public money. Oxfam (2013) estimated that the cost was £141 billion. The initial bailout took place under the Brown administration, which followed standard Keynesian principles by stimulating demand in the economy. For example, VAT was reduced and capital spending on schools and social housing was increased. In the period 2008–10, the poorest fifth of the population saw incomes grow at a rate of 3.4% per annum (Oxfam, 2013).

Austerity as a policy involves huge cuts in public and welfare spending. Krugman (2015) notes that austerity marks a significant departure from traditional management of the economy as a fiscal stimulus would normally be introduced in an economic downturn. The standard approach would be to reduce government spending and public projects during a boom.

Austerity cannot be understood as purely or solely as a matter of economics. It was a clear political project by the coalition and later Conservative governments to recast and reduce the role of the social state (Cummins, 2018). The coalition government successfully put forward the message that the crisis in the public finances was the result of the previous administration's failure to control public spending during a period when the economy was experiencing sustained growth. In an oft repeated ministerial phrase Labour 'did not fix the roof when the sun was shining'. The measures that the coalition introduced were ones that would reduce welfare provision but also shrink the social state permanently. Blyth (2013) is highly critical of austerity on economic terms but also the morality of the poor being made to pay for a situation created by the one of the wealthiest groups in society. As Taylor-Gooby (2012) concludes, the result of austerity is that the UK public sector has shrunk to the smallest among major economies – including the US. Taylor-Gooby (2012) concludes that the attack on the welfare state was the most sustained that it had faced.

Alongside reductions in welfare state spending, the coalition changed the relationship between local and central government as well as seeing increased private sector involvement in key areas such as health and education (Crossley, 2016). These moves are based on the notion that the welfare state, as seen by its critics, is both a drain on the public finances but also rewards anti-social behaviour and creates dependency. Cameron's (2010) notion of a leaner more business-like 'smarter state' involves a recasting of the relationship between individuals, communities and the state.

The impact of austerity and the retrenchment of the welfare state falls disproportionately on poorer members of society. A Joseph Rowntree Foundation (Bramley et al, 2016) report shows that the majority of the poor are actually in work. The extension of zero hour contracts, the 1% cap on public sector pay rises and the cuts in services combine to increase inequality but also the sense of precariousness in employment. The Institute for Fiscal Studies (IFS) (2012) has calculated that there will be a reduction of over 900,000 public sector jobs in the period 2011–18. The public sector, as well as doing vitally important work for the wider society, is also an area that employs more women than other sectors of the economy. Therefore, the impact of austerity has to be viewed through the prism of gender alongside race, class and disability. The May government has stopped using the term austerity and is attempting to distance itself from the Cameron/Osborne years. However, there are more cuts to public services planned, alongside welfare reforms that will impact disproportionately on the poorest, particularly families with children (Crossley, 2016). Far from being 'all in it together', it is clear that the most vulnerable have paid the greatest price. Beatty and Fothergill (2016) calculate there will be reductions in welfare spending of £27 billion a year by 2020–21. The coalition's commitment to localism and the withdrawal of funding linked to deprivation means that the local authorities with the highest levels of need have had to manage the most significant reductions (Innes and Tetlow, 2015). This is Tudor Hart's (1971) inverse care law as government policy with those in most need being allocated fewest resources.

Crossley (2016) concludes that the largest cuts were experienced in those areas that had officially been identified as being poorer and having increased local needs. There is a vicious circle here as individuals and families in these areas are less likely to have the economic and social capital to replace the resources and community assets that are not sustainable without state funding. Bourdieu et al (1999) conclude that the poorest areas of our cities become characterised by 'absence' – they have been abandoned by the welfare and other institutions of the state. Austerity is neoliberal social and welfare policy in tooth and claw. The fiscal crisis provided a cover for an attack on the welfare state that previous Conservative governments could have only dreamed about.

Karban (2016) highlights the need for a health inequalities approach to mental health. Such moves should be particularly attractive to social workers for two interrelated reasons. The first is that they inevitably involve a challenge to the dominance of a biomedical model of mental illness. Such an approach requires a broad analysis of social policy that produces increased inequality but also a critical perspective towards the way that mental health services are configured and delivered. The second is that this is an approach implicitly based on notions of social justice that remain at the core of social work.

As outlined above, austerity has had a profound impact on the welfare state and those who are most reliant on the services it provides. The coalition government's policies, therefore, inevitably had the most impact on the most vulnerable. Fifty per cent of the cuts in spending fell in two areas – benefits and local government spending (Centre for Welfare Reform, 2015). These areas account for 25% of government spending. Austerity led to a 20% cut in benefits – the majority of which are paid to people with disabilities and people living in poverty. As outlined above, the cuts in local government spending have disproportionately affected the poorest and the poorest communities. People living with severe disabilities bear 15% of the cuts in welfare spending. Welfare in the debates around austerity was a very specific term and was always linked with dependency (Garrett, 2015). It meant payments to those not in work. Pensions were seen as having a different status – also the recipients were seen as an important political constituency. The government's triple lock meant that the level of pension payments were protected.

Impact of welfare reforms

One of the key ideas in the neoliberal attack on the welfare state is that it creates dependency. In addition, it is felt that the payment of benefits allows the claimant to avoid responsibility. It has long been the aim of these critics of the welfare state to place more conditions on benefits – the reforms to the welfare system introduced by the coalition government building on initial moves by the Brown government did this. In particular, the WCA scheme meant that individuals who were claiming the Employment and Support Allowance (ESA) underwent a fitness to work assessment. The WCA has been very controversial. It was introduced in 2008. Originally, the scheme was managed by ATOS, which won the contract from the Department for Work and Pensions (DWP). This is an example of the processes whereby state functions are privatised and then managed for profit by commercial companies. It also highlights the way that the state contracts have become key markets for private sector companies.

As discussed earlier, there are clear barriers to employment that people living with physical disabilities or mental health problems face. Access to employment with good pay and conditions is clearly an aim that the majority would support. The WCA scheme was presented by the DWP as an attempt to help people off benefits and into employment. This is a laudable aim but the experience of the scheme was somewhat different. It was an essentially punitive experience. In the assessment process, there are three possible outcomes:

- fit for work
- unfit for work but fit for pre-employment training
- fit for neither work nor training

One of the most significant criticisms of the WCA is that the assessment is a functional one. It is often carried out by staff who have little understanding or professional experience of mental health problems. By their nature, mental health problems are complex, fluctuating and therefore difficult to assess. The impact on an individual's ability to work may vary across various forms of employment. It will also change because of the nature of the difficulties that they face. For example, low mood or anxiety are symptoms of illness that would be difficult to evidence in the way that bureaucracies demand. All these factors combine to put people with mental health problems at a disadvantage if a testing regime is a functional one – focusing on physical capabilities. There have been concerns not only about the outcome of the WCA – in terms of people being deemed fit for work whose mental health was still such that they were not – and the impact of the whole WCA process.

An analysis of the introduction of the WCA process by Barr et al (2016) provides a clear insight into the impact of this new system. The study examines the programme in the period 2010–13. There were just over a million assessments in this period. The number of assessments varied across the country. The study concluded that, in those areas with higher rates of reassessment, there was an increase in suicides, antidepressant prescribing and self-reported mental health problems. The authors concluded that across England, the WCA process was linked to:

- 590 suicides
- 279,000 additional cases of self-reported mental health problems
- 725,000 additional prescriptions for anti-depressants.

Those in the lowest socioeconomic groups are more likely to be in receipt of these benefits. The social gradient in health (Marmot, 2010) means there is a greater prevalence of mental and physical health problems within this cohort. The WCA process thus has a double impact as it is more likely to affect vulnerable individuals in more marginalised communities. In addition, this research focused on those who were subject to the WCA process. The wider social impacts also need to be examined. The 590 people who ended their own lives were all members of families, communities and wider social networks. The impacts of such policies are even broader than is sometimes allowed for. Barr et al (2016) regard the whole WCA process as an experiment in public health that had disastrous consequences for individuals, families and communities. The authors conclude that any benefits in terms of reduced welfare spending are far outweighed by the personal and wider damage that the policy caused. It may have actually led to increased public spending in terms of greater calls on mental health and other agencies. Such policies do not tackle the exclusion of people with mental health problems from the labour market. It might well be that they increase rather than decrease this exclusion.

Mental health and social capital

Social capital

This section will examine the outline approaches to social capital and the use of the term as a tool of analysis. Portes (1998) notes that social capital is a term that has been imported into everyday language and debates. The idea that society is more than a group of atomised individuals and that there is benefit in group participation is not new. The benefits accrue to individuals but also to the wider society. Durkheim (1984) presents group membership as a buffet against the anomie of modern life. Marx (1894) makes a distinction between an atomised class and a more mobilised and effective class that brings about political change. Social capital focuses on the positive benefits that accrue from group or social activity.

Bourdieu

Pierre Bourdieu (1930–2002) has become on the most influential thinkers and widely cited writers in sociology and the modern humanities. His analysis of the functions of class in liberal democracies (Bourdieu, 2010) can be read as a foregrounding of these issues. It is also a counter to those such as Beck (1992, 2008) who saw class as diminishing. Far from being the 'zombie category' that Beck claimed, Bourdieu suggested that class divisions had become more deeply entrenched. He also noted that the daily significance of class increased just as many were marking its decline. Bourdieu was a critic of neoliberalism and its attack on the foundations of a social state.

Bourdieu's notion of social capital has to be placed within the broader context of his political and sociological thought. I will briefly outline these before examining the notion of social capital in more depth. Bourdieu's analysis of class is based on a *Capital, Assets and Resources* model (Savage, 2016). He identified three models or types of capital – *economic, cultural and social*. Economic capital is clear – financial assets and wealth. Cultural and social capital are related to economic capital. Bourdieu sought to examine the way that economic elites also create a cultural language of taste and artistic value that reinforces and reproduces their dominant position. Cultural references such as music, food, newspapers and TV programmes are all part of these processes. Elite schools and universities not only reinforce existing social divisions, they enable elites to create the social connections that will serve them well in adult and professional life. Bourdieu outlines the ways in which the social world is a system of power relations but also a symbolic system. Taste or cultural preferences are not simply neutral – they become a basis for social judgement. An appreciation of so-called high culture – art, opera and classical music – becomes a requirement for and a signifier of the membership of an elite. The experiences of working class children like Bourdieu, who become members of these institutions, can be a profoundly dislocating one (Hanley, 2012, 2016). Milanovic (2016) has been critical of Bourdieu's emphasis on cultural activities as markers of membership of elites, arguing that this is a particularly French approach.

Bourdieu emphasised that the forms of capital that he identified were interrelated. For example, you clearly need a certain level of economic capital to purchase seats at Sadler's Wells to watch a performance of a ballet. This purchase will also potentially open up access to other forms of capital – you may make social or business contacts that then increase your economic capital. Your attendance is also an important cultural signifier. It marks you as a member of a certain group and you are seen to possess a level of taste and sophistication. A review of the performance will appear in broadsheet newspapers, it will be discussed on BBC Radios 3 and 4. These signifiers are intertwined and self-reinforcing. At the same time, you may the economic capital but feel culturally and socially excluded. You might attend but feel socially awkward. The functioning of networks is at the core of this argument. Networks are, by their very definition, processes of inclusion and exclusion. Bourdieu was particularly interested in the ways that education operated in these areas. Elite institutions – public schools, Oxbridge and other elite universities – provide not only academic credentials but also access to social networks. These become self-perpetuating. Littler (2016) demonstrates the current dominant narrative of meritocracy, which commits to a more open society, actually reinforces the position of elites and inequality.

Bourdieu (1986: 248) defines social capital as

> the aggregate of the actual or potential resources which are linked to possession of a durable network of more or less institutionalised relationships of mutual acquaintance or recognition.

There are two elements to this. These relationships provide claims to access to resources. As part of a social elite network, individuals can gain access to resources or other networks. The other aspect of social capital is the extent and quality of the resources that networks possess. The notion of social capital thus provides an analytical framework to explore notions of social mobility but also the functions of social elites. Loury (1977) used the notion of social capital as a way of challenging the individualism that is at the heart of much orthodox economic theory. The focus on individualism ignores social and historical inequalities – for example, issues of race and gender. Loury (1977) shows that an analysis of unemployment rates among African Americans has to include the poverty of black parents and its impact on educational achievement. In addition, African Americans face discrimination in the labour market. Finally, Loury (1977) concluded that African Americans did not have the informal links with the labour market that social capital generates. This applies at all levels but is particularly the case where entry to elite professions – law, medicine, academe – is smoothed not only by graduating from particular universities but also by informal social and other contacts such as unpaid internships.

Bourdieu's notion of social capital provides a critical perspective. It is also one that recognises that social capital is a tool of analysis that can be used across social groups. It is not only elites that have access to forms of social capital. Wacquant and Wilson (1989) show that one of the impacts of the deindustrialisation that took place from the 1970s onwards was that it removed sources of effective social capital from urban, largely African-American communities. In Drake and Cayton's (1993) classic study, the ghetto is described as a 'black city within the white'. This is clearly not to deny the impact of Jim Crowism and racial segregation. However, it acknowledges that there were communal aspects and social organisations such as the Church that acted as a buffer against the wider society. The ghetto was thus a socially, ethno-racial defined space with clear psychological and physical boundaries (Slater, 2009). Wacquant (2008) notes the ghetto was home to both professional and working class African Americans. Ghettoization is a 'distinctive modality of racial domination that encompasses all members of a group'. Thus, it can help to develop communal solidarity but also increase access to various forms of social capital. One of the most important impacts of neoliberalism is the fact that it means the creation and maintenance of such social institutions is much more difficult. Traditional patterns of employment also helped to foster community welfare organisations – unions, sports and social clubs, and so on. Some of these institutions might be now viewed as rather paternalistic. The replacement of Fordist patterns of employment has meant that they have largely disappeared. More precarious forms of employment make it much more difficult to organise unions as well as welfare and social clubs.

Bourdieu's notion of social capital can thus be used as a means of examining the sources of social support that exist within communities and groups. Social capital is a measure of the links that individuals have to the wider society, and also the extent to which the groups that they are part of are able to exercise influence. The application of its use within in the field of mental health is discussed in more detail below.

Putnam and social capital

The relationship between the individual and the wider society is one of the key areas for debate and analysis across the social sciences and humanities. In his (1903) classic text *The metropolis and mental life*, Simmel set out the fundamental dilemma as follows:

> The deepest problems of modern life flow from the attempt of the individual to maintain the independence and individuality of his existence against the sovereign powers of society, against the weight of the historical heritage and the external culture and technique of life. The antagonism represents the most modern form of the conflict which primitive man must carry on with nature for his own bodily existence.

There have been constant shifts between the poles of community solidarity and individual autonomy since that point. Putnam is an American political scientist. In his most famous work *Bowling Alone* (2000), he charts what he sees as a decline, since the 1950s, in social and civic values in the US. Putnam's description of a more atomised and fragmented community – encapsulated in the title's reference to the disappearance of the bowling leagues that had been so popular in his youth – became very influential. Both the Clinton and Blair administrations accepted the key premises of his analysis. The communitarian thread that runs through this approach had a particular influence on the Blair government's social policy.

Putnam (1993) carried out his initial research in Italy contrasting what he saw as the different approaches to government in the north and the south. He argued that there was a fundamental difference between attitudes to civic participation in the two areas. In the north, Putnam suggested that people viewed themselves as citizens. In the south, in contrast, they saw themselves as subjects. He suggested that the difference between the two areas could be explained in terms of the fact that the north had a strong economic system and a high level of integration. He saw the source of this as being the region's successful accumulation of social capital. Putnam identifies three aspects to social capital:

- Social norms and moral obligations
- Shared sense of social values – trust is a key value
- Social networks – particularly voluntary associations and clubs

Putnam is part of a communitarian tradition that sees the causes of modern social problems as lying in an alleged decline in civic norms and social capital. In this schema, social capital is both self-reinforcing and cumulative. It also provides a circular explanation of cause and effect. Greater community cohesion is explained by higher levels of social capital, which is the result of greater community cohesion.

Putnam's work has been criticised for being a recast version of 1950s or 1960s functionalism. His measures of social activity – reading newspapers, participation in voluntary associations and sports clubs – can seem somewhat outdated. He was writing before the development of social media. It is, of course, a moot point as to whether social media has increased or decreased political engagement. In addition, the period that is seen as being the height of civic activity was one that effectively denied full citizenship to African Americans, women, and gay and lesbian people. In the area of mental health, the asylum system and the associated social stigma functioned in such a way to exclude those deemed to be mentally ill from the wider society (Scull, 2015). Putnam does not address these important issues. He ignores about how community cohesion can be based and usually is based on the creation and exclusion of the 'Other' – be that racial, sexual or other minorities. Putnam does not explore in any depth the political tensions and differences that exist in or between voluntary associations. There is an inherent danger that these groups are dominated by middle class voices.

Social capital – a comparative approach

There is a fundamental difference between the approaches that Putnam and Bourdieu take to social capital, reflecting the contrasting sociological traditions from which they emanate. Bourdieu views society as being made constructed of a range of social fields. He sees social capital as having a symbolic character. Economic capital exists as money, investments and so on. Cultural capital can be evidenced by the diplomas and examination certificates that one obtains from elite institutions and so on. Bourdieu sees economic, cultural and social capital as becoming meaningful via processes of symbolic translation (Bourdieu and Wacquant, 1992).

Putnam largely ignores any conflicts between civil and political society and the state. Bourdieu is much more concerned with the role of the state. He sees the state as a field that is increasingly the site of struggles over legitimate symbolic power. Bourdieu and Wacquant (1992: 167) argue that symbolic violence is the violence which is exercised upon a social agent with his or her complicity... I call misrecognition the fact that recognising a violence which is wielded precisely inasmuch as one does not perceive it as such.

Bourdieu's use of social capital is, therefore, a more radical critique of social structures and how they function. Putnam's work is more conservative in both its scope and conclusions. There is scope for both approaches to be applied in the area of mental health. Putnam's work would support approaches to mental health that focus on community based responses. Bourdieu was a noted critic of neoliberalism who called for a greater investment in the social state. Part of this investment would result in the development of social capital.

Mental health, poverty and social work

In a previous work, I outlined what I termed social work's 'poverty paradox' (Cummins, 2018). This was an attempt to capture a contradiction. Poverty is a hugely significant factor in the lives of many people accessing social services. However, poverty itself was largely absent in debates about the nature of the profession. One of the impacts of austerity has been to push these issues further up the agenda. There is a growing literature that seeks to rekindle a more radical approach to social work practice and address structural issues of inequality and poverty (Backwith, 2015; Krumer-Nevo, 2015). This work can be read alongside a wider 'literature of austerity' (O'Hara, 2015 Garthwaite, 2016a), which details the impact of these policies on the day-to-day lives of those in poverty. These works are not specifically concerned with mental health issues. However, what they all share is a commitment to social justice. In addition, all these works demonstrate that poverty is inextricably linked with poor physical and mental health.

Krumer-Nevo (2015) proposes a new model of social work education and practice that she terms a 'poverty aware paradigm'. I think that this is an approach that has real potential across social work but, perhaps, particularly in the area of mental health social work. The fundamental for Krumer-Nevo is that poverty should be viewed as an issue of human rights. As noted earlier, Somers (2008) outlines the way that the poor are systematically denied full participation in major capitalist societies. Civil rights exist in the abstract but without a framework or the resources to claim them or seek their enforcement, many groups are denied meaningful rights. Austerity did not remove the right to vote from marginalised groups but, as detailed earlier, the policies have had a hugely disproportionate impact on the poorest and potentially the most vulnerable members of society. The introduction of the WCA is an example of an effectively discriminatory policy that puts the government in breach of its international treaty obligations to protect citizens regarded as living with disabilities. I note here that the language of these United Nations(UN) documents is problematic and would not ideally be used as it is regarded by many as oppressive.

Krumer-Nevo (2015) seeks to challenge the notion that poverty is the result of individual mistakes, misfortune or immoral and anti-social behaviour. This is the essence of Murray's (1990) underclass argument where inequality is seen as both an inevitable and desirable outcome of a market economy that rewards some and not others. From this point of view, society cannot be equal because skills and other attributes are not distributed equally across society. Any attempts to create a more equal society will fail because of this. They also require restrictions on the liberty of some. One of the more dispiriting aspects of recent social policy, particularly since the summer 2011 riots has been the *Othering* of those living in poverty (Tyler, 2014; Cummins, 2018). These views have unfortunately seeped into areas of social work practice. For example, in the area of child protection, issues of poverty have been recast as ones of parental neglect. This has led to an increase in the number of child referrals to social services departments (Bilson and Martin, 2016). Krumer-Nevo's starting point is that social work educators and practitioners have to start from a position that rejects individualised explanations of poverty. Poverty and inequality have to be viewed as structural issues. This is, of course, does not deny individual agency. It is rather a recognition of the power of societal inequalities and their influence on the life opportunities and chances that citizens have.

Krumer-Nevo's work, alongside others such as Mantle and Backwith (2010) and Backwith (2015), is part of broader moves to reclaim social work from approaches that are bureaucratic and focused on risk management. One concern is that social work interventions are experienced more as punitive than empowering (Tobis, 2013; Featherstone et al, 2014; Gupta, 2017). There are some differences in the emphasis in these approaches but what they have in common is that while they recognise that social work is often about individuals or families, it also has to be about communities. Social work seeks to change the broader society, as well as working alongside individuals and families to improve their own circumstances and increase life chances. This is an area where social work practitioners need to be 'facing both ways at the same time', being involved in wider campaigns such as

Boot Out Austerity and opposition to the WCA assessment process, as well as working alongside individuals experiencing poverty to mitigate the impact of the policies of austerity that they oppose. For many, this might appear to an obvious statement of social work's traditional role and purpose. On one level it is just that; however, in the current practice environment that it is still largely dominated by a procedural form of practice, it is somewhat of a radical departure. A 'poverty aware paradigm' would require a shift to a much more relational focused form of practice. Gill and Jack (2007) coined the term 'poverty blindness' to capture the way that poverty, such a feature of the lives of service users and thus the practice landscape, has become marginalised. From my viewpoint, the poverty paradox is apparent in social work education where, in my experience, these issues are given less prominence in social work curricula. The result is an atomised view of the nature and context of social work practice.

Conclusion

This chapter has examined the complex links between mental health issues and poverty. It starts from the premise that we need to take a broadly social view of the causes of mental health problems. The Marmot Review (2010) shows that the social gradient is particularly significant in this area. The higher rates of mental illness experienced by people living in poverty cannot be explained by the notion of social drift – the idea that the impact of mental illness on employment and life chances increases the risks of experiencing poverty. There are wider factors at play – poverty has significant impacts on physical health, educational and employment opportunities, as well as the potential exposure to other forms of trauma – and all these in turn are relevant to the development of mental health problems.

The aims of the policy of deinstitutionalisation were based on notions of active social citizenship. Poverty has to be viewed as the denial of citizenship and as an issue of human rights (Somers, 2008). In the context of mental health services, poverty is both a result of and an addition to the structural discrimination that individuals and groups face. In this area, social work needs to reject the formulaic risk management approaches that marginalise the keys of good social work – building relationships, advocacy and interprofessional practice. The lessons of Lipsky's (1980) classic text need to be revived. He argued that so-called street level bureaucrats exercised significant discretion and were often opposed to formal government policies, which they recognised had a negative impact on the communities they served.

Whatever the demands of the bureaucracy, there is always space for social workers and others at street level to be creative and subversive. There is a danger that the current structures of CMHT marginalises social work's identity and in so doing blunts some of this subversive edge. Krumer-Nevo's (2015) *poverty aware paradigm* offers the basis for a more critically engaged model of practice that challenges structural inequality as well as working alongside individuals and communities to develop 'social capital'. Such approaches should have wide appeal across social work as they are based on a restating of fundamental social work values. They are also in line with the commitment to social justice that is at the heart of both the International Federation of Social Workers definition of social work and the domains of the Professional Capabilities Framework.

FOUR

Contemporary mental health services

This chapter will examine some of the key issues in mental health services. One of the most important developments in mental health services is the belated and far from complete recognition of the importance of service user perspectives. The chapter begins by a consideration of these issues and then goes on to examine a range of contemporary concerns within services and mental health social work.

Surviving psychiatry

Sick role

Parsons (1975) identified four main elements to the 'sick role'. One approach to understanding service user responses to the psychiatric system is to regard them, whatever form they take, as a challenge to Parsons. He outlined four key elements to the role:

- The person is not responsible for assuming the sick role.
- The sick person is exempted from carrying out some or all normal social duties (e.g. work, family roles).
- The sick person must try and get well – the sick role is only a temporary phase.
- In order to get well, the sick person needs to seek and submit to appropriate medical care.

The *sick role* is a binary, paternalistic model. Modern medicine takes a rather different approach to the causes of ill health. There have been significant changes in societal and professional attitudes. For example, being sick is no longer necessarily a temporary phase but also it does not exempt one from usual social obligations. Shifts since Parsons outlined the sick role include the fact that there is greater ambiguity about responsibility for the adopting the sick role. For example, public health campaigns emphasise that diet, exercise, smoking and drinking are all potential factors in the development of long-term conditions. Patients have a much greater role, including the exercise of choice, in the management of illness. The idea that the patient must simply submit to the treatment regime that is outlined by the medical profession is an outdated one in almost all areas of medicine. Wagner et al (1996) outlined a *Chronic Care Model* and the changes that the health care system would be required to undergo to produce a health care culture and delivery system to promote patients' priorities. This model flips the doctor-patient relationship and the patient becomes the expert. The patient and medical staff act work in partnership to identify goals and select the combination of treatments and services most likely to achieve them. It is interesting to reflect that some of these themes, which are now taken as a given in most areas of medicine, are still struggling to be accepted or become effectively embedded in the mental health arena.

This section will examine the emergence of what might be termed the 'modern user/survivor movement'. The use of language is very important as it reflects not only changing social attitudes but also the political shifts that underpin these moves. I feel that I should share some personal information here. In 2011, I had treatment for depression and stress brought on by the toxicity of modern academic life. However, I would not identify myself as a survivor in the terms that are discussed here. Porter (1987) notes that for as long as people have been defined as 'mad' by the medical profession and wider society, individuals have resisted or challenged the diagnosis and label. The refusal to accept the label is, of course, often seen as further evidence of the correctness of the diagnosis. Porter (1987) quotes the English playwright, Nathaniel Lee (1653–1692) who was admitted to Bedlam and afterwards remarked "They called me mad, and I called them mad, and damn them, they outvoted me." This is an observation that has echoes of Laing and Goffman's later criticisms of the nature of psychiatric diagnosis (Cummins, 2017b).

Crossley (1999, 2004) identifies the features of a social movement that are present in the user/survivor challenge to the power of psychiatry. A social movement consists of a network of agents and groups which can develop, sustain and transmit a culture or set of views. In this case, the culture is one of resistance and challenge. However, it is important to recognise that, within any social movement, there will be different and often opposing viewpoints. These will be explored later in this chapter. Crossley (1999, 2004) identifies the anti-psychiatry movement of the late 1950s and 1960s as a 'revolution from above'. The 'leaders' of the revolution were academics and psychiatrists. Crossley (2004) notes that the anti-psychiatry 'revolt from above' preceded and gave some impetus or ideological support to the 'revolt from below' that created the modern user/survivor movement. The Scottish Mental

Patients Union was established in 1971, followed by the Mental Patients' Union in 1973. There then followed the Community Organisation for Psychiatric Emergencies (COPE), which campaigned for local and ward changes but also established 'crash houses' as alternative safe places for those members who were experiencing crisis. In Italy, the work of Basaglia led to the establishment of the campaigning movement *Psichiatra Democratia* (Foot, 2015). These movements were all influenced by the radicalism of Laing and his challenge to the basis of diagnosis and the practice of institutionalised psychiatry. These groups and campaigns all share a commitment to challenging the medical model and thus the authority of psychiatrists and other mental health professionals. Diagnosis can be understood here as a form of *symbolic violence* (Bourdieu, 1998).

Bourdieu's notion of the field can be used as an approach to the analysis of the mental health policy. Bourdieu's notion of the field was a way of exploring the different positions and shifting alliances that occur in any area of public policy. Actors or agents within the field have to be aware of the history that led to the foundation of particular groups, their political positions and their alliances. He calls these 'the rules of the game'. This approach opens up the approach to analysis allowing for a more sophisticated understanding but also a recognition that these areas can be very complex and often contradictory. There are competing claims for authenticity among groups but also opposition. Crossley (2006) identifies the user/survivor movement as a field within itself. Within the field, he describes four poles: *anti-psychiatry, survivor, civil rights* and *paternalistic.* Crossley includes groups such as National Schizophrenia Fellowship (NSF) and SANE in his discussion. Both these groups essentially set out to represent the views of families, not necessarily those of patients. Their criticisms of psychiatry were founded on a belief that it had become too liberal – too influenced by Laing's notion that the root cause of what we term mental illness is the result of oppressive family dynamics. This is diametrically opposed to groups such as Recovery in the Bin (RITB) who argue that the original radical challenge to psychiatry has been marginalised. RITB makes much bolder political statements about the causes of mental illness.

The radical challenge to psychiatry that groups, such as the *British Network for Alternatives to Psychiatry* established by Laing and Cooper, represented can be seen as part of the wider 1960s counterculture. In 1986, *Survivors Speak Out* was established. The use of the term 'survivor' represents not just a change in language but a shift in approach. One only becomes a survivor after a traumatic experience. The use of the term at that point was most closely associated with the Holocaust. From the early 1980s onwards, it was used more widely, for example, in the context of childhood sexual abuse. Patients are not usually referred to as 'surviving medical care'. The term thus captures the political perspective that psychiatry is a form of social control, which involves the institutionalised abuse of individuals. The term also indicates that the mental health system, from this perspective, should not be seen as a humanitarian intervention to relieve suffering. It should be viewed as a damaging and corrupting system that relies on coercion including forcible medication but also barbaric treatments such as ECT. ECT remains a very controversial treatment even within psychiatry. In the discourse of surviving psychiatry, it becomes a cipher for the wider legally sanctioned abuses that psychiatric systems perpetrate.

The above represents what Crossley terms the *anti-psychiatry* and *survivor* poles of a field that Sedgwick (1982) termed *psychopolitics*. These two perspectives clearly have much in common. However, within the field of mental health activism, it is important to acknowledge that there are other more reformist or conservative traditions. Mind was founded in 1946 and adopted a reformist approach until the late 1970s. It was not opposed to the fundamental basis of psychiatry in the way that the Laing-influenced more radical groups were. With the appointment of the American lawyer Larry Gostin in the mid-1970s, Mind moved to a more civil rights/patients' rights agenda. This can be seen as part of a wider move that saw mental health issues being recast in terms of the broader civil rights and equalities agenda. Clearly, there were differences in the way that racial and gender discrimination operated at that time when compared to the experiences of mental health patients. However, alongside the discrimination that gay men and lesbians faced, there are clear overlaps or intersections. As well as social discrimination, all faced legal and other barriers to full citizenship. The civil rights perspective is based on this broader notion of citizenship (Somers, 2008; Sayce, 2016).

Crossley's (2006) final pole of the activism field is termed paternalism. I am not sure that this is an accurate description of the position of groups such as NSF, SANE and the Zito Trust. These groups have campaigned against what they see as the failings in community care. NSF was founded by Jonathan Pringle who wrote to *The Times* exasperated at the lack of support that was being offered to his family. SANE was established by the well-connected journalist Marjorie Wallace. SANE's name is an indication of its founding premise that there was a need to reform mental health policy. It saw argued that the focus on patients' rights had gone too far. A combination of liberal social workers and other mental health professionals were refusing to intervene in individual cases of real distress. In addition, SANE in particular felt that mental health professionals were reviving the Laingian theme of family blaming. Jayne Zito established the Zito Trust following the murder of her husband Jonathan Zito in 1992. The trust campaigned for reform of the MHA – it closed when CTOs were introduced – and supported families where there had been a homicide committed by a person in contact with mental health services. SANE and the Zito Trust received wide media coverage for their campaigns (Cummins, 2012). These organisations were very influential in the construction of a narrative of community care that saw its failings being the result of a liberal mental health legislation. From this perspective, it was argued that the MHA was written in such a way that it prevented intervention until individuals were severely mentally ill. The result was to put vulnerable people at risk and cause unnecessary suffering and distress to them and their families.

Bourdieu (2010) argued that language is not only a means of communication, it is also a medium of power. User/survivor may not be a term that is widely used by psychiatrists; doctors will, on the whole, use the term patients. This is, of course, a reflection of what they see as the power dynamics of these relationships. The term user/survivor did have important ramifications and influence in the broader mental health field. In health generally, there has been a shift towards a more consumerist approach. This is partly a reflection of wider cultural trends. However, as Karban (2016) notes this also has the potential to create a narrative of individual responsibility that hides the structural causes of health inequalities. The consumer movement in health helped to create a space for the 'survivor' in mental health. Crossley (2004: 167) argues that:

> survivors have been able to convert their experiences of mental distress and (mis)treatment into a form of cultural and symbolic capital. The disvalued status of the patient is reversed within the movement context.

Recovery

The modern version of the recovery model has its roots in the radical perspectives that challenged the power of psychiatry, particularly institutionalised coercive psychiatry. Rather than a humanitarian intervention, psychiatry was seen as abusive, stigmatising and based on flimsy scientific evidence (Cummins, 2017b). Activists argued that psychiatric interventions were damaging and not based on notions of respect and dignity. These treatments were seen to reduce or deny agency. The power of diagnosis was emphasised by mental health activist, Campbell (1996). She argued that psychiatric diagnosis becomes a destiny – one imposed or created by mental health services and the wider society. The implication of diagnosis is that it will map out a future of medicalisation, hospitalisation and social exclusion.

The recovery model became a new paradigm for mental health services from the 1990s onwards. Recovery, in its early form, was seen as an alternative to top down approaches. Its focus was on developing a different paradigm which was based on the following principles:

- A fundamental belief in the idea that recovery from severe mental illness is possible.
- Recovery is based on a holistic view of mental illness – focus is on people not symptoms.
- Recovery is a journey.
- Recovery is not a linear process.
- Recovery means different things to different people.
- Recovery does not necessarily involve getting back to where you were before.
- Recovery is based on people's expectations and attitudes.
- It requires a system of support from family, friends, professionals and the wider community.
- Recovery requires innovative and new ways of working.[6]

Recovery became one of the buzzwords that dominate services. The basic principles are one that most, if not all, of those involved in mental health services can sign up to support. At its core is a recognition – really a call for a paradigm shift – that diagnosis is not destiny. Such a shift requires a commitment to the involvement of service users in the design and development of services. The recovery paradigm should be an essentially optimistic one.

The success of the recovery model has led to some groups becoming critical of the way that it became subsumed in mental health services. There is a danger that the radical edge of such moves is lost as they become absorbed into mainstream thinking. Radical groups, for example Recovery in the Bin,[7] argue that mainstream services have used terms such as recovery to mask the actual impact of the retrenchment of mental health services. This radical perspective is summed up in the

---

[6]   Adapted from www.mentalhealth.org.uk/a-to-z/r/recovery

[7]   https://recoveryinthebin.org/

group's outline of its key principles. It is worth quoting these at length to demonstrate the unashamedly political nature of these statements. RITB makes an explicit link between the current economic and social policies of austerity and neoliberalism and mental health systems.

> This User Led group is for Psychiatric Survivors and Supporters who are fed up with the way colonised 'recovery' is being used to discipline and control those who are trying to find a place in the world, to live as they wish, while trying to deal with the very real mental distress they encounter on a daily basis. We believe in human rights and social and economic justice!

What we believe

1 We believe that the concept of 'recovery' has been colonised by mental health services, commissioners and policy makers.
2 We believe the growing development of this form of the 'Recovery Model' is a symptom of neoliberalism, and that capitalism is at the root of the crisis! Many of us will never be able to 'recover' living under these intolerable social and economic conditions, due to the effects of circumstances such as poor housing, poverty, stigma, racism, sexism, unreasonable work expectations, and countless other barriers.
3 We believe that the term 'UnRecovered' is a valid and legitimate political self-definition (not a permanent description of anyone's mental state) and we emphasise its political and social contrast to 'Recovered'. This doesn't mean we want to remain 'unwell' or 'ill' but that we reject the new neoliberal intrusion on the word 'recovery' that has been redefined, and taken over by market forces, humiliating treatment techniques and homogenising outcome measurements.
4 We believe that there are core principles of recovery that are worth saving, but that the colonisation of 'recovery' undermines those principles which have so far championed autonomy and self-determination. These principles cannot be found in one size fits all models, or calibrated by outcome measures. We also believe that autonomy and self-determination can only be

attained through collective struggle rather than through individualistic striving and aspiration, as we are social beings.

5 We propose to spread awareness of how neoliberalism and market forces shape the way mental health 'recovery' is planned and delivered by services, including those within the voluntary sector.[8]

This makes a clear, radical statement. Mental health is presented as an overtly political issue. From this perspective, the treatment of people with mental health problems cannot be divorced from the social and political contexts in which it takes place. In addition, the psychiatric system is seen to form part of a wider system of social control that is a buttress to the wider economic inequality that has increased under neoliberalism. These approaches have much in common with the radical challenge that Basaglia posed to established mental health systems (Foot, 2015).

Mad Studies

Since the publication of *Mad matters: A critical reader in Canadian mad studies* (LeFrançois et al, 2013), Mad Studies has gained an increasingly high profile. In 2014, the first Mad Studies stream at Lancaster Disability Studies Conference was convened at Lancaster University, bringing together critical scholarship and activism. Costa (2014) notes the term Mad Studies is not a school or group in the traditional sense of those terms. The focus is on survivor research but also exploring representations of madness in popular culture as well as current policy and legal issues. The term Mad Studies represents a clear paradigm shift from a positivist focus on 'mental illness' or the 'mentally ill'. In this model, experiential knowledge (Webb, 2008) is placed in a privileged position whereas psychiatry as a discipline would seek to minimise its significance or exclude it (Russo, 2012). Mad Studies challenges this quantitative paradigm where single or perhaps extreme experiences are viewed as just that. Here, these experiences can and should be used as a means of exploring wider concerns and issues. Mad Studies is a growing field that brings together a number of themes in the process of challenging the power of institutionalised psychiatry. It also provides an alternative standpoint that challenges the colonisation of user/ survivor movements by mainstream services. These processes are seen to

---

[8] https://recoveryinthebin.org/ritbkeyprinciples/

neutralise the radical edge and challenge that such movements present by incorporating them into a corporate and managerialist discourse.

Beresford and Wallcraft (1997) set out five key ways in which user/survivor research can challenge the established biomedical approach. The research comes from an explicit value base which is reflected in the following characteristics:

• Illness is replaced by concepts such as crisis or distress.
• Medical explanations are secondary to social or other models of understanding.
• The idea of symptoms, for example hearing voices, as a sign of illness is replaced by other possible explanations and constructions of such experiences.
• Psychiatric treatment – certain forms, for example ECT, or processes such as compulsory admission – are seen as types of abuse or torture.
• Diagnosis and the stigmatising labels it produces are seen as damaging.

The Mad Studies approach is one that appears to have a great deal of instinctive appeal to mental health social workers. It is clearly based in emancipatory and social justice paradigms of research and practice. In addition, it is focused very much on the experiences of user/survivors. It has a radical, political cutting edge. There is a danger that mental health social workers will fail to see that Mad Studies also carries with it an explicit radical and damaging critique of social work's role in mental health services and institutionalised psychiatry. The focus may be on psychiatrists but social workers and other mental health professionals have to look deeply at their own position. Larson (2008) in a discussion of anti-oppressive practice commented that social work in the area of mental health was still heavily committed to biomedical models, which were viewed as being incompatible with social justice aims. Reid and Poole (2013), in calling for a new approach in social work education, note that many mental health courses remain focused on issues such as intervention, medication and treatment. I would add that, in the context of England and Wales, one might add the role of the AMHP. It is not to say that these issues are not important, they are. It is to highlight the danger that such approaches potentially lead to a:

> divisive us and them mentality in social work where we the rational social work educators, decide on and distance ourselves from them, the irrational 'ill' users of mental health/social work services (Reid and Poole, 2013: 212).

One of the most significant changes in mental health services since the late 1970s has been the growth in user/survivor movements and groups. Mental health policy and services do not develop in a linear fashion. It would be naive to see the closure of the asylums and the development of community care as being simply driven by a paternalistic sense that the injustices of a previous age need to be addressed. One significant factor in this has been the increased presence of a range of critical radical user/survivor voices and perspectives. The field of political action has shifted from a focus on the institutional response to a much broader analysis of mental health and mental health policy. Groups such as RITB make an explicit link between neoliberal social and economic policy and mental health issues. The group also highlights the danger that mental health services will respond to user/survivor groups in a tokenistic or patronising way. It is much easier for an organisation to have a mission statement that commits itself to working with 'experts by experience' than it is to achieve the organisational and cultural shifts that are required for this to become meaningful. This is a classic dilemma for community and other groups: how do they ensure that they engage effectively with the mental health system without being colonised by it? Recognition and becoming part of the official discourse is a double edged sword. There is an inherent danger that the survivor voice becomes marginalised by or subsumed within processes that nominally recognise it.

Social work's relationship with user/survivor movement is a complex and shifting one. Social work and social workers would, I think, naturally seek to align themselves with the anti-psychiatry/survivor poles of the field of mental health activism that Crossley (2004) outlines. This is a fit in terms of social work's values and professed commitment to social justice. It also neatly side steps any debates about the role of social work in mental health services. Statutory social work, in particular, has certainly played a role in the symbolic violence that mental health institutions have inflicted. However, in examining these questions, it has to be recognised that social workers work in a range of settings and carry out a variety of roles. In addition, social workers, as with academics, can identify as survivors and be doubly located within the mental health system and the survivor movement.

Contemporary issues

The chapter will now go on to examine some contemporary concerns across mental health services.

Life on wards

Psychiatry and all mental health social work can be seen to take place in the shadow cast by the use of the formal powers of the MHA. It is a constant source of surprise to me how little real consideration is given to the impact of the use of compulsory powers but also how mental health units remain hidden or closed institutions. They generally only appear in the media spotlight when there have been difficulties or examples of abuse and poor practice. This appears to me to be part of the long-standing fear and stigma that is attached to mental health services and key institutions.

Sexual violence and mental health units

Foley and Cummins (2018) report the findings of a scoping study that set out to explore the extent of recorded sexual violence perpetrated on mental health units. Using Freedom of Information Act (FOI) requests, data was obtained from both police forces and subsequently Mental Health Trusts on the number of recorded offences of rape and sexual assault by penetration for the five years 2010–15. Before discussing the results of the study, it is important to place them in the context of the increased vulnerability to victimisation of people with mental health problems and the current approaches to ensuring patient safety.

Sexual violence

Estrich and 'real rape'

Estrich (1987) coined the term 'real rape' as a way of capturing the dominant stereotype that pervades social and cultural attitudes to the offence. She argues that 'real rape' is constructed as a crime where a white, attractive, young victim is attacked at night by a stranger. The motivation for the attack is sexual gratification. This stereotype is very powerful in that rape cases that are reported in the media tend conform to the key elements of it (Franiuk et al, 2008). It is also the imagine of the offence of rape that dominates in popular culture. ONS (2015) data suggests that only 15% of rapes would fit the 'real rape' stereotype, in that they involve an attack perpetrated by a stranger. Kelly et al's (2005) research concluded that women are most likely to be assaulted by a partner or someone they know. These rapes often following social situations involving alcohol. The impact of the 'real rape' construct is such that victims of rape that occur in different circumstances – the overwhelming majority of cases – feel that the starting point of the investigation is a questioning of the legitimacy of their experience or their behaviour and/or sexual history (McMillan and Thomas, 2009). Work by Brown et al (2007) indicates that the prosecution of a case is more likely if it has the characteristics of 'real rape'. Victims who do not fit the 'real rape' stereotype are thus less likely to be believed when they report that they have been raped. Women with mental health problems might not fit the stereotype of the 'real rape' victim. These factors combine to produce an environment where it may be even more difficult for women who experience mental health problems to report assaults or give evidence in court (Foley and Cummins, 2015).

Sexual violence is a worldwide occurrence. It has huge social, personal and political implications. Reactions to it reflect wider cultural and other attitudes. The impact of sexual violence clearly varies from individual to individual. Browne and Finkelhor (1986) explain these variations can be linked to individual psychosocial factors but also the nature of the sexual violence and the support that is offered to the survivor in the aftermath of the assault. Black et al (2011) found that 1% of US women reported that they had been raped in the previous 12 months. The dominance of the construct of 'real rape' acts as a barrier to the prosecution of offences that do not fall within it. In these cases, the focus, particularly within the Criminal Justice System (CJS) and trial settings then shifts to the behaviour of the victim. Black et al (2011) highlight that stranger attacks are much rarer than those by intimate partners. In their study, 0.6% of US women reported that they had been raped by a partner. The traumatic impact of sexual violence can be manifested in a range of mental health issues. These include depression, alcohol and substance misuse, suicidal ideation, self-harm and PTSD. Women in the CJS and prisons are much more likely than other groups in the population to have been subjected to sexual violence. The Corston Inquiry (2008) into the use of imprisonment for women in England and Wales highlighted this. A third of women in prison have also attempted suicide at some point in their lives.

The potential impact of sexual violence is such that it must be a priority issue for mental health services. There are two elements to this. The first is that those using mental health services may have been subjected to sexual violence. The second is that inpatients may be at greater risk. All patients are owed a duty of care – this extends to ensuring personal safety while an inpatient. There have been ongoing concerns about the physical environment of mental health wards. Quirk and Lelliott (2001) found that patients were concerned about life on the wards – they reported concerns about the lack of meaningful activity.

Alongside this, wards were described as dirty and the food was poor. In addition, patients reported that they were concerned by the availability and use of street drugs on the wards. Patients in this study reported that they were concerned for their physical safety. The personal safety of patients has to be a priority issue for all those working in mental health care. In the inpatient setting, if patients are concerned that they are not physically safe, then this will almost certainly have an impact on their mental health.

Stenhouse (2013) uses the term 'sanctuary harm' to capture the potentially damaging impact of abuse or violence that occurs to patients who have been admitted to a mental health unit. The study highlighted that patients wanted to feel safe as one of the basic aspects of inpatient care. Nursing staff have a key role to play here. This study found that patients felt safer with more male staff on duty as male nurses were seen as being able to respond to and deal with physical violence and aggression. Jones et al (2010) see wards as both safe and unsafe places. It should be noted that people with mental health problems are much more likely to be victims of crime and abuse than the general population. Therefore, the mental health unit might be a safer place, particularly if individuals have good relationships with staff and are familiar with the environment and other patients. Jones et al's work (2010) indicates that factors such as unfamiliarity with the staff group and witnessing the use of restraint and seclusion were factors that increased anxiety among patients. Ellison et al (2015) identify higher rates of victimisation among adults with 'psychosocial disabilities'. There have been a series of concerns about the way that the CJS responds to people with mental health problems who have made complaints about sexual violence (Mind, 2007; Pettitt et al, 2013). Hester (2013) highlights that women with mental health problems are less likely to be believed when they make a complaint of sexual violence. In their discussion of the Serious Case Review (SCR) that examined the suicide of Mrs A, Foley and Cummins (2015) highlight the way that Mrs A's mental health problems were used by the defence to suggest that the allegations were fantasy. Despite some progress in this area including the use of special measures for victims giving evidence in court, it remains the case that there are additional barriers to the reporting and investigation of sexual crimes where the person making the complaint has mental health problems. These barriers made be greater if the assault takes place on a mental health unit when the victim's mental health is such that they have been detained under the MHA (1983).

Choe et al (2008) note that people with mental health problems are at greater risk of victimisation than the general population. Violence and sexual violence have to be areas of concern for all mental health professionals because of their potential impact on the development of mental health problems but also because of the potential victimisation of service users. Bengsten–Tops and Ehlisson (2011) carried out a study involving 174 patients: 67% of this cohort had been victims in adulthood; 39% had been threatened at some point; 51% had been assaulted and 32% had been the victims of sexual assault; 33% of the cohort had been a victim in the previous 12 months – 15% had been subjected to sexual violence in that period. Women reported greater exposure than men. As Khalifeh et al (2014) note, the focus of research on violence and serious mental illness has been on debates around whether people with mental health problems are more likely than other groups to commit such offences. This is clearly a very important area but it does divert attention from the experiences of people with mental health problems as victims of serious violent crime. The authors note that the relationship between serious mental illness and experiencing violence is a complex one that is most likely to be bi-directional. These patient histories of trauma are often not acknowledged by professionals (Howard et al, 2010) or where they are there is not an appropriate response (Nyamie et al, 2013). Khalifeh et al (2014) conclude that men and women who experience severe mental illness and are in contact with psychiatric services are 2–8 times more likely to experience domestic violence or sexual assault. The study also concluded that these experiences of violence could be a potential trigger for suicidal ideation. In addition, this violence is often not disclosed to health care professionals.

Mind (2007) conducted a survey of people with mental health problems and their experiences of crime: 71% of respondents with a mental health problem had been a victim within the previous two years. This compared with 22% of the general population. There was a very definite perception among victims and witnesses with a mental health problem or a learning difficulty that both the police and the Crown Prosecution Service (CPS) made judgments about the case based on whether the complainant would be able to go to court and give evidence. In a thematic review (HMCPS Inspectorate, 2016) of CPS study of decision making , a case file review of 45 cases showed that in 38 cases it was the police which was the first agency to make the CPS aware of that a victim or key witness had a mental health problem or learning difficulty. In 15 cases, there was a 'no prosecution' decision by the CPS. The most common causes were evidential issues including the reliability and or credibility of the victim or concerns that it would be detrimental, in some way, to the health of the victim or key witness to pursue the case.

In the report *At risk yet dismissed* (Pettitt et al, 2013), 9% of victims reported crimes that had taken place in psychiatric settings. This study is based on a series of interviews with people with mental health problems who had been victims of crime. The interviews reveal the impact of violence with participants reporting that they felt fear, shame and embarrassment in the aftermath. The negative impact on mental health was also documented with participants reporting feelings of distress. In some cases, the mental health of victims deteriorated and the crime triggered a relapse and subsequent admission to hospital. The issue of reporting was also examined in this study. Participants reported that one of the factors in their decision not to report was a fear that they would not be believed. Those who decided to report the assault to the police indicated that support from friends, family and professionals was a factor alongside a previous positive experience with the police. In addition, the concern that the offences might escalate and the wish to protect others were all positive factors in this process. This study also highlighted the concerns that individuals had that would prevent them reporting incidents to the police. A previous negative experience with the police was a factor here. However, the overarching concern was that they would not be believed. The interviewees were extremely conscious that the fact that they had a mental health problem might potentially be used as a basis for discrediting their account. It is particularly regrettable that many thought that they may even be detained under the MHA if they reported a crime.

Patient safety

The National Patient Safety Agency (NPSA) has a key role in the monitoring of incidents that put any patients at risk in any way. This applies across health service providers. In its guide *Seven Steps to Patients Safety*, the key factors to the creation of a culture of patient safety include the promotion of reporting, involving and communicating with patients and public, and learning and sharing safety lessons. In addition, staff should report 'near misses' or 'no harm'. The NPSA recognises that there is a need for a greater awareness of the potential vulnerability of those experiencing mental health problems when they are inpatients. It is not the main focus of this paper but the NPSA notes that this includes an acknowledgement that sexual disinhibition is a not uncommon symptom of serious mental illness. Therefore, mental health professionals have to manage a number of different aspects of this problematic issue. However, it is vitally important to emphasise that the focus of interventions needs to be based on the potential victimisation of patients. NPSA guidance starts from the premise that reports of such incidents must always be taken seriously. As noted above, one of the biggest barriers to the reporting of such incidents is the belief that victims hold that they will not be taken seriously and that this is, in part, due to their mental health problems.

As well as emphasising that any allegations will be taken seriously and crimes investigated, the guidance highlights that patients should have access to appropriate sexual health advice and support services. The physical layout of the wards should also be considered. There has been a move to single sex wards more generally within health services. This appears to be of particular importance in this area. The DH issued guidance recommending single sex sleeping, toilet and bath accommodation in 2000. In 2004/05, 99% of institutions had completed these changes. The NPSA also notes that units that are in areas of high demand should resist the pressure to admit patients of the opposite sex to single sex wards in times of acute bed shortages. The wider pressure on mental health services makes this an increasingly common problem that mental health service providers have to face. The guidance does not explicitly discuss sexual violence but emphasises the importance of ensuring the physical safety of patients. It also highlights that separate toilets and sleeping accommodation for men and women is also an important standard and a government policy. In themselves, these guidelines will not necessarily prevent incidents of sexual violence. However, they are all important in creating a culture that recognises the potential increased vulnerability of an inpatient, takes step to prevent incidents and provides appropriate support to those reporting any incidents of sexual violence.

The National Reporting and Learning System (NRLS) exists to collate all reports of incidents where a patient's safety has been put at risk in any way. There is a general underreporting of incidents. The categorisation of incidents includes patients' accidents – for example slips and falls, disruptive and aggressive behaviour, self-harm and absconding. In 2006, incidents categorised under these headings accounted for 84% of all reports. It should be noted that there is not a specific category of sexual assault or violence – either as a victim or perpetrator. The NRLS carried out an analysis of a sample of 200 incidents of disruptive or aggressive behaviour. Five incidents in this sample concerned sexual safety. As a result, a further search of the whole data set of incidents of disruptive and aggressive behaviour was undertaken. There were 122 reported incidents where concerns were the result of sexual behaviour – 19 rapes, 20 cases of consensual sex, 13 cases of exposure, 18 cases of sexual advances, 26 touching and 26 other. The report notes that there was significant variation among trusts in how they approach and report these incidents. When an incident is reported, the organisation has to assess the degree of harm that the impact has had on the patient. In 114 of these cases, 'no harm' was reported. Even if one allows for the fact that this an assessment of physical rather than psychological needs, this is a startling assessment. The impact of such incidents has to include the potential trauma and that such incidents may well be examples of revictimisation. The nature of these crimes, particularly that there are 19 rapes included, means that there must have been a level of physical violence involved. In the cases of rape, eight attacks were perpetrated by patients and eleven by staff. In addition, the 20 cases that are described as being consensual sex raise a number of important questions about the nature of consent in such circumstances. They also beg the question why consensual sex would be described as disruptive or aggressive behaviour.

Improving mental health units

Having raised serious concerns about some of the aspects of the experiences of patients in mental health units, it would be wrong not to acknowledge that there is a great deal of work being undertaken to improve the situation. This is vitally important in not only ensuring that all patients are treated with dignity and respect, but also in challenging the stigma that attaches itself to mental health. If the experiences of a mental health unit are poor, they play into that wider social narrative about the nature of mental illness and what the response should be. In 2011, the Royal College of Psychiatrists (RCP, 2011) published a guide called *Do the right thing: How to judge a good ward*.

The RCP guide had ten standards against which a psychiatric ward should be judged:

- *Bed occupancy rates of 85% or less:* Bed occupancy rates are a main driver of inpatient care standards. A higher bed occupancy rate will mean delays in admission but also that it is difficult to provide patients with periods of leave.
- *Ward size maximum of 18 beds:* A larger ward creates a more institutionalised environment.
- *A physical environment that is fit for purpose:* There needs to be access to fresh air as well as private and quiet spaces. Separate toilets and

sleeping accommodation for men and women is also an important standard and government policy.

- *The ward as a therapeutic space:* The purpose of any admission has to be a therapeutic one. Therefore, wards need to provide a range of therapeutic activities alongside leisure and other activities that will have a positive impact on patients' mental and physical health.
- *Proportionate and respectful approach to risk and safety:* The ward environment has to ensure the safety and dignity of the patients. This requires a whole systems approach to risk ensuring that appropriate procedures are in place but also that there is an acknowledgement that recovery will involve some risk. Individuals need to be involved in decisions about their treatment.
- *A recovery-based approach:* The ward should be seen as one aspect of the wider mental health systems.
- *Access to psychological interventions.* Psychological therapies are an integral part of the recovery process.
- *Personalised care:* This cannot be provided unless there is adequate staffing and the appropriate mix and levels of skills among the staff.

Star Wards

Star Wards was founded in 2006 by Marion Janner, who was awarded the OBE for her work in this area. The project, by sharing good practice and ideas from across the sector, seeks to challenge the notion that it is inevitable that mental health units will be bleak, unforgiving places that are as likely to increase mental distress as tackle the issues that patients face. It is committed to ensuring that wards have sufficient resources to ensure that acute inpatient units have the greatest opportunity to create an environment of therapeutic engagement, while at the same time maintaining links with service users' support networks and community. This is an approach that challenges the sorts of issues highlighted in the CQC(2015) review of the MHA. It looks at ways of fostering a creative, dynamic and improved therapeutic environment.

Perinatal mental health

Perinatal mental health problems are those that occur during pregnancy or in the first year following the birth of a child. It is estimated that such problems affect between 10% and 20% of women during pregnancy. The Maternal Mental Health Alliance (MMHA) is a grouping of 60 organisations. Its campaign – *Everyone's Business* – highlights the often patchy provision so services in this area. It calls for all women throughout the UK who experience perinatal mental health problems to receive the care they and their families need, wherever and whenever they need it. It is a sobering thought that National Confidential Enquiry into Maternal Deaths (Oates and Cantwell, 2011) reported that while suicide is the most common cause of death among pregnant women and mothers in the first year after giving birth, in the overwhelming majority of such tragic cases the women were not being cared for by specialist mental health teams.

Closing the Gap – priorities for essential change in mental health (DH, 2014) identifies maternal mental health as a key area for service improvement. There is a hugely significant public health issue but appears to have been neglected. MMHA reports that only 3% of clinical commissioning groups (CCGs) have a specific strategy for commissioning specialist perinatal mental health services (CMH/ LSE, 2014). They estimate that perinatal mental health issues such as depression, anxiety and psychosis cost about £8.1 million for each annual cohort of births. MMHA outlines the extent of these concerns. For example, 7.4% of women experience symptoms of depression in the first trimester, 11.4–12.8% in the second trimester and 13.1–14.8% in the final trimester (CMH/LSE, 2014). The work of Heron et al (2004) and Bennett et al (2004) conclude that symptoms of post-natal depression were experienced by 7.4–11% of women in the first three months after the birth of their child, 7.8–12.8% of women in the first six months and 8.5–12.0% of women in the first nine months. All mental health problems are potentially serious. Postpartum psychosis (or puerperal psychosis) is a severe episode of mental illness which begins suddenly in the days or weeks after having a baby.[9] It affects approximately one in 1,000 new mothers. Symptoms include high mood or mania, delusions and hallucinations.

Specialist perinatal mental health services are required for women who have complex needs or those who are experiencing severe episodes such as postpartum psychosis. These will include specialist mother and baby units – a normal psychiatric ward would be a totally inappropriate for a mother and her newly born baby. NICE (2007) reported a shortfall of 68 specialist beds in mother and baby units. MMHA highlights that there are only 17 such units in total across the UK. There are none at all in Wales and Northern Ireland or the Southern or Eastern health regions. The potential for intervention in perinatal mental health is very significant. It is clearly a very important public health issue with

---

[9] www.rcpsych.ac.uk/healthadvice/problemsdisorders/postpartumpsychosis.aspx

implications for the health of women and children. In addition, it is very unusual for women not to be in some form of contact with health services during their pregnancy. There are some groups of women where this is more difficult – for example, women who are homeless. However, only 41% of new mothers reported being asked specifically about their mental health by midwives or health visitors (Hogg, 2013).

Howard et al's (2013) work shows that domestic violence is more likely to occur in pregnancy. Symptoms of depression, anxiety and trauma responses are also significantly associated with the experience of domestic violence during pregnancy. NICE guidelines suggest that women should be asked questions about related to domestic violence during consultations with their midwife. This work also highlights other difficulties such as breaks in the continuity of care, which can create barriers to the establishment and maintenance of good relationships. This might make it more difficult for women to discuss any issues that they are experiencing. In addition, there are strong cultural attitudes that mean there is a reluctance to discuss these areas of pregnancy. There is a national shortage of midwives and health visitors. *Closing the Gap* (DH, 2014) outlines ambitious plans to recruit 5,000 additional midwives and 4,200 additional health visitors.

Karban (2016), in outlining a health inequalities approach to mental health, emphasises the impact of structural factors. In the area of perinatal mental health care where social factors and health inequalities combine to mean that poorer women face greater risks. Edge (2007, 2010) highlights the experience of women from BAME backgrounds. Edge (2010) emphasises that there is a danger of using this group as a proxy or representative of all BAME women. This ignores the particular cultural and social experiences of the different groups of women who make up the totality of BAME women. These differences include language barriers, cultural practices and the experiences of migration. This is an important issue. Edge (2010) notes that, in the same way, 'white' is also a catch all term that obscures or ignores huge variations in experiences between groups including people of Irish origin, recent East European migrants to the UK and non-European white people.

Edge's (2007, 2010) work demonstrates that the needs of pregnant BAME women are often overlooked and do not receive an appropriate response from services. There are social factors that need to be acknowledged here. BAME women are more likely to come from poorer backgrounds. Almost half of Black Caribbean women who give birth in the UK are lone parents. Edge (2010: 22) argues that '…even settled migrants who were born in the UK and are living in circumstances that are known to increase their risk of perinatal depression might have their needs overlooked'. The issues that create barriers for Black Caribbean men accessing mental health services and led to their over-representation (Keating et al, 2002), of course, apply in perhaps slightly different fashion to women. There are very important messages here for social work and health agencies about how they need to take steps to ensure that there is a more open approach to these issues.

Young people and mental health issues

One aspect of the increased difficulties that mental health services face has been in providing appropriate support for young people in crisis. In August 2017, these issues were brought to wider public attention when Sir James Munby said he felt 'ashamed and embarrassed' that no hospital place could be found for a 17-year-old girl who was about to be released from youth custody. The judge warned the nation would have ' blood on its hands' if a suitable hospital placement could not be found for the young woman who had a distressing and complicated history, including attempts to take her own life. The judge concluded that:

> We are, even in these times of austerity, one of the richest countries in the world. Our children and young people are our future. X is part of our future. It is a disgrace to any country with pretensions to civilisation, compassion and, dare one say it, basic human decency, that a judge in 2017 should be faced with the problems thrown up by this case and should have to express himself in such terms. (Rawlinson et al, 2017)

This is clearly an unusual case but it did highlight a range of concerns about not only the pressures that young people face but also the struggles that services and community groups face. Sir James's intervention forced agencies to act and eventually a suitable placement was found. However, this is one, perhaps extreme, example. It should not require the intervention of a judge to resolve such matters. It would be impossible in all cases. One also has to wonder what the potential impact of the delays and uncertainty had in this case – firstly on the young woman and her family but also on those involved in or with responsibility for her care.

In 2015, the coalition government published *Future in mind* (DH, 2015a), which sets out a policy framework for children and young people's mental health and wellbeing. The report acknowledges that there has been historically an underinvestment in mental health services for children and young people. This situation has been exacerbated by the retrenchment in youth services and other provision for young people that have an impact on health and wellbeing.

Future in mind has five key themes or areas:

- promoting resilience, prevention and early intervention
- improving access to effective support – a system without tiers
- care for the most vulnerable
- accountability and transparency
- developing the workforce.

The report notes that over half of mental health problems in adult life, excluding dementia, start by the age of 14 and 75% by the age of 18. It goes on to suggest that, though mental health problems are relatively common, young people do not get the help that they require as quickly as they should. As well as the pain and distress that mental health problems create for young people and their families, there are obvious knock on effects in areas such as education, which can restrict the opportunities that young people have as adults. There is, therefore, an economic and moral case for investing in these services. For example, children with conduct disorder are twice as likely to leave school with no qualifications (DH, 2015a: 13). The structure of the education system and modern economy mean that it is increasingly difficult to make up these skills and qualification gaps but also that the range of employment opportunities is limited to low paid precarious work.

The taskforce that completed the work for this DH report was made up of specialists and influential figures from the range of relevant children's services. It reported the following key areas of concern:

- *Gaps in data and information:* A failure to collect systematic data makes reform and appropriate service configuration increasingly difficult. This is particularly the case in the complex world of NHS commissioning and other developments.
- *A treatment gap:* Green et al (2005) suggested that only 25–35% of young people with a diagnosable mental health problem accessed support. Since that time, there have been increasing concerns about issues such as eating disorders and the increase in the number of young people who self-harm.
- *Difficulties in access:* As with adult services, there are concerns about accessing services and waiting times. Service providers also highlight

the fact that they are dealing with an increasing complex range of issues.

- *Commissioning:* The current complex structures create real risks that children and young people will fall through safety nets. This has been a recurring issue documented in a series of reports.
- *Crisis services:* As in adults services, access to crisis services is at best patchy.
- *Vulnerable groups:* There are a range of barriers that some of the most vulnerable young people – for example, those in the care of the local authority or unaccompanied asylum seekers – face.

Future in mind outlines the programme of investment that has been undertaken, including:

- £60m into Children and Young People's Improving Access to Psychological Therapies (CYP IAPT) programme over the period 2011–15/16
- £150m over the next five years (2015–20) in England to improve services for children and young people with mental health problems with a particular emphasis on eating disorders
- £15m is being invested in the Children and Young People's Secure Estate by NHS England.

There are ongoing concerns about the impact of much wider societal pressures on children and young people, which have implications for mental health. Eating disorders and depression among young girls have been linked to social media and other pressures. Half of young people who die by suicide are not known to services. NICE (2010) reported that 60% of children and young people in the care of the local authority have a diagnosable mental disorder.

Schools are key institutions in the lives of children and young people. DH (2015a) notes that many schools are developing a whole school approach that aims to promote emotional wellbeing. This includes support around particularly stressful times such as public examinations but also in moves to support the development of resilience and to tackle issues such as bullying. Schools are also involved in interventions to promote positive physical health – healthy eating, drug education and anti-smoking work – that have been demonstrated to have a positive impact on self-esteem and mental health. This is also true of work that is focused on sexual health and education, which focuses on positive relationships. Taggart et al (2014) found that pupils in 86% of the secondary schools that they surveyed has access to a trained or qualified counsellor. These should not be seen as an alternative to specialist mental health services but clearly they have a key role in supporting children and young people in the often pressurised school environment.

Young people in crisis

This section began with the discussion of a case where a young person was clearly in a crisis and in need of intensive specialised inpatient care. The problems in this area of provision for young people reflect some of the concerns that have been discussed about adult services. This includes young people being admitted to adult wards, for example a study by the BBC and Community Care magazine (Limb, 2014), based on information from 51 trusts, that in 2011/12, 242 young people were placed on adult wards; in 2012/13 the figure was 257; and in the six months to December 2013, it was 350. In addition, there are many examples of young people being placed out of area – often hundreds of miles away from their families, friends and schools. Any admission to a mental health unit is likely to have a disruptive effect on the lives of a young person and their family. This will be exacerbated in such circumstances.

Transitions

The issue of transition – moving from child and adolescent mental health services (CAMHS) to adult services – is one that has been a long-standing cause of concern. A young person who took part in the one of the taskforce's engagement sessions for *Future in mind* outlined their experience as follows:

> 'I had a very bad transition from CAMHS to adult services. One day I was in CAMHS with plenty of support and then the next, the only support I knew of was a crisis number. It took over 6 months for me to have a proper assessment and be assigned a care co-ordinator, by which time I had suffered a complete relapse in my condition.' (DH, 2015a: 48)

This is one example but it brings together a number of broader concerns. In addition, it should be recognised that it is at the time of transition – from school to higher and further education or work or moving into adulthood – that young people need the most support. All young people find these moves potentially stressful in one way or another. Those with mental health concerns face increased pressures.

Within this cohort, the taskforce identifies particularly vulnerable groups, for example, care leavers or those in contact with the CJS. The taskforce report (DH, 2015a) makes few direct references to the role of social work in the new vision of mental health services. However, the public health approach that is adopted and the recognition of the importance of social and peer group factors mean that is an area where social work can and should make a key contribution.

Mental Capacity Act 2005

The Mental Capacity Act (MCA) 2005 was introduced in 2007. It provides a legal framework for the assessment of individual capacity. Where individuals are deemed as lacking capacity to make a particular decision then those doing so on their behalf must act in their best interest. The MCA applies to anyone over the age of 16. In law, capacity means having the ability to make a decision and to take actions. There is a presumption in favour of a capacity: there has to be evidence to prove that an individual can be deemed to lack capacity. Capacity is fluid – a person's capacity may well fluctuate over time. Any assessment of capacity must be time and decision specific. This acknowledges the fluid nature of the concept but also that there may be other factors, such as the level of complexity in the decision making process or the impact that need to be taken into consideration. A person cannot be said to lack capacity simply because of an illness or disability.

There are five key principles that underpin the MCA:

1. Presumption of capacity
2. Individuals being supported to make their own decisions
3. Unwise decisions
4. Best interests
5. Least restrictive option[10]

Combined, these principles mean that it is not possible to second guess –i.e. if someone is viewed as having capacity, one cannot use the decision they make to argue that this assessment was incorrect. People can and do make decisions that others see as unwise, foolish or just plain wrong. This is a fact of adult life.

---

[10] www.scie.org.uk/mca/introduction/mental-capacity-act-2005-at-a-glance

Decisions about capacity

There is a two stage test to decide whether an individual has the capacity to make a particular decision.

Stage 1. Is there an impairment of or disturbance in the functioning of a person's mind or brain? If so:

Stage 2. Is the impairment or disturbance sufficient that the person lacks the capacity to make a particular decision?

The MCA states that a person lacks capacity if one of the following applies:

- A person cannot understand information given to them.
- They cannot retain that information long enough to be able to make the decision.
- They cannot weigh up the information available to make the decision.
- They cannot communicate their decision – this could be by talking, using sign language or even simple muscle movements.

In this schema, every effort should be made (and documented) to show the processes that professionals have followed in reaching a decision that the person lacks capacity. This is particularly important if it is felt that the person is not able to communicate their decision. In making a decision that is in someone's 'best interests'. The 'decision maker' has to consult widely.

The MCA aims to enhance personal autonomy (Manthorpe et al, 2009). Part of the process of doing this was the creation of a new framework and roles where individuals wished to make advanced care and treatment decisions. The Lasting Power of Attorney allows nominated individuals to make decision in key areas such as finance, welfare and health on behalf of the person who has nominated them to take this role. The key roles in this framework are:

- *Lasting powers of attorney (LPAs):* The MCA allows people over the age of 18 to formally appoint one or more people to look after their health, welfare and/or financial decisions
- *Court of protection and deputies:* The MCA created a new court and a new public official to protect people who lack capacity and to supervise those making decisions on their behalf.
- *The public guardian:* The role of the public guardian is to protect people who lack capacity from abuse. The public guardian is supported by the Office of the Public Guardian (OPG).

- *Independent mental capacity advocate (IMCA):* IMCAs are a statutory safeguard for people who lack capacity to make some important decisions. This includes decisions about where the person lives and serious medical treatment when the person does not have family of friends who can represent them.[11]

The MCA also introduced new offences of wilful neglect and mistreatment of people who lack decision making capacity. Manthorpe et al (2009) note that, while the Act is not solely written with people with dementia in mind, it is clearly this group of people that are likely to be most affected by the introduction of the MCA.

Deprivation of Liberty Safeguards (DOLs)

Article 5 of the Human Rights Act 1998 – the right to liberty – states that 'everyone has the right to liberty and security of person. No one shall be deprived of his or her liberty [unless] in accordance with a procedure prescribed in law.' The MCA 2005 allows for the use of restraint where it is felt that this is necessary to ensure the safety of the individual. The Supreme Court in the case referred to as *Cheshire West* clarified an 'acid test' for what constitutes a 'deprivation of liberty' in 2014. The test established that a person is deprived of their liberty if they:

- lack the capacity to consent to their care/treatment arrangements;
- are under continuous supervision and control; and
- are not free to leave.

The Supreme Court further held that the following factors such as the person's compliance or lack of objection to the proposed care/ treatment and the reason or purpose behind a particular placement are not to be considered in reaching a decision. In 2013/14 there were approximately 13,700 applications. In 2014/15, the year after Cheshire West there were 137,540 (DH, 2015b). The Deprivation of Liberty Safeguards (DoLS) can only be used if the person will be deprived of their liberty in a care home or hospital. In other settings the Court of Protection can authorise a deprivation of liberty. Care homes or hospitals must ask a local authority if they can deprive a person of their liberty. Best interest assessors (BIAs) carry out an assessment role in overseeing the use of these powers.

---

[11] www.scie.org.uk

In March 2017, the Law Commission published a report *Mental capacity and deprivation of liberty*. Since the *Cheshire West* judgment, there have been concerns that the demands of the system are unsustainable. In submissions to the Law Commission, the system was described as being overly bureaucratic and distressing for individuals and families. The demands on the system were such that there was a backlog of cases and people, or the circumstances in which they were living were left being unassessed.

The Law Commission final report called for DoLs to be replaced. The replacement scheme proposed is called *The Liberty Protection Safeguards*. The Commission set out the proposed conditions to authorise arrangements where:

- the person lacks capacity;
- a medical assessment confirms that the person is of unsound mind within the meaning of the European Court of Human Rights (ECHR);
- the arrangements are proportionate to any likelihood of harm;
- there has been a consultation with the friends and families; and
- any authorisation would not conflict with a valid decision as to where the person should live or receive care or treatment.

The Law Commission proposed the creation of a new role – the *approved mental capacity professional* (AMCP). This role would build on the best interest assessor role. The AMCP role clearly has echoes of the AMHP role. There would be a significant difference in that it would be to provide written approval of the care arrangements, ensuring that they are proportionate. The AMCP would be a similar position to the AMHP – independent but acting on behalf of a local authority. Independence would ensure that an AMCP could not be directed to reach a particular conclusion. There would be a system of registration and approval by the Health and Care Professions Council both of AMCPs and courses that provide training.

At the time of writing, it is not clear how these reforms will be pursued, if at all. However, it is apparent that the DoLs in their current format are under tremendous pressure but also that the legislation is not meeting the aims original framers envisaged.

Care Act 2014

The Care Act 2014 was heralded by the coalition government as marking a fundamental change in social care in England. Norman

Lamb, UK Minister for Care, stated that the Act represented the most significant change since the creation of the structures of the modern welfare state after World War II. He argued that the Act introduced changes that would result in people and their carers taking control of their care and support (DH, 2014). The Act creates a new legal framework for how systems should seek to protect adults at risk of abuse or neglect.

Key principles of the Care Act 2014

Section 1(1) of the Care Act 2014 placed a general duty on local authorities to promote the wellbeing of the individual. Slasberg and Beresford (2014) note that this alongside the guidance issued subsequent to the Act, which states that any assessment must begin from 'the assumption that the individual is best placed to judge the individual's well being' seems to put service user in a much more powerful position. However, as they conclude, the guidance gives the local authority the trump card as the guidance makes clear that the local authority ultimately makes decisions about what a person's needs are. Even for individuals who self-assess, the council has to be 'satisfied that the individual's self-assessment has accurately captured their needs' (para 6.58). These changes were introduced in a period of austerity and welfare retrenchment, during which services and benefits for people with disabilities were particularly severely hit (Cummins, 2018). The introduction of the Act also saw the introduction of the concept of a national 'minimum eligibility threshold'. This replaced the previous policy *Fair access to care services* (DH, 2003). The aim was to provide consistency and transparency in this area. However, Slasberg and Beresford (2014) argue that the new guidance is a rehashed version of the old that will essentially replicate existing practice whereby need is defined by the resources available. Critics of the Care Act argue that the message of the Act that these changes will lead to people gaining more control through personal budgets and that practitioners will be able to work in a more person centred way are misleading. These welcome aims crash on the rocks of a system that still leaves need being defined by resources and the overall policy of austerity with its impact on people with disabilities.

Safeguarding

No secrets (DH, 2002) is an important document in the development of adult protection and safeguarding policy. Some regarded it as an important step in raising awareness of the issues of 'vulnerable adult protection' (Penhale et al, 2017). In particular, there was some optimism that this would be another stage in the process of putting the abuse and exploitation of vulnerable adults on a par with the organisational responses that were required when children are subject to abuse or neglect. There was one major flaw in that *No secrets* was issued as guidance so local authorities did not have to respond in the way that child protection procedures and legislation require. This is indicative of the long-standing differences in response to the neglect of adults.

No secrets was subject to further criticism. This included that the use of terminology such as 'vulnerable adult' was seen as patronising and potentially discriminatory. Some local authorities interpreted 'vulnerable adult' in such a way to mean that the person had to be in current receipt of community care services. This definition runs the risk of excluding significant numbers of people. In addition, the definition of abuse was very vague. For example, it did not include any reference to self-neglect. There was no duty to act but also local adult social services departments (SSDs) actually had few powers under which they could intervene. Finally, 'vulnerable adult protection' was seen as an SSD matter (Penhale et al, 2017). The result was an incoherent and often contradictory response to these issues. Neglect and other issues such as financial abuse are difficult to investigate and subsequently prosecute via the courts. Other legislation such as the MHA 1983 was not designed to address some of these issues.

Safeguarding is based on the following principles:

- *Empowerment:* People are supported and encouraged to make their own decisions and give informed consent.
- *Prevention:* It is better to take action before harm occurs.
- *Proportionality:* The least intrusive response appropriate to the risk presented.
- *Protection:* Support and representation for those in greatest need.
- *Partnership:* Local solutions through services working with their communities – communities have a part to play in preventing, detecting and reporting neglect and abuse.
- *Accountability* and *transparency* in safeguarding practice.[12]

---

[12] www.scie.org.uk/safeguarding/adults/introduction/

Safeguarding Adults Boards

Local Safeguarding Adults Boards (SABs) have an overall responsibility to lead adult safeguarding. This will include overseeing and coordinating the safeguarding arrangements of its member and partner agencies. This is partly about creating cultures which support and encourage raising awareness of safeguard issues – for example, supporting whistle blowers but also a no blame culture where it is possible to be frank and open about 'near misses'. This is much easier said than done. In addition, the organisations involved in safeguarding – housing, the police, NHS, residential care homes and adult social care – often have conflicting or competing agendas. SABs have three core duties:

- Develop and publish a strategic plan setting out how they will meet their objectives and how their member and partner agencies will contribute.
- Publish an annual report detailing how effective their work has been.
- Commission safeguarding adult reviews (SARs) for any cases which meet the criteria for these.[13]

SABs have to focus a broad range of issues including:

- the safety of people who use services in local health settings, including mental health;
- the safety of adults with care and support needs living in social housing;
- effective interventions with adults who self-neglect, for whatever reason;
- the quality of local care and support services;
- the effectiveness of prisons in safeguarding offenders; and
- making connections between adult safeguarding and domestic abuse.[14]

Conclusion

This chapter has explored the challenge that the service user/survivor movements have posed to mental health services. One of the key aspects here is that services have has to respond to quite proper demands for inclusion and for the service user voice to be heard and respected.

---

[13] See note 12.

[14] www.scie.org.uk/safeguarding/adults/reviews/

There is an ongoing concern that the radicalism of the service user movement is colonised by mental health agencies. The recovery model is an excellent example of these concerns. If it loses its radical and combative edge then recovery becomes another managerialist buzzword. Who could be against recovery? The devil is in the detail. Those who make explicit links between mental ill health and the condition of late modern capitalism might be very well be against recovery – if it means returning to work in precarious conditions for a tax avoiding multinational. In examining the context of mental health services, the chapter has discussed some of the key contemporary policy changes. There are ongoing concerns about the quality of care provided in mental health units. The recently published interim review of the MHA[15] reported that mental health inpatients were not consistently treated with the levels of dignity and respect that other areas of modern mental health take as a given.

---

[15] https://tinyurl.com/y8o69pqv

FIVE

Contemporary mental health social work

Introduction

In common with other areas of practice, mental health social work can on occasions struggle to define its professional role, vision and contribution to services. The argument put forward that in mental health social work brings a uniquely valued focused approach (Gould, 2010) seems to me wholly inadequate and inaccurate. Social workers are not the only professionals with a value base. The social work value base is not without its critics or failings. I would argue that the role of social workers is to work alongside people with mental health problems and in so doing they can bring a social and community based perspective that a purely medical model lacks. Social work as a profession and discipline has social inclusion at its core. Social work practitioners seek to support social inclusion on both an individual and organisational level. The danger is that in the current political, organisational and economic climate these core contributions are lost. As Karban (2016) notes, there is a danger that mental health social work will be reduced to a bureaucratic exercise in risk assessment and risk management, rather than a dynamic relational form of practice.

Mental health social work in context

Mental health social work is concerned with challenging the individual and social barriers to full citizenship. The journey that Sayce (2016) described as being from 'patient to citizen' has some way to go despite the increased legal protections and changes in social attitudes. The potential for a new form of mental health social work that shakes of the shackles of manageralism is hinted at in some recent key policy documents: *The role of the social worker in adult mental services* (Allen, 2014), *The knowledge and skills statements for social workers in adult services* (DH, 2015) and *Social work for better mental health* (DH, 2016). All these policies emphasise the importance of co-production – that is, working with individuals and communities, not tokenism, and building

111

community resources to prevent the development of mental health problems. There are concerns that co-production like the recovery model will lose its radical edge and become colonised by professionals to create a discourse that results ironically in the exclusion rather than the inclusion of service users.

Mental health social work: a Bourdieusian analysis

The work of the late French sociologist Pierre Bourdieu can used as the basis for a critical analysis of the role of social workers in the area of mental health. Bourdieu provides three main conceptual tools – *field, habitus and capital* – that can form an intellectual arsenal to examine these issues. Here, I will focus on the notions of *field* and *habitus*. Garrett (2015) describes Bourdieu as a critical public intellectual, a staunch critic of neoliberalism and a staunch defender of public services. In *Weight of the world* (1999), Bourdieu with a range of colleagues outlined the impact that neoliberalism was having on the social and working conditions in France. This work can be read as a series of individual case studies that illuminate the way that, in the name of flexibility or other commonly used terms, the social contract between French workers and capital was being eroded. Bourdieu and later Wacquant (Cummins, 2015a) use the term *doxa* for phrases, such as 'flexible working conditions' or 'free market', and terms that restrict the contours of any debate. Chopra (2003) notes that *doxa* function as if they were objective truths or commonly accepted and agreed assumptions. Examples in the mental health context would include *empowerment, service user, recovery* and *personalisation*. Social work generally, and mental health social work in particular, seems very prone to the generation and use of *doxa*. Bourdieu argues that it is the role of critical intellectuals working alongside others to question and interrogate *doxa*. He sees academic work as inevitably political. This approach in itself is one that should recommend him to social workers.

Bourdieu's conceptual framework of *field, habitus* and *capital* provides a series of tools to analyse the development of mental health policies. In this context, I would argue that mental health policy and practice would meet Bourdieu's (1998) definition of a field as 'a structured social space, a field of forces' (Garratt, 2007). Bourdieu argues that a field has three key elements within it. The first is the impact that it has on the development of the habitus of individuals within it. He then goes onto suggest that a field seeks to maintain its own autonomy but there is competition between the actors within that area. Within this area, one can identify a number of key actors who seek to dominate or control key areas of the field. However, one can see that elements within this bureaucratic field have been jockeying for position. The result is the constant ebbing and flowing of policies and approaches. Using the notion of field allows for these policies to be seen not as contradictory but as competing elements of a strategic battle. The notion of field encourages us to examine the influences on the development of policy in nuanced fashion. The interaction between the notions of *field* and *habitus* is crucial. Wacquant (1998) argues that in themselves they do not have the 'capacity to determine social action'. It is the interplay between the two that needs to be considered. Even if we assume that there is agreement across a field, it does not mean that all individuals in a given position within that field will act in the same way. Field has a key role to play in the development of the habitus of any individual located within it.

The 'mental health field'

Any attempts to draw a 'mental health field' will be partial. One of the dangers of the field metaphor is that it becomes a sporting or military one: two sides fighting or in competition. This is particularly important to avoid in an area such as mental health where there are many unresolved historical and other issues. With this proviso, I think that the notion of the field provides a way of examining the development of policy but also the impact of social, cultural and political issues. There is potentially a wide range of actors in the mental health field. These might include: service users and service user groups; charities; mental health trusts and third sector organisations; government departments including the DH, the Home Office, the DWP and the Treasury; professional bodies such as the British Association of Social Workers (BASW), RCP and Royal College of Nursing; and the courts. Another attractive feature of this approach is that it allows for the recognition of influential individuals. The mental health field will, therefore, include significant political and legal figures alongside professional leaders and chairs of inquiries. Theresa May, Sir James Munby, Professor Louis Appleby and Lord Adebowale have all made very significant contributions to the debates in the mental health field and the development of policy. The concept allows for a consideration of much broader cultural or theoretical figures such as Michel Foucault or Erving Goffman, who continue to exert an influence through the ongoing engagement with their ideas. Finally, any modern field has to consider the role of social media and the key figures there. Overall the field produces a fluid, dynamic analysis rather than a static one.

In addition, it allows for a much broader consideration of the factors and actors in any given field.

Habitus

Bourdieu's notion of habitus is a complex one and often difficult to define (Hillier and Rooksby, 2002). However, it can provide a critical way of examining the values, dispositions and attitudes of individuals. Bourdieu used it as a part of an attempt to move away from what he saw as two poles of the structure /agency debate. Bourdieu felt that structuralism presented humans as automatons subject to and behaving within 'laws' that they knew little of or did not recognise. Such an approach fails to address the question of agency or issues of subjectivity. The other pole of this debate where the focus is solely on the philosophy of the subject fails to take account of the structural context in which people live their lives. The notion of habitus is there an attempt to overcome the emphasis on individualism in one tradition and the focus on social structures in another. Bourdieu was suspicious of the meta narratives of Althusserian Marxism which did not seem to allow for or explain individual agency. Hall (2017 b) notes that these approaches tend to conclude that it is possible to read individual political and ethical positions from their position in the class structure.

Habitus is the reworking or reformulation of a notion that has long philosophical roots (Wacquant, 1998). Bourdieu described habitus as a 'dynamic system of disposition'. It is therefore a combination of values, experiences and social attitudes. It is not a static concept – habitus will change over time, depending on individual experiences and social and cultural changes. In discussing habitus in the context of social work, Houston (2002: 157) concludes that it should be seen as ' a very loose set of guidelines permitting us to strategise, adapt, improvise or innovate in response to situations as they arise'. It should not be seen as rigid or as providing solutions to all moral or other questions that arise in a given circumstance. Alongside the notion of habitus, we also have to consider doxa. As noted above, doxa operate as forms of objective truth. They act to construct and demarcate areas of debate or challenge. It is important to acknowledge or recognise that there is a relationship between doxa and habitus. Doxa are generated across fields – part of the struggle for social capital within a field cannot be seen as the relative strengths or positions of the doxa of groups within it. What is seen as a doxa for one group is not necessarily so for others within the field.

Towards a mental health social worker habitus

Having set out the notion of field and habitus, I will now move on to examine features of the habitus in mental health social work. The starting point has to be that social workers are … social workers. This might seem an odd statement to make – what else could they be? I make this statement to emphasise that while social workers may carry out different roles within the mental health field – for example, care co-ordinators, AMHP or acting as an Appropriate Adult under the Police and Criminal Evidence Act (PACE) 1984 – they do so from a particular perspective and having undergone a particular form of training and education. One of the concerns that I share with others is that the social work identity is being lost in the establishment of CMHTs and a particular approach to case management (Morriss, 2016a).

The use of habitus as an analytical tool allows us to move away from the position where social work either defines its contribution to this area in negative terms – *we are not psychiatrists or mental health nurses* – to a more positive definition and outline of the role. This would include an emphasis on the development of critical perspectives on the current structure and provision of services – including social work but also a focus on a broader social justice approach. This would include being part of national campaigns such as *Boot Out Austerity* or highlighting the injustice of and damage caused by the WCA regime but also individual and community work. For social workers, the challenge is often as much about tackling the impact of the bureaucratic systems within which they are forced to work. Bourdieus note that social workers are agents of the state but 'shot through with the contradictions of the state' (Bourdieu in Bourdieu et al, 1998: 184). This is a restatement of the classic debate around care and control that lies at the heart of social work. In Bourdieu's formulation of the right and left hands of the state, where the right represents agencies of discipline such as the police and the courts, and the left more welfare-oriented functions, then social work sees itself as very much on the left. Garrett (2007) highlights that Bourdieu's notion is too arbitrary in that welfare and disciplinary functions are part of a number of state agencies – the police and social work being two clear examples.

Bourdieu et al (2002: 190) notes that there is a tension between 'the logic of social work which is not without a certain prophetic militancy or inspired benevolence and that of bureaucracy with its discipline and its prudence'. They go on to suggest that there is a paradox at the heart of bureaucratic systems in that they actually rely on the initiative and inventiveness of those who work within them to function adequately: 'If bureaucracy were left to its own logic ... then bureaucracy would paralyse itself' (Bourdieu et al, 2002: 190). The habitus of a mental health social worker will have at its root a critical perspective towards institutionalised and coercive forms of mental health care. While acknowledging the progress that has been made in mental health services, it acknowledges that there is a need for an understanding of the historical, social, political and cultural factors that combine to produce the current system. Bourdieu saw social workers and other public sector workers as fighting on two fronts. The first was clearly to work alongside service users to tackle the barriers they face to full citizenship. The second was the battle within the bureaucracies in which they are inevitably forced to practice.

Street level bureaucracy

Social work as a profession commits itself to working with marginalised communities and individuals. As well as work at this level, it is part of wider campaigns for social justice. Social work takes place in a specific, social and political context. Howe (2014) talks about the practice of social work taking place in a social space between the individual or family and the state or wider society. The impact of social and economic policy alongside specific social work legislation constructs the contours of that social space. Lipsky's (1980) concept of street level bureaucrats summarises the way that frontline public sector workers influence how policies are implemented. For example, children and families experience the Children Act 1989 not as an abstract piece of legislation but in the way that social workers, the courts, the police and other services use the powers that it creates.

Lipsky notes that political figures are rarely, if ever, involved in the day-to-day implementation of policy. This falls to relatively low level staff. This creates a potential disconnect between the aims of the policy as it is designed on a national level and the way that it is rolled out. Lipsky highlights the way that street level workers use their discretion on a daily basis. This can result in the aims of a policy being subverted or even resisted. He sees this as part of a process whereby workers adapt the policy to meet the complex work and the complex lives of the public who their agencies are in contact with. Social workers can be viewed as street level bureaucrats par excellence. One of the tensions in contemporary social work is the attempt to create an environment that restricts the scope of social workers' autonomy (Munro, 2011; Featherstone et al, 2014; and Cummins, 2018). It is a very important aspect of mental health social work and is discussed further later, but there is a danger in focusing on the AMHP role. Allen (2014) suggests that the current structure of services and debates about mental health have created an environment where there is a danger that mental health social work becomes care coordination plus AMHP work. The dominant focus in both these roles is on risk and risk management. Care management was originally presented as a move away from paternalistic social work. However, in practice it became part of the moves towards a more bureaucratic and risk averse form of practice. As a result, it becomes more paternalistic and potentially more restrictive. In addition, the notions of independence and choice can be used as cover for the failure to provide services.

In some senses, mental health social work has become too timid in its claims and too narrow in its focus. If we return to the core definitions of mental health and social work, we can see that there is synergy between the two. Good mental health has been defined as 'a state of wellbeing in which the individual realises his or her own abilities, can cope with the normal stresses of life, can work productively and fruitfully, and is able to make a contribution to his or her community' (WHO, 2012). The IFSW definition of suggests social work aims to promote 'social change, problem solving in human relationships and the empowerment and liberation of people to enhance wellbeing'. These two definitions should and do intersect. Allen (2014) argued that there were five key areas for social work practice within in mental health:

A: Enabling citizens to access statutory social care and social work services and advice to which they are entitled, discharging the legal duties and promoting the personalised social care ethos of the local authority.

B: Promoting recovery and social inclusion with individuals and families.

C: Intervening and showing professional leadership and skill in situations characterised by high levels of social, family and interpersonal complexity, risk and ambiguity.

D: Working co-productively and innovatively with local communities to support community capacity, personal and family resilience, earlier intervention and active citizenship.

E: Leading the Approved Mental Health Professional workforce. (Allen, 2014: 6)

Social work increasingly takes places outside statutory settings. I may be in a minority in welcoming such developments. One of the reasons for this is that the statutory environment has become too dominated by risk paradigm. When visiting students on placement in CMHTs over the past two or three years, I have been increasingly struck by the way that these shifts play out in practice. There is a greater emphasis on clinical symptoms and the use of traffic light systems to categorise risk – red zone being for service users seen most at risk. I should emphasise that I am not being critical of students or my colleagues in practice here. It is more a reflection on the change. These systems are examples of Webb's (2006) notion of manufactured risk and the way that a broader discourse of security replaces a focus on individual need. The system then becomes an almost self-generating bureaucracy – if you have a traffic light system then the status of each individual has to be reviewed daily. Within these systems, the individual service user – the person, a fellow citizen – can be lost. Morriss (2016b) highlights the potential for the social work perspective to be lost in the new organisational culture of the CMHT.

The role of the social worker in adult mental services (Allen, 2014) can be read as a statement or more accurately a restatement of fundamental social work values in the context of mental health provision. It emphasises that social work is, at its core, concerned with relationships. It involves the understanding and application of legislation, knowledge of community resources and the provision of practical support and assistance as well as working with a range of professionals and community groups but the core is – or should be – building relationships. The fundamentals of a relational approach are *dignity, warmth, trust, respect, openness, honesty* and *reliability.* There is a tension between these key concepts and the bureaucratic approach that focuses on risk. Pressures on services and lack of resources combine to create an environment where it becomes increasingly difficult to develop and sustain positive working relationships.

Role of the AMHP

The AMHP was created by the reform of the MHA in 2007. These reforms meant the role of the ASW was removed. The AMHP role is essentially the same as the ASW one. The fundamental shift is that the role is now open to other mental health professionals. The majority of AMHPs are from a social work background. DH (2012) indicated that of 936 individuals undertaking AMHP training, 84% were social workers; 14% were nurses. The majority of the AMHP workforce will be made of social workers for the foreseeable future.

The role of the AMHP is outlined in the MHA Code of Practice (DH, 2015) The AMHP has overall responsibility for the coordination of assessments under the MHA. This can involve a range of tasks potentially involving: arranging two doctors to carry out the required medical assessments; deciding whether police support is required; attending the magistrates court to obtain a warrant under Section 135 MHA; and arranging an ambulance to convey the person to hospital. Section 26 MHA defines a person's nearest relative (NR). There is a legal obligation for the AMHP to identify the NR and then consult with that person and other significant individuals in that person's life. In carrying out an assessment, an AMHP has a duty to interview the person in a 'suitable manner'. The AMHP can only make an application for compulsory admission to hospital if they are satisfied that the statutory criteria for detention are met. In reaching this conclusion, an AMHP must be satisfied that, in 'all the circumstances of the case', a detention in hospital is the most appropriate way of ensuring that the person receives the care and treatment that they are deemed to need. The AMHP role is an independent one. They are employees of a mental health trust but they must make a decision exercising their own professional judgement. The role of the AMHP is to provide a social perspective as well as an independent decision as to whether there are alternatives available (DH, 2015). The MHA Code of Practice (DH, 2015) enshrines the 'least restrictive principle' at the heart of these processes. Thus, the AMHP has to decide that the only available option to resolve the crisis is a compulsory admission to hospital.

Watson (2016) notes the AMHP role does not really exist in other jurisdictions. It places social workers and a social dimension at the heart of decision making in the area of compulsory admissions to hospital. For all the discussion of the dominance of the medical model, in the overwhelming majority of cases, the decision about detention is made by a social worker. AMHP undertake additional professional training for the role. This includes a consideration of the law alongside ethical issues as well as approaches to mental illness and critical perspectives on psychiatry. Alongside this, there is a requirement to undertake placement work in a mental health team and shadow AMHPs undertaking MHA assessments and lead on assessments. The ASW role was the only one in statutory social work where there was a requirement to undertake such formal additional training. The Post Qualifying Framework when it was introduced was not role specific but more concerned with overall professional development.

The AMHP role requires a particular set of professional skills and knowledge. As well as being able to organise the usually complex logistics of an assessment, AMHPs also have to a knowledge of the law and it should be said the ability to remain calm in pressurised situations. In addition, the role of the AMHP requires excellent communication skills, empathy and a clarity of thinking. From this perspective, the AMHP role seems to fit or overlap with the core skills of social workers. There has always been a question as to whether aspects of the ASW/ AMHP role fits with the broader aims of social work. It can hardly be said to be empowering to deprive someone of their liberty. One of the persistent criticisms of institutionalised psychiatric care has been that it is too reliant on coercion. As we have seen, the conditions on mental health units are of real concern. Though AMHPs make the application for admission to hospital and ultimately have the final say in the MHA, the assessment process should be a joint one. For an assessment to be truly holistic it requires a social dimension – surely a role for social workers. In fact, one of the concerns about the AMHP role is that professionals from mental health nursing or other backgrounds is that they will have narrower social perspectives. At this early stage, it is impossible to reach any conclusion on this point.

Morriss (2016a, 2016b) in her study of mental health social workers working as AMHPs in CMHTs examines not only attitudes of staff to the role but also their position within the team. Social work, as a profession, always seems to face a battle to establish itself within an area of practice. This is particularly the case in the area of mental health. Morriss (2016b) shows that the relatively recent configuration of CMHT and Mental Health Trusts has added to this social work existential crisis of confidence. Social workers feel professionally isolated and occasionally overwhelmed within the CMHT, which is dominated by medical professionals but also a clinically focused ethos. These trends have been hardened by the focus on risk and risk management (Turner and Columbo, 2008).

Morriss (2016a) contrasts the role of the AMHP with other aspects of the social work role. Hughes (1971) introduced the concept of 'dirty work'. He noted that there are what he terms 'in and out groups'. Hughes argues that the greater the social distance between the in group and the out group, the more that the 'management' of that group is obscured or left to professionals with a societal mandate – doctors, police, social workers and others. Following Hughes, Morriss (2016a) argues that the severely mentally ill are an out group and the social control mandate falls to the AMHPs in the MHA process. For Hughes, 'dirty work' is a term that captures those aspects of an occupation that 'may be a symbol of degradation, something that wounds one's dignity' In Morriss'(2016a) study, what one might term the day-to-day of mental health social work – welfare, housing and negotiating with other bureaucracies – was regarded as having a different status to AMHP work. AMHP work was held in much higher prestige and seen to confer a level of professional regard. This is the result of the further training, the complex range of skills required to become an AMHP and the significance of the decisions that they make. This is a very important but to my mind a potentially troubling finding. It seems to reflect a downgrading of all that social workers do that is not AMHP work. The institution and coercion remain deeply embedded within the structure of mental health service provision.

The practitioners interviewed for the Morriss study also expressed the tensions within the AMHP role as they were keenly aware not only of the personal impact on individuals and families but also that the hospital environment was often a bleak one. From my own personal experience, the MHA assessment process is always in Hughes' phrase 'dirty work' – I was less convinced that carrying out the role conferred a new professional status. Assessments mean that you are naturally seeing individuals and families who are experiencing acute distress. Alongside this, as the pressure on mental health services increases, the alternatives to hospital admission seem to reduce. The decision to deprive someone of their liberty is one that always heavy on the mind of professionals involved. @DrEm_79's BMJ piece (2017) brings home forcefully and movingly the impact that it has on those who are detained. This has to be at the forefront of our thinking. Evans et al (2005) examined the potential impact of ASW work on social workers and concluded that burnout rates for this groups were significantly higher than for mental health social workers generally. Watson (2016) indicates that AMHPs face additional pressures such as more lone working and the potential that they face more aggressive or violent behaviour that other workers. He noted that the current crisis including an increase in MHA assessments, the reduction in the number of beds and the involvement of the police and ambulance services that face their own pressures, all have an impact on the AMHP role. Many participants in this study found the work 'challenging but emotionally rewarding' – challenging being a great social work euphemism. The AMHP role is one that creates a great deal of stress but also is often carried out with a lack of supervision or a reflective space (Evans et al, 2005; Gregor, 2010; Buckland, 2014).

Risk

It is impossible to consider the work of AMHPs without some consideration of risk. On one level, the role can be examined through a prism of risk and risk management. One of the concerns is that, while this may be understandable in the context of the MHA assessment, it has become a dominant paradigm for all social work including mental health social work (Webb, 2006; Webber et al, 2015; Featherstone et al, 2014). The retrenchment in services means that eligibility criteria become narrower and more restrictive. The overall result is that services become much more responders to emergencies or crisis. It should be noted here that austerity has the pincer effect of increasing the social factors that contribute to mental distress – poverty, inequality and family pressures – while at the same time reducing the resources available to support or work alongside people. Race and gender were important factors in the construction of the narrative that community care had failed and put the wider society at risk (Cummins, 2010, 2013). Warner and Gabe's (2008) study of risk and detention highlighted the impact of gender issues. Male workers were seen by themselves and others as being in a better position to work with 'high risk' service users. The majority of those deemed 'high risk' service users were male. Warner and Gabe (2008) concluded that this area was highly gendered as the focus was on the risk was posed by male service users to others. In addition, female service users demeaned high risk were more likely to be allocated a female worker. Social work is traditionally a female profession and the majority of staff and students are women. However, mental health work is an area where more male social workers can be found. The status of the AMHP role and the nature of the work might provide some of the explanation for this.

Motivating factors

The picture that is painted above of the AMHP role does not make it appear that attractive. An obvious question that arises is why do social workers and others take on the role? It is a particularly intriguing one for social workers as many aspects of the role seem to run counter to core social work values – for example, empowerment. I would strongly argue that it is possible, indeed vitally important, to carry out an MHA assessment and treat people with dignity and respect. I fully accept that there is a counter view that would suggest that the potential outcome – detention in a bleak poorly resourced mental health unit – renders this impossible. Despite the fact that MHA assessments are, clearly, concerned with decisions about admissions to hospital, Watson (2016) found that one of the key motivating factors was to provide a social perspective in assessments. Gregor (2010) suggested that the protection of individual rights, resolving crises and the status of the role were motivating factors. Buckland (2014) highlighted the difficulties in bringing a social perspective to an area that is still largely dominated by medical professionals. In Morriss' work (2014, 2016a, 2016b), the social workers who are undertaking the AMHP role see it very much as a way of maintaining a role for the profession within mental health services. This is in a period when the restructuring of services and the development of CMHTs have combined to create a feeling of professional isolation for many mental health social workers.

As noted above, the AMHP role or an equivalent does not exist in other jurisdictions. The involvement of a professional – usually a social worker – to provide a social perspective has to be welcomed. One of the most consistent and powerful criticisms of psychiatry is that it remains wedded to coercion (Cummins, 2017b). On the surface then, it might seem surprising that social workers are embedded within these processes. This overlooks something of the fundamentally contradictory nature of social work. Elements of the role have always been linked to mechanisms of social control. The AMHP can be seen as a Janus-faced one – as well as being involved in the deprivation of liberty, the role does provide a means for protecting vulnerable people and supporting them and their families. The research explored here highlights the complex nature of the role but also the tensions that this creates. The root of these tensions might be seen to lie solely in a clash between medicalised and social approaches to illness. However, one of the increasing concerns is that mental health units are not providing a safe, secure and supportive environment for individuals in acute mental distress. One of the most powerful arguments for compulsory treatment is a paternalistic one – it is in the best interests of the individual. For that to hold, there has to be a significant improvement in the environment in which people are detained under the MHA.

Mental Health Act 1983

This section will examine trends in the use of the MHA 1983. It is important to state that mental health social work is much broader than statutory assessment and work related to them. However, the MHA stands like one of Powell's Asylum Watchtowers, a brooding presence dominating the mental health policy landscape.

The MHA 1983 that applies in England and Wales allows for the detention of an individual. Part II of the MHA relates to detention in hospital. As outlined below, the courts also have powers to sentence people to detained under Part III of the MHA. There are two sections that are most commonly used under Part II – civil detentions Section 2 and Section 3 – this is the origin of the phrase 'sectioned' – a phrase that I personally have a strong aversion to. The MHA creates the framework for the compulsory admission of individuals to hospital – the act uses the term 'patient' throughout. This section is not, in any way, a definitive guide to the MHA. It rather outlines the main areas where it will impact on social work practice. There then follows a detailed discussion of the role of the AMHP. In addition to the MHA, practice in this area has to be in accordance with the principles outlined in the MHA Code of Practice (DH, 2015). The most important overarching principle is the 'least restrictive' one. This means that compulsory powers should only be used as a last resort and for as short period as possible. If someone is detained under the MHA, the least restrictive principle means that they should be in the most open conditions as possible taking account of their health needs and the safety of others.

Assessment under the MHA

I will focus here on assessment under Sections 2 and 3. The emergency provisions of Section 4 allow for the assessment by a Section 12 doctor and the AMHP and for detention up to 72 hours. These are or should be very rare uses of the MHA where there is some imminent risk that means it would not be prudent to wait for the third mental health professional to be available.

For both Sections 2 and 3, the assessment involves:

- an AMHP
- a Section 12 MHA approved doctor – a consultant psychiatrist or a registrar
- a registered medical practitioner, usually the GP.

The medical professionals have to decide that the person is suffering from a mental disorder within the meaning of the Act. The next question for all involved is whether an admission to hospital using compulsory powers is the most appropriate course of action. In reaching this conclusion, they have decided that the patient's own health or safety are at risk, or that there is a need to protect other people.

Definition of mental disorder

The reform of the MHA in 2007 included a new definition of mental disorder which is now defined as 'any disorder or disability of mind'. Substance misuse is not classified as a disorder under the MHA. Person with a learning disability can only be subject to the provisions of the MHA if their behaviour is additionally considered abnormally aggressive or seriously irresponsible.

Nearest relative

Section 26 MHA defines who someone's NR is. This is an important role and it is one where the law is very prescriptive. NRs have to be consulted before a Section 3 assessment and can object to one being carried out. NR can technically complete an application for admission to hospital. However, the Code of Practice (DH, 2015) is clear that this is a situation that should be avoided in most circumstances. The NR role is under review as part of the wider MHA review process. It seems outdated and at odds with an individual rights based approach.

Section 2

Section 2 can last for a period of up to 28 days. It is designed for a period of assessment. A Section 2 cannot be renewed. A person who is detained under Section 2 might be assessed for admission under Section 3 during this period. Patients detained under Section 2 have a right of appeal to the Hospital Managers and the Mental Health Tribunal. It cannot be renewed.

Section 3

Section 3 can last for a period of up to six months. It can be renewed for a period of six months and then for 12 months. Patients have the right of appeal to the Hospital Managers and the Mental Health Tribunal.

Independent mental health advocate

Patients detained under Sections 2 and 3 have the right to support from an independent mental health advocate (IMHA). Legal aid is available for mental health review tribunals.

Section 5(2)

If staff are concerned about the health of a voluntary patient, this section allows for an emergency detention for a period of up to 72 hours. During this period, an MHA assessment with view to an admission under Section 2 or 3 must be completed.

Mental health review tribunals

First tier tribunals in England hear appeals against compulsory admission. A mental health review tribunal (MHRT) comprises:

- a lawyer, who chairs the hearing;
- a 'lay' member who is experienced in the area of mental health; and
- an independent psychiatrist, who examines the patient before the panel hearing.

The MHRT can decide that the grounds for detention no longer apply and the patient should be discharged.

Supervised CTOs

CTOs can be imposed when a patient who has been detained under Section 3 is discharged from hospital. Conditions that can be placed on the discharge might include:

- having to live in a certain place;
- being tested for alcohol or illegal drugs; and/or
- attending appointments for treatment.

The CTO introduced the power of recall to hospital if the responsible clinician has concerns that:

- the patient needs medical treatment in hospital for a mental disorder; and
- there would be risk of harm to the health or safety of the patients or of others

The patient can be recalled for up to 72 hours where decisions are made about future treatment plans and support.

Section 117 MHA aftercare

Section 117 MHA provides that certain groups of patients who have been detained under the MHA are entitled to aftercare. The biggest group is those patients who have been detained under Section 3. Patients cannot be charged for services provided under Section 117 MHA.

Trends in the use of the MHA

Trends in the use of the MHA are based on information collected via the NHS Digital online on Omnibus KP90 collection system. This collects from organisations in England that are registered to provide mental health services and use the MHA.

There has been a worrying increase in the use of the MHA. In 2015/16, there were 63,662 detentions. This is an increase of 9% from the 2014/15 figure of 58,399. There has been an increase of nearly 50% in detentions in the ten years since 2005/06, when they were 43,361. As has been noted, there are increasing concerns about police involvement in mental health issues. The use of Section 136 MHA rose by 18% to 22,965 in the year to March 2016. There was a fall in the use of police cells as a place of safety from 3,996 to 1,764.[16]

At the end of March 2016, there were 25,577 people subject to the provisions of the MHA. Of these, 20,151 were detained in hospitals. There has been an increase in the number of people who are detained under the MHA but are actually resident in facilities that are managed by independent sector providers. On 31 March 2016, 5,954 patients were detained in private hospitals. This represents 30% of all detained patients. This is the highest percentage since 2006, when 17% of patients were detained in private hospitals. There has been a particularly significant increase in the use of Section 3 following an initial admission under Section 2. In 2015/16, there were 12,462 such incidences. This represents an increase of over 80% on the previous four years. There were 4,361 CTOs were issued in 2015/16. This was a decrease of 4% compared with the 4,564 issued in 2014/15. There were 2,294 recalls to hospital, a slight fall compared with 2014/15. In 2015/16, there were 3,120 either revocation or discharges of CTOs (CQC, 2018).

---

[16] Figures provided by the National Police Chief's Council (https://news.npcc.police.uk/releases/use-of-police-custody-for-those-in-mental-health-crisis-falls).

Section 136 MHA

Section 136 MHA is a police power. It authorises any police officer to remove someone who appears to be mentally disordered from a place to which the public has access to a 'place of safety'. This is an emergency power and is generally used in circumstances where a person is putting themselves at immediate risk. Examples would include people who are threatening suicide or someone who is behaving in a very disturbed or disinhibited fashion. The use of Section 136 MHA relies on the assessment of the individual police officers involved. There is no need for a formal medical diagnosis. The purpose of Section 136 is for a mental health assessment to be carried out by a psychiatrist and an AMHP. The Section lasts up to 72 hours. However, the MHA Code of Practice (DH, 2015) and locally agreed protocols emphasise that these assessments should be completely as quickly as possible. The recent Home Office review of Section 136 reduced that this time limit to 24 hours. This is the case with the equivalent Scottish legislation. The place of safety should normally be a hospital. It can be a police cell but this is widely recognised as being far from ideal – this is discussed in more detail below. Many Mental Health Trusts have developed Section 136 suites at mental health units to tackle these issues.

Use of Section 136 MHA

The monitoring of the use of Section 136 has been generally poor. However, it is widely accepted that there has been an increase in its use over the past 20 years. There is a body of literature (Rogers and Faulkner, 1987; Dunn and Fahy, 1990; Bhui et al, 2003) that highlights the over-representation of BAME groups, particularly young black men, in Section 136 detentions. This is a crucial issue as it means that in a number of cases the first contact that this group has with mental health services is via the police or other areas of the CJS. Section 136 MHA is much more likely to take place outside of standard office hours when normal support services are less likely to be available. Borschmann et al (2010) indicate that the 'typical' Section 136 patient is a young, single working class male with a past history of mental illness – a group that is much less likely than others in the population to access general health care including mental health services. Borschmann's study also noted that this group tended not to be registered with a GP. The IPCC carried out a major study of the use of Section 136 in 2005/06 (Docking et al, 2008). In this study, 11,500 patients were assessed in custody and 5,900 in a mental health setting. The report highlighted significant variations between forces. Some of these can be explained by local conditions – for example, Sussex Police covers Beachy Head, a spot to which people with suicidal ideation are often drawn. This study also confirmed Browne's (2009) finding that black people were almost twice as likely as other groups to be subject to Section 136.

Use of police cells as a place of safety

Police custody is a pressurised, busy and often chaotic environment. There is clearly the potential for this to have a negative impact on an individual's mental health. Police officers are called upon to manage very difficult situations such as self-harm or attempted suicide often with little training or support (Cummins, 2007, 2008; Cummins and Jones, 2010). The physical environment of a police cell also needs to be taken into account when considering the potential impact of custody. A police cell should only be used as a place of safety in exceptional circumstances. Hampson (2011) argues that in practice exceptional means that the patient is 'too disturbed to be managed elsewhere'. HMIC et al's (2013) study, *A Criminal Use of Police Cells?*, examined in detail 70 cases where a cell had been used as a place of safety. The report estimated that 36% of all Section 136 detentions involve the use of police custody . There are significant variations between or even within forces. This is the result of different local service provision. The most common reason for a police cell being used was that the person was drunk and/or violent or had a history of violence.

Service user perspectives

There is very limited research which examines service user perspectives on the experience of being detained under Section 136. This is true of other uses of compulsory powers under the MHA. As the HMIC review (2013) notes that, if the individual is taken to police custody, the experience can be almost the same as being arrested. In custody, they are treated in the same way as any other person. The booking in process is the same – it would include being searched. On occasions, because of concerns about self-harm or suicide, clothing may be taken away from the detained person. There will almost certainly be periods of delay in custody or an A&E department. Jones and Mason's (2002) study highlighted that for from a service user perspective this is a custodial not a therapeutic experience. In this study, service users made clear that the routine of being booked into custody was a dehumanising one. They also felt that police officers were too quick to assess that they were at risk of self-harm, meaning that there was an increased risk that they would be placed in a paper suit. Riley et al (2011) confirm this dissatisfaction with the process. In particular, the participants in their study felt that they were being treated like criminals for experiencing distress. Some felt that their mental health had worsened because of their time in custody.

MS v. UK

The case of *MS v. UK*, which was decided in the ECHR in 2012, demonstrates illustrates the potential difficulties that can arise. MS was detained under Section 136 MHA following an assault on a relative. When he was assessed at the police station, it was decided that he needed to be transferred to psychiatric care. There then followed a series of delays and arguments between mental health services as to which unit would be the most appropriate to meet MS's mental health needs. This argument went on for so long that the 72-hour limit of Section 136 (MHA) was passed. MS was still in police custody and this had a dramatic impact on his mental state. For example, as a result of paranoid delusional ideas, he refused food. The ECHR held that the treatment of MS constituted a breach of Article 3, which prohibits inhumane and degrading treatment. This is clearly an unusual case but it illustrates the potential issues that arise. The judgment made it clear that the initial decision to detain MS under mental health legislation was valid and justified. It is clear that the police cannot hope to tackle the root causes of these problems in isolation.

Section 136 outcomes

Data provided by NHS Digital[17] shows that, in the majority of cases, those individuals assessed following the police use of Section 136 were not formally admitted to hospital – that is, detained under Section 2 or 3 of the MHA 1983. One of the major difficulties when examining the use of Section 136 is the danger that there is too narrow a focus on outcomes. It is a fallacy to argue that Section 136 has not been used appropriately if the person is not detained. The test of Section 136 is whether the officer thinks 'that it is necessary to do so in the interests of that person or for the protection of others'. Police officers have to respond to the emergency that they face; if mental health professionals

---

[17] https://digital.nhs.uk/data-and-information/data-tools-and-services/data-services/mental-health-data-hub/mental-health-act-statistics

carry out an assessment and an alternative to hospital is organised then that does not mean the police officer's decision was incorrect. The whole purpose of Section 136 is for an assessment to be carried out, not for a formal admission to hospital. Borschmann's (2010) study is an analysis of the use of Section 136 in a South London trust: 41.2% of these did not lead to hospital admission, 34.4% led to admission under the MHA, and 23.1% to an informal admission.

The use of Section 136 MHA is a very important area. It raises very important civil liberty issues as well as wider ones about the treatment of people experiencing mental health problems. As Latham (1997) points out, it allows for an individual who has no formal mental health or qualifications to detain someone. Unlike Sections 5(2) and 5(4) of the MHA, the person with the power has no medical training and no medical evidence is required for the power to be enacted. In fact, the purpose of detention under Section 136 is for psychiatric assessment. However, it is important to bear in mind that this is just one area of mental health work in which police officers are potentially involved. There is a danger that debates about the workings of Section 136 overshadow the whole debate in this field.

Forensic mental health services

As noted above, there are fundamental ethical issues that arise in this area. The first concerns the problem of trying to unravel what links exist, if any, between the mental health problems that the individual experiences and their offending. Following on from this, the issue of the status of the individual has to be considered. A patient in a forensic setting is that but also a prisoner. Thus, there is a conflict between the therapeutic aims of an institution and the needs of security. For example, the standard ethical positions of patient confidentiality cannot be applied in the same way in these settings as the professionals involved will have a much wider duty of ensuring public safety and so on. In addition, this is an area that attracts a great deal of media attention with the focus on a very small number of high profile offenders.

The link between mental illness, violence and other offending remains an area of controversy. The debate can become polarised around two extremes: that no such link exists, or the mentally ill as a group are violent. The media portrayal of community care in the 1990s is virtually all based on cases of homicide or serious injury (Cummins, 2010, 2012). This style of reporting, particularly from the tabloid press, was very influential in undermining wider public confidence in mental health services. This is very much an ongoing issue. For example, the

National Confidential Inquiry report (Appleby et al 2013) showed that in 2010 there were 29 homicides by mentally ill people in 2010, the lowest since 1997 when this data was collected for the first time. This was reported in *The Sun* in lurid terms (Cummins, 2013). There are a number of pathways into forensic services. Patients may be admitted directly from prison, from community services, or following conviction and sentence by the courts. A network of Regional Forensic Secure Units (RSUs), increasingly private provision and the three English high secure or special hospitals – Rampton, Broadmoor and Ashworth – plus Corsairs in Scotland, exists to meet the complex needs of this group. The RSUs and the special hospital are thus a mix of a therapeutic institution and a prison. It is possible to be admitted to these institutions without having committed an offence – for example, if a psychiatric intensive care unit cannot safely nurse a patient then they will be transferred to more secure environment. However, the majority of patients in these institutions have been convicted of the most serious offences such as manslaughter, rape and arson. Section 37 MHA allows for detention on conviction. The nature of these offences means that they are heard in the crown court. When sentencing under Section 37, judges have the power to impose a restriction order under Section 41. The effect of the restriction order is that the patient can only be discharged by a Mental Health Tribunal or the Ministry of Justice. Those who are detained under the most secure conditions are deemed to 'pose a grave and immediate danger to the public'.

There has been an increase in the number of patients detained in secure forensic settings, which have around 3,500 beds. Around 35% of those beds are now provided in the private sector. As noted above, the image of this sector is dominated by a gothic-style focus on the details of particularly violent and brutal crimes. There is reinforced in popular culture and the media. In addition, the media focuses on high profile individuals such as Brady and Sutcliffe. This ongoing fascination was emphasised by Brady's appearance via TV link at his MHRT hearing in 2013 (Cummins et al, 2016). Brady's death in 2016 served to confirm this media obsession (Cummins et al 2019). In his seminal work, *Wound culture: Trauma in the pathological public sphere*, Selker (1997) argues that public culture, particularly in the US, has become addicted to violence. He used the term 'wound culture' to refer to this fascination with the public display of defiled bodies. Trauma is used here in both a physical and psychology sense. Wound culture is thus extended to our fascination with the public display of distress. One of the key features of the modern celebrity narrative is the point at which they publicly address their own traumas – be it that alcohol or drug addiction, childhood sexual abuse or an eating disorder. The consistent examination of the wound is a key feature of post–modern culture (Selker, 1997).

Social work in forensic settings

Fifty per cent of forensic patients are discharged within five years and 34% have an admission of under two years (Cummins, 2016) These facts alone indicate that there is a clear social work role in this field. There may be a slightly different emphasis in practice but the issues that mental health social workers are concerned with on a daily basis are all factors in the lives of those who have been in forensic mental health units. One of the themes of this work is the idea that services have become dominated by notions of risk and risk management – this is perhaps the one area where there is greater justification for this approach.

Social workers based in secure settings face a particular set of ethical and professional dilemmas and challenges. As a member of staff in these settings, they are part of and have a responsibility for security. Having taken that into account, it does not change the fact that patients in these settings have a range of social care needs. It has to be emphasised that the impact of violent offending is widespread. Families have to cope with the shock that a loved one has committed such an offence – the victims may have been other family members or they may face community hostility and so on. When a patient appeals to a MHRT, then social workers will complete a social circumstances report which examines a broad range of areas – views of family members and the community to the original offence, child protection or adult safeguarding issues, and what support needs the individual has. Section 37 of the MHA creates an entitlement to Section 117 MHA aftercare in the same way that Section 3 does. The provision of this aftercare takes place within a particular context and with a greater emphasis on the management of risk but it does not alter some of the fundamentals of the social work role.

Social supervision

Patients detained under Section 37/41 can be conditionally discharged. The conditions will include living at a particular address, attending for treatment and cooperation with mental health professionals. The patient is subject to recall if they do not keep to these requirements or if there are particular concerns about their behaviour. A social supervisor is appointed – usually an AMHP – as part of the team involved in the care and supervision of the individual. I use those terms deliberately in an attempt to capture the potentially conflicting nature of these roles. The Ministry of Justice guidance for a social supervisor states that 'over 50% have been convicted of offences against the person and a further 12% convicted of sexual offences' (MoJ, 2009: 5).

As well as the day-to-day aspects of social work, the social supervisor is required to submit regular reports to the Ministry of Justice that outline the progress of the individual who has been conditionally discharged. The power dynamics in the relationship mean that the term service user is somewhat redundant here. The nature of the offences mean that this group will also be subject to the multi agency public protection arrangements (MAPPA). The MAPPA system was introduced by the Criminal Justice and Courts Services Act 2000. The system brings together all the relevant agencies involved in the management of offenders who are considered to pose the greatest risk to the wider community. MAPPA panels have to ensure that they have carried out risk assessments on the offenders in their areas who meet the criteria outlined above. The panel then decides on the level of risk and the appropriate arrangements to manage those concerns. Social workers will be involved in these processes of risk management – in the discussion of the imposition of conditions and then the monitoring of them. For example, an offender may be excluded from the area where the original offence was committed or from contact with particular individuals. These are complex and demanding cases for all professionals including social workers. There is the inevitable concern about reoffending. In addition, many social workers are somewhat uneasy with the more overt exercise of power that is allowed or even perhaps required here.

Social work, certainly in England and Wales, needs to more actively re-engage with issues raised by the CJS and the increased use of imprisonment (Cummins, 2015). The recent history of the Probation Service in England and Wales reflects decline of the belief in rehabilitation and reform (Garland, 2001). It has moved from a 'social work agency in the CJS', focusing on tackling the social problems that were seen as being as the root cause of offending to a risk management agency. With the introduction of Community Rehabilitation Companies (CRCs), these reforms almost totally sever the link between probation and its social work roots. CRCs will supervise 160,000 offenders who are deemed to be a medium to low risk while the National Probation Service will retain responsibility for high risk offenders. The economics are fairly clear here: contracts for the supervision of low-risk offenders are much more attractive to companies as the costs will be lower. A Public Accounts Committee report (2106) by British MPs concludes that the timetable for the introduction of these complex changes has not allowed for the new arrangements to be fully piloted. These reforms follow a pattern of other welfare reforms elsewhere in the world where private companies have been given large contracts to deliver services.

Cavadino et al (1999) coined the term 'punitive manageralism' to describe the shifts that had occurred within UK penal policy outlined above. Official research has shifted from the social causes of crime to an emphasis on crime prevention and the management of individual offenders (Gregory, 2007). These trends are particularly important when examining mental health issues. If we do not address the fact that, as a society, we are seemingly addicted to the use of imprisonment then we cannot hope to move on to then provide effective mental health care for those caught up in the CJS. Fyodor Dostoyevsky famously observed in his novel *The House of the Dead* (1862) that 'The degree of civilization in a society can be judged by entering its prisons. In this section, I have extended that observation to a broader consideration. There are too many examples, such as the suicide of Sarah Reed (Gentleman and Gayle, 2016), where the state has failed in its basic duty to ensure the safety of those in its care.

Conclusion

The significant organisational changes that have taken place within mental health services have combined to marginalise the role of social work. That is not to say that individual social workers are not working on a daily basis in a way that is congruent with wider social work values. Such a claim would be too broad and too insulting to dedicated professionals who work alongside service users to challenge both the impact of austerity but also the managerialism that combine to suck the last vestiges of humanity and decency from mental health services. My concern is that the social space (Howe, 2014) within which social workers are practising has become increasingly restricted. Mental health social work has to be more than the AMHP – important though that is.

SIX

Mental health social work reimagined

Introduction

In this concluding chapter, I will summarise the key themes of the book and then move on to consider different approaches to the role of social work and social workers in the mental health field. I began work on this project shortly before Theresa May made her speech that the treatment of mental health problems was one of the injustices that she would seek to rectify in *her* period of Prime Minister. Professor Sir Simon Wessely, formerly president of the RCP, was appointed to lead a review of the MHA. Whether the legislation is the key area that needs to be addressed to resolve the issues that mental health services face is a very debatable point. The fact that the past president of the RCP was appointed to lead the review is itself a source of concern for many – not because of Sir Simon's personal qualities or integrity – because of the symbolism of it being led by a psychiatrist.

Narratives of reform

In 1998, when he introduced *Modernising mental health services* (DH, 1998), Frank Dobson then Secretary of State for Health stated that 'community care has failed'. Whether one agrees with that statement or not, the document provides an interesting and to my mind coherent analysis (with one huge exception) of the factors that need to be addressed to reform mental health services. The exception is the need for legal reform, which resulted in the introduction of the CTO. Reforms were needed to ensure that the legislation would remain compatible with the soon to be introduced Human Rights Act. *Modernising mental health services* (DH, 1998: 2) identified the causes of the failings of community care:

Failures of the past

Although with staff dedication and commitment, the policy of care in the community has benefited many, there have been too many failures. Failure has been caused by:

- inadequate care, poor management of resources and underfunding;
- the proper range of services not always being available to provide the care and support people need;
- patients and service users not remaining in contact with services;
- families who have willingly played a part in providing care have been overburdened;
- problems in recruiting and retaining staff;
- an outdated legal framework which failed to support effective treatment outside hospital.

The document then goes on to outline the steps that will be taken as part of the reform.

We will modernise mental health services by providing safe, sound and supportive services:

- services should be safe, to protect the public and provide effective care for those with mental illness at the time they need it;
- services should be sound, ensuring that patients and service users have access to the full range of services which they need;
- services should be supportive, working with patients and service users, their families and carers to build healthier communities.

Modern mental health services will assess individual needs, deliver better treatment and care whether at home or in hospital, enable 24 hour access to services, ensure public safety, and manage risk more effectively.

Modern mental health services will have a firm base in primary care.

Primary Care Groups will work closely with specialist teams to integrate service planning and delivery.

Information systems will support the delivery of care and the management of resources, and there will be close partnerships with education, employment and housing.

Patients, service users and carers will be involved in their own care, and in planning services.

Services will be delivered in the most efficient and cost effective way with clear guidance from the National Institute for Clinical Excellence.

Secure hospital services will be improved. Public protection will remain our first priority at all times. (DH, 1998, p 2)

One is immediately struck by three things. The first is the number of times that safety and public protection are mentioned. There is no challenge here to the deeply engrained cultural attitudes about mental illness and violence. The second is that the focus is very much on organisational service issues. The values that should underpin the reform of mental health services are virtually absent. Finally, one cannot fail to notice that, 20 years on, a number of these goals have not been achieved – 24-hour access and consistent service user involvement in their own care and planning services being two areas that the Wessely review should address. Following the publication of *Modernising mental health services*, the tortuous process of the reform of the MHA began. One hopes that the Wessely review will not be as complicated a process. Perhaps more importantly, there followed a period of investment in mental health and public services more generally.

Narratives of reform within mental health have, for far too long, failed to address fundamental issues of dignity. For example, in 2011, the RCP described psychiatric wards as overcrowded and understaffed. Professor Dinesh Bhugra, the college's outgoing chair, accepted that these failures meant that inpatient care – often imposed against an individual's will – was not of an acceptable standard. He had previously stated that he would not personally use such facilities or allow a member of his family to do so. The report showed that wards were often not a safe, let alone therapeutic, environment – highlighting poor physical conditions, limited contact with staff or access to psychological therapies, and a lack of constructive activity. This has echoes of a survey carried out by mental health charity Mind (Baker, 2000) in London in 2000 . Its conclusions paint a picture of dirty wards, poor food, lack of stimulating activities and minimal contact with staff.

The following gives a flavour of its main findings:

- 30% of patients found the atmosphere on the wards unsafe and frightening;
- 62% of patients said illegal drugs were easily available on the wards;
- 16% of patients said they had experienced sexual harassment on the ward, and 72% of those who had complained about this said no action was taken.

There is much positive work going on in inpatient settings but there remain concerns. These include the pressures on beds. The reduction in inpatient beds has not been matched by the provision of community alternatives. This, combined with the wider retrenchment in welfare services, has had a ratchet like effect in this area. The result is that people who need inpatient care are denied access to it or a bed is 'out of area'. Out of area is a phrase that can mask the real impact that being detained in hospital far from home can have on an individual and their family. In addition, these distances make discharge and aftercare arrangements more difficult to put in place. The provision of out of area beds also has financial implications for trusts.

In August 2013 the House of Commons Health Committee produced a report on the functioning of the then relatively new 2007 reforms, including the operation of CTOs. The Committee was chaired by Stephen Dorrell, a former Secretary of State for Health. On publication of the report he stated that:

> Many psychiatric wards are over capacity and there is huge pressure on beds, nevertheless, we were shocked to learn that there is evidence that patients who need hospital treatment are being sectioned unnecessarily in order to access a bed. This represents a serious violation of patients' basic rights and it is never acceptable for patients to be subjected to compulsory detention unless it is clinically necessary.[18]

---

[18] https://tinyurl.com/y5wphgyh

Dorrell also suggested mental health services were more in danger of local health care cuts because commissioners thought they were easier to cut than 'more politically sensitive acute services'. The Select Committee also concluded that the lack of hospital beds was driving an increase in the number of CTOs, supposedly to reduce hospital admissions. The danger is that the reform narrative marginalises these issues to focus on legal issues, which, are of course important but can distract from the fundamental problems within the mental health system.

Austerity, neoliberalism and mental health services.

Beresford (2013) produced a devastating critique of the position of mental health services. He noted that there was a seemingly ever widening gap between mental health policy documents, which consistently promised the completion of a mental health revolution, and the reality of service provision. For all the talk of a complete shift in focus in the structure and values in services, a series of issues needed to be addressed.

A report from LSE (2012) concluded that mental illness now constitutes nearly a half of all ill health suffered by people under 65 – yet only a quarter of those involved are in any form of treatment. Mental illness accounts for 23% of the total burden of disease. Yet, despite the existence of cost-effective treatments, it receives only 13% of NHS health expenditure. The LSE report highlighted the following:

- Pressures on services made them increasingly difficult to access. People in mental health crisis face real barriers to access appropriate support.
- BAME service users were more likely to be subject to the MHA and at the same time were less likely to have access to talking therapies or other alternatives to medication.
- People with learning difficulties and older people continue to be poorly served by both mental health and physical care services.
- Welfare and benefit reforms, including the WCA, bedroom tax and housing benefit cap, all had a direct impact on the mental health of individuals.

This work takes a health inequalities approach to mental health issues. Such a perspective argues that the roots of many of the issues that we now classify as mental illness fundamentally have their roots in poverty, social inequality and injustice (Marmot, 2010; Karban,

2016). The impact of austerity has been to deepen these inequalities. A UN (2016) report, which was damning of the impact of austerity, specifically mentioned the poor provision of mental health care, alongside related issues such as the increased use of food banks and the rise in homelessness. The conclusion of the report was the policy of austerity had had a disproportionate impact on the most vulnerable. This is an inevitable conclusion that includes such drastic retrenchment. It is a statement of the obvious but one that bears repeating – welfare services, which were targeted, are designed to support those facing the most difficult situations. Any reduction in services will have its greatest impact on the poor and vulnerable. This is not by chance, it is a deliberate government policy – a war on the poor. The impact in the area of mental health is twofold. First, such policies have a disproportionate impact on those with mental health problems. Second, such policies are bound to lead to higher levels of depression and anxiety among those are subjected to them. There are future costs as these policies increase the numbers of children living in poverty. There is a great deal of evidence that shows that growing up or living in poverty has long-term implications for the onset of adult mental health problems.

Ways forward?

There is a danger of presentism, in that we assume that the current situation is one that has no parallels or that there is nothing that can be done in the face of political and economic forces that are much more powerful than the user/survivor movements, social work and social workers. This represents to me a counsel of despair and actually goes against much of what we know about the nature of the way that deeply entrenched political positions are challenged.

The current landscape of mental health service is a bleak one. The damage that nearly a decade of austerity has done to mental health services is apparent in a number of areas, including: the pressure on inpatient beds, out of area placement, the response to individuals in crisis, the increased use of the MHA, the position of the CJS as a default provider of mental health care, and the personal toll that policies such as the WCA have inflicted. There is an alternative, which is to see the current position as an opportunity or an opening to create a new debate about the structure and role of mental health services. This position is influenced by Hall's revival of the term 'conjuncture'. In his discussion of Gramsci's analysis of revolutionary political analysis, Hall (2017a) pays particular attention to the notion of conjuncture.

In particular, Hall emphasises that an economic explanation is never complete – it is a vitally important factor but we also need to look at wider cultural factors. Hall argues that Gramsci's work requires us to explore the social, cultural, political and economic forces that are present at one given time and the way that they combine to create a new politics.

The challenge to the power of institutionalised psychiatry has created new forms of resistance but also counter practices that open up the potential for new responses to the mental distress. There is clearly much to do. However, it seems to me if the distinguished psychiatrist Sir Robin Murray (2017) accepts that one of his errors was to underestimate the impact of social factors in the development of schizophrenia then we have potentially reached a new point in the development of mental health services.

In applying this approach, there are many examples from the field of mental health both historical and current that can be used as an inspiration. Laing may have ended his career in disgrace but this should not undermine his earlier achievements in challenging the appalling conditions that he encountered in his first posting as a psychiatrist (Cummins, 2017b). Basaglia appeared to have been sent into exile at the asylum in Gorizia. He not only revolutionised care there, he used it as a base from which he transformed psychiatric care across Italy and the rest of Europe. The history of the user/survivor movement is full of examples of courageous individuals who were subjected to treatments that should be viewed as abuse but challenged the psychiatric system. There is a danger, which has probably receded, if not disappeared, since the Brexit vote and the rise of Trump, of assuming that we live in some sort of post racial, post gender, post queer liberal utopia where these issues have been settled. This is clearly not the case. Not only is the history of psychiatry scarred by its treatment of women and members of ethnic and other minorities, these remain issue of ongoing concern. @DrEM_79's work (2017) in highlighting the impact of detention is another example of the potential for opening out debates. As noted earlier, there are downsides to the development of the consumer movement but it does open a discourse that can be used to push an agenda that challenges across a range of service provision and issues.

Mental health social work needs to develop a model of practice that challenges some of the key assumptions which underpin current approaches that have become far too closely aligned with a biomedical model. It might appear utopian but I would begin by a radical overhaul of the CMHT which, as Morriss (2016b) clearly demonstrates, has led to the marginalisation of social work values. The CMHT model is too deeply entwined with a bureaucratic form of practice. Alongside this, there needs to be a concerted challenge to the risk/risk management paradigm. There is much for mental health social work to learn from Munro's (2011) review of child protection social work. It is impossible to remove risk and we need to have sensible discussions about these issues. The risk paradigm, far from protecting service users, means that they face greater restrictions but also that services become more and more bureaucratic. This is not only frustrating for individual workers, it is very inefficient but most importantly of all it creates another barrier between 'service users' and workers. This is a circular process because this binary opposition then further undermines the core values on which services should be based – dignity and respect.

This work has examined the impact of structural inequalities and their relationship with the development of mental health issues. In the current environment, poverty and inequality have increased. Backwith (2015) makes the point that in several areas – for example, policy towards asylum seekers – poverty and destitution is not an unintended outcome of policies: it is the policy. The 'poverty aware paradigm' that Krumer-Nevo (2015) outlines can be adapted or applied within the mental health settings. This is a good example of social workers 'facing both ways' – working with individuals and within communities. The poverty aware paradigm starts from the proposition that poverty is a fundamental violation of individual human rights. It can also be viewed as the denial of human rights to groups of citizens. This approach would involve shifts in social work education that is very much focused on individual pathologising narratives of poverty. The impact and experiences of poverty remain a fundamental but often neglected aspect of the lives of those who are using services. Social workers find themselves in a position where they are often seen as representatives of a state policy that they themselves do not support – either on a personal or professional level. They can and do have a campaigning role in bringing these injustices to wider attention.

The reform of the MHA provides an opportunity for social work to challenge the workings of the law in this area. In my opinion, there is a danger of concentrating on the legal processes to the detriment of asking broader questions about psychiatry – and mental health services' reliance on coercion. The well documented rise in the number of detentions under the MHA can be seen as one indicator or symptom of a more fundamental issue – the lack of community based services that can provide appropriate support to those in crisis. It is only with a properly resourced network that alternatives to admission to hospital make sense. This then leads to another series of debates about what these alternatives to admission might look like. The reform of the MHA should also examine whether CTOs should be retained. In her speeches about the need for reform, Theresa May has used the language of injustice and rights. The CTO is, in my opinion, an area where people with mental health problems are placed in a different category – on the basis of being detained. There is growing evidence that the CTOs are ineffective on their own terms – it is difficult to exercise the power of recall in such a stretched system. More fundamentally, the argument that this ensures aftercare has to be exposed as a condemnation not a justification. It adds to the stigma attached to severe mental illness. It will be interesting to see if the Wessely review examines these issues.

New approaches

I think that there is a danger that although attitudes have shifted to incorporate wider perspectives on the social factors that cause mental distress, the responses or solutions are viewed in terms of very traditional service models. Two examples of alternative approaches demonstrate that there are ways of tackling taboo issues in new ways. Both the initiatives involve suicide prevention.

Preventing suicide on the railways

Network Rail, the organisation that has overall responsibility for managing the railway system, is a signatory of the Mental Health Crisis Care Concordat (2014). The Concordat was signed by 22 national bodies. It acknowledged that there was a need for a new approach from services in their response to those in acute mental distress. The railway industry is complex with a web of different operating companies that employ over 100,000 staff across the country, with millions of passengers each day. Network Rail has a pivotal role working with other organisations such as the British Transport Police and Samaritans to reduce the number of suicides on the railway. Samaritans organise to visit after an incident to offer support to staff and passengers. It has been involved in training over 11,000 rail staff on how to identify, approach and support a potentially suicidal person. The aim of the course is to give staff the skills and confidence to intervene. Network Rail in partnership with the British Transport Police and Samaritans have identified priority locations. A range of responses are being developed. These include physical changes, such as more fencing, barriers at the end of platforms and alterations to the design of stations. Other initiatives include motion-activated speaking signs, and the use of blue LED lights that can have a calming effect. Responses also include links with local groups.

A State of Mind

The State of Mind programme[19] was established in rugby league following the death by suicide of well-known ex-professional player Terry Newton. Rugby league is intensively competitive, physically demanding and at times brutal. Its traditional base in the north of England along the M62 corridor is in working class communities that have been severely hit by the problems associated with deindustrialisation. The programme seeks to use sport as a way of reaching out to individuals and groups who are potentially at risk but who traditional service models and approaches have struggled to engage. The programme involves education sessions throughout the UK to professional and amateur clubs as well as colleges and community groups, aimed at raising awareness of mental health issues within sport. Professional sport is clearly highly competitive and there are concerns that these environments make it difficult for individuals to show any sign of what might be considered a 'weakness'. In addition, professional sport is an environment with inbuilt huge swings of emotion, often within the same game. The State of Mind programme aims are:

- to promote positive mental health among our sportsmen and women, fans and wider communities, and ultimately to prevent suicide;
- to raise awareness of the issues surrounding mental health and well being and deliver education on the subject to all levels of sport, business, education and community groups;
- to signpost individuals to where they can receive care and support in their area.[20]

The programme has become very well-established and each of the Super League clubs is involved in outreach work as well as there being a round of matches in each season that supports and raises awareness of the programme.

These are examples of a broad social capital approaches to mental health. The challenge for mental health social work is to rediscover its roots in relational and community work. These are examples of non-

---

[19] http://rugbyleague.stateofmindsport.org/
[20] www.stateofmindsport.org/

medicalised community based and organic developments that were once the core of mental health social work that saw itself as outside and a challenge to institutionalised psychiatry.

Conclusion

Morriss (2016a) argues that social work has struggled to maintain its identity within the new structure of mental health services. There is a paradox here. It seems that as social models of mental illness, or at least a recognition of the importance of social factors, have become more widely accepted, the influence of social work as a discipline within the field has diminished or been marginalised. Duggan et al (2002) identified the skills and knowledge that workers need in the new mental health environment. These included what appear to me to be key social work skills, such as a commitment to building individual and community capacity, and a willingness to challenge practices that are not in the interest of communities or individuals. This is the essence of a community-oriented form of social work practice. In this area, poverty looms over social work practice but there is still a reluctance to engage with these issues. The IFSW definition of social work contains an implicit view that poverty is a structural problem rather than the result of individual failings of the poor.

Mantle and Backwith (2010) identify three very broad approaches and responses to the issues of poverty. An approach that can be termed a bureaucratic or functionalist one focuses on individuals or families. Bureaucratic approaches have become more dominant in recent times. An alternative approach would be focused on building community links and resources. This recognises the structural nature of poverty but also the potential strength of individuals and communities

There are new areas or approaches, such as TIAs and the building of social capital, that have potential to make further progress in attitudes and responses to mental distress. These can only be successful in the context of the development of a broader range of policies that are committed to reducing social inequality and tackling social injustice. This is the core of social work values and practice. The optimism of the initial period of deinstitutionalisation was replaced during the 1980s and 1990s by wider societal concerns that focused on risk. As services have come under increasing pressures, systems have developed that focus on these issues and marginalise user/survivor voices.

The Professional Capabilities Framework offers an opportunity for social work generally, and for the mental health social worker in particular, to re-engage in these debates and reject a bureaucratic managerialism that focuses on risk assessment and risk management. If mental health social work is not a critical voice based on the fundamental values of dignity and respect, then it is nothing.

POSTSCRIPT

Review of the Mental Health Act 1983

The announcement by Theresa May that there would be a review of the Mental Health Act 1983 (MHA) was somewhat unexpected. The review was chaired by Professor Sir Simon Wessely and completed in December 2018 (DHSC, 2018). The review process included a series of stakeholder events and examining literature and other research to explore key themes that emerged. Theresa May was explicit in identifying the crisis in mental health care as an issue of social injustice – while at the same time not making any links between broader social policy developments and their impacts (Cummins, 2018).

In his foreword to the final report, Simon Wessely outlines the case for change. One of the fundamental drivers of the review was the increasing rate of detentions under the MHA. Within mental health services there have been long-standing concerns about the processes of admission under the MHA and patients' experiences on inpatient units. The review notes that the patient's voice is often lost or ignored within mental health services and services being experienced as bureaucratic, uncaring and coercive. The review was also charged with addressing the long-standing over-representation of people from black and minority ethnic groups who are detained under the MHA. The experiences of people with learning disabilities and or autism within mental health services were also examined. Finally, there were concerns that the current mental health legislation in England and Wales did not comply with international standards on human rights. None of these issues is new. There are several echoes from New Labour's review of mental health law 20 years previously.

The review reports that there were 49,551 detentions under the MHA in 2017/18, excluding short-term orders such as Section 5(2) (DHSC, 2018: 44). There was a 40% increase in detentions in the period 2005/06 to 2015/16. Black people were four times more likely than white people to be detained under the MHA.[21] The risks of black patients, particularly young men, of being subject to community treatment orders (CTOs) were also noted. Black people were eight time more likely to be subject to a CTO than their white fellow citizens.

---

[21] https://digital.nhs.uk/data-and-information/data-tools-and-services/data-services/mental-health-data-hub/mental-health-act-statistics

The research carried out for the review highlighted black service users' experiences of coercion, stigma, racism and discrimination. This bleak picture reinforces long-standing concerns (Keating et al, 2002) that black citizens' experiences of mental health services is institutionally racist. Despite the efforts outlined earlier in Chapter Two, there seems to have been little, if any, shift in this area. In his introduction, Simon Wessely outlines the way that service users and carers had brought home to him the often poor standard of care and support that was being provided in mental health services, including inpatient units.

The review proposes a number of significant changes to the MHA. It starts from the position that we need to move to an approach that is fundamentally rights based. In doing so, it proposes four key principles to underpin a new Mental Health Act. In addition, the call for a reinvigorated mental health system based on fundamental values of dignity, respect for persons, mutuality and reciprocity emphasises the potentially damaging impact of current approaches. Lack of dignity inevitably results in a lack of trust between service users and professionals. The review notes:

> Lack of dignity, and a lack of a trust that patients will be treated kindly and with respect, inspires fear. We have heard how many service users fear that being compulsorily admitted to hospital will worsen, not improve, their mental distress. (DHSC: 17)

The review accepts this point. It concludes that such fears of poor and coercive treatment mean that engagement with mental health professionals suffers. This may well put an individual's mental health at some risk. It also increases the possibility of coercive interventions – someone is clearly at greater risk of being detained if his or her mental health deteriorates. Such a cycle reinforces the negative connotations and stigma that are attached to seeking mental health care and treatment. This is not simply about the legal process of assessment under the MHA. Changes to the MHA will not alter the poor conditions of inpatient units. However, the MHA is a key element of mental health services. The structure and underlying principles of mental health legislation makes a key statement of the values that should underpin services.

Four principles of a reformed Mental Health Act 1983

The review proposes the following as new underpinning principles for a reformed MHA:

Principle 1: Choice and autonomy

- The review argues that shared decision making between service users and mental health professionals should be the basis for the development of care plans. As far as possible, this should extend to decisions about treatment as well. The review argues that it should be more difficult for any decisions where service users refuse treatment to be overridden by mental health professionals. In a radical shift, the review proposes the creation of statutory advance choice documents (ACDs). ACDs would allow service users to make choices and statements about the sort of treatment they will receive if or when they become inpatients. The review also suggests that the decisions about medication should reflect service user's wishes. Patients should have a right to challenge treatments that do not reflect their choices. In addition, the review argues that more detailed care and treatment plans should be drawn up when patients are admitted to hospital. These plans would be a key document. Patients would be to request a second opinion appointed doctor (SOAD) review of the initial care and treatment plan or whenever significant changes are proposed. The review has suggested that the government should consult widely on a potential change to the law that would allow a person to consent in advance to admission. In effect, such a move would allow a patient to agree to be a voluntary patient at some future point. This would remove the need for the use of the MHA in these circumstances. However, the review notes that it is an area fraught with potential difficulties. In particular, it raises questions about what safeguards should be put in place.

- The role of the nearest relative (NR) is outlined in Chapter Five. It is an area of the MHA that is most in conflict with other areas of health care. In other areas, there is no statutory obligation to consult with NRs. In fact, in the area of mental health the NR has a series of potential rights relating to admission and discharge. The review proposes that the NR role is replaced by a new role, that of the nominated person (NP). Patients would be able to nominate a NP of their own choice. In circumstances where a person has not nominated a NP or lacks the capacity to do so, an interim NP will be nominated. NPs will be consulted on care plans and patients will have greater rights to disclose confidential information.

- The review recognises the important role that advocacy plays in mental health services. The current statutory right to an independent mental health advocate (IMHA) should be extended to all mental health patients – including informal patients. The review argues that the IMHA should also be available to those who are being transferred from a prison or immigration detention centres. Finally, those who are preparing ACDs should include choices about detention under the MHA. The review recommends that Section 132 MHA is amended so that there will be a requirement on hospital managers to provide information on complaints procedures. In addition, it proposes a series of changes to the way that complaints are dealt with, including greater training on the potential impact of detention under the MHA for those staff dealing with such matters.

- The review makes important recommendations regarding how mental health services respond to deaths that occur when the patient is detained under the MHA. It argues that a formalised family liaison role should be created to support families whose loved ones die unexpectedly in detention. In addition, in these tragic circumstances, families should receive non-means-tested legal aid so that they can be represented at inquests and other hearings. Finally, the review argues that those deaths that occur when the patient is subject to DoLS should be regarded as a death in state detention. This would mean that there would need to be a coroner's investigation and an inquest with a jury.

Principle 2: Least restriction

- This is, or should be, a core principle of current mental health practice. The concerns about the rising detention rates and the involvement of the police and other criminal justice system agencies in mental health mean that this principle is being eroded. The review suggests that there needs to be research that examines the rising rates of detention under the MHA. In addition, it calls for a drive to tackle what it terms the risk averse culture that permeates mental health services. It should be noted that mental health services are not alone in facing this charge. However, some would challenge the notion of risk averse services. For example, For example, Professor Louis Appleby tweeted that in his role on the National Confidential Inquiry into Homicide and Suicide he had received many letters from relatives pointing out concerns had been raised but agencies did not act or respond. This indicates that organisations were not risk averse but reluctant to become involved due to a combination of factors, including wider pressures on services.

The review emphasised that people should be treated with their consent wherever possible. In a new MHA, it suggests, the section that allows for voluntary admission (currently Section 131) should be placed above Sections 2 and 3 in the schedule of the Act. The process of assessment and admission under the MHA inevitably involves the potential for the overriding of an individual's rights. This does not and should not mean that an individual cannot be treated with dignity and respect. I fully accept that many would regard this as at best naive or at worst a failure to appreciate the nature or impact of detention. The review suggests that the capacity to consent must be always be assessed and recorded as part of any MHA admission. If a person is detained under the MHA he or she must be an informal patient or subject to the provisions of the Mental Capacity Act, if appropriate. The review calls for a strengthening of the criteria for admission. This would mean that the patient would be only detained if

- treatment is available which would benefit the patient, and not just serve public protection, which cannot be delivered without detention; and
- there is a substantial likelihood of significant harm to the health, safety or welfare of the person, or the safety of any other person, without treatment.

The review recommends that detention should require a comprehensive statutory care and treatment plan (CTP). The CTP would be in place within seven days and reviewed after 14 days. The CTP would include, among other elements, an outline of why compulsory elements of the treatment are needed, any cultural needs and planning for discharge.

The review makes a number of recommendations as regards the length of detention. The first is to suggest that if a person has been detained under Section 3 within the last 12 months then Section 2 should only be used if there has been a significant or material change in the individual's circumstances. This would be introduced via a change in the Code of Practice. In addition, the Code of Practice would be clarified so that Section 3 rather than Section 2 should be used if the person has been subject to Section 2 in the last 12 months. It is not clear how many assessments this will affect as practice in these areas varies quite significantly. The review sees the current processes as too restrictive. It therefore recommends further changes including reducing the initial maximum period of detention under Section 3 to three months instead of the current six. A Section 3 would be renewable after three months then after six months. After that, as is the case now, it would be renewable on a 12-month basis. The least restriction principle also generates changes to the tribunal system. The review recommends that the tribunal should, when a patient applies for discharge, should have the power to grant leave, direct a transfer to a different hospital and a limited power to direct the provision of community services. In addition, IMHAs and NPs would have the power to apply for discharge on behalf of a patient.

Community treatment orders have been the subject of much debate. The review stops short of recommending their complete abolition. However, there are a number of recommendations that would alter the use of the CTO. The criteria for the CTOs would be revised in line with the changes that are suggested for the application of Sections 2 and 3. There is a shift in the evidence threshold that would need to be passed for the CTO to be used. The responsible clinician (RC) would need to demonstrate that there had been a previous disengagement with services and that this had led to a mental health relapse. The practical implications of this shift would reduce or even possibly exclude entirely the use of CTOs following a first hospital admission. The application for the CTO would be made by the RC along with the community supervising clinician and an AMHP. A CTO would last initially for six months and be renewable at six months and then 12 months. The CTO should end after 24 months, though it would be possible to make a new application. The recall process and criteria should be reformed to make it simpler. The review suggests that the impact of their recommendations should be reviewed in not more than five years' time. If the outcomes for CTOs have not improved at that point then they should be abolished.

Principle 3: Therapeutic benefit

- When the interim review was published, it highlighted that the standard of care provided in a number of settings was poor. Newspaper reports highlighted that patients were abused and treated in a degrading fashion. This is clearly a broader organisational issue. This review echoes previous research (discussed in Chapter Four) that identified the poor physical environment of many units, the use of blanket bans and the imposition of often petty rules. Alongside this, as noted above patients and family members has consistently complained that they do not feel physically safe on wards. The review addresses this issue calling for an improved CQC inspection regimes for inpatient units. It also calls for patients to have daily one to one sessions with (permanent) staff as per NICE guidelines. The review also calls for a significant capital investment in mental health units. As part of this process, the design of wards should be considered. The review emphasised that this review should be co-produced with people with lived experience.

The therapeutic benefit principle also generates recommendations that apply across community and inpatient settings. The review calls for the creation of statutory care plans (SCP). A SCP would be created for anyone in contact with a CMHT as well inpatients and/or social care services. The review calls for there to be a statutory duty on clinical commissioning groups (CCGs) and local authorities to work together to ensure that the services identified in the SCP are provided.

Principle 4: The person as an individual

- The focus throughout the review is for a reshaping and refocusing of mental health care. Some expression of the explicit recognition of the fundamental dignity of all those who use mental health services is to be found in the professional ethics and values of those who work in this field. It is, therefore, something of an indictment of the current position in the provision of services that the review identifies the need to restate this core value. In calling for person-centred care , the review recommends that the CQC revises its approach to inspection and monitoring. The review highlights that the CQC inspection process needs to ensure that the views of groups of patients who be more marginalised are properly taken into account. This would include those with more complex needs, for example learning disabilities or autism, but also those who are placed out of area – in other words, away from their local mental health unit. The person as an individual is a theme that runs through recommendations in the whole of the report. In this section, the report highlights the need for additional training for tribunal panel members. In addition, there is a need for the collection of more robust data on the 'protected characteristics' of those who apply to tribunals and the outcomes of such hearings.

The history of mental health services has been scarred by racism. The review highlights that the current experiences of many BAME mental health service users have not necessarily changed significantly from those of the early 1980s. Over-representation and stereotyping have been constant scars on mental health services. In announcing the review, Theresa May was, for a political figure, unusually blunt in saying that institutional racism was one a cause of the issues discussed here. The review calls for culturally appropriate advocacy and citizens of black African and Caribbean heritage. Interestingly, the review calls for research into early interventions to prevent the exclusion from school of young people who are at risk. Alongside these recommendations, the review calls for regulatory bodies including the CQC to use their powers to support greater equality in access to service and improved treatment outcomes. Finally, there is a call for improvement in the collection of data about race, ethnicity and the use of the MHA. This should take place along research to examine the factors that lead to mental disorder in people from minority ethnic backgrounds and interventions which improve outcomes.

Principle 4 generates further recommendations with regard to the treatment of children and young people. The review suggests that young people aged 16 or 17 should not be admitted or treated on the basis of parental consent. If a young person is admitted, then an initial review should take place within five days of an emergency admission. If the admission is to an adult unit, the review should take place within three days. The review calls for an amendment to the Children Act 1989 so that any child admitted to a mental health unit is automatically regarded as a *child in need*. This would mean that parents and carers would be able to request services from their local authority. The panel is concerned about the experiences of people with learning disabilities, autism or both within mental health services. This is an area of growing concern. The panel argues that there needs to be greater monitoring the number of detentions with autism, learning disabilities or both.

The final area that the review considers is policing and mental health as well wider issues in the CJS. The review shares many of the concerns that have been have discussed in recent reports such as *Policing and mental health: Picking up the pieces* (HMICFRS, 2018). These reports argue that the police are being asked to take on too much mental health work. The review notes that by 2023/24 investment in mental health services will mean that it will possible to remove police cells as places of safety within the meaning of the MHA. The review also notes that the investment will mean that the majority of people detained under Section 136 should be conveyed to places of safety by ambulance rather than in a police van. The review calls for improvement in the ambulance fleet and the commissioning of specialist mental health vehicles to respond to these mental health emergencies. The use of police cells as places of safety has been declining. The review suggests that NHS England should take responsibility for the commissioning of health services in police custody.

The final areas considered here are patients in the criminal justice system. The review recommends that magistrates courts should have the same powers as crown courts. This would mean that magistrates would be able to remand for an assessment under Section 35 MHA and remand for treatment under Section 36 MHA. The review recommends that prisons should never be used as places of safety. The panel recommends the creation of a new independent role to manage transfers from prisons and immigration removal centres to mental health facilities.

The review takes a clear rights-based approach. This is to be welcomed. However, some of the initial responses to the review question whether it goes far enough in the rights-based direction. The concern is that the caveats which are included will allow mental health professionals will be able to overturn advanced treatment decisions more easily than the panel allows for.

There is a much more fundamental concern, however. The review of the MHA identifies some very serious concerns about the current structure and delivery of mental health services such as the poor quality of inpatient care, abusive practices and the experiences of BAME service users. These will not be resolved by changes to legislation. They require investment in mental health services but also organisational and cultural changes. One of the recurring themes of this book is that the provision of mental health care cannot be divorced from wider social and political issues. The panel acknowledges that there needs to be radical improvements in the design and building of mental health units. I do not think that anyone could seriously dispute that. The question will be whether the government, which appears to accept the recommendations of the review, will do so in their entirety. The process of reform of mental health legislation can be an arduous and complex one. The previous reform of the MHA took the best part of ten years from beginning to end. The reforms to the MHA here are, on first analysis, not as controversial and are likely to receive broader support. However, the legislative and parliamentary timetable over the next three to five years, if not longer, will be dominated by one issue – Brexit. This may well squeeze out other business.

References

@DrEm_79 (2017) What it feels like to be compulsorily detained for treatment. *BMJ 2017*, 358(j3546), https://doi.org/10.1136/bmj.j3546

Agamben, G. (2003) *Stato di eccezione: Homo sacer, II, I*, Vol. 3. Turin: Bollati Boringhieri

Allen, R. (2014) *The role of the social worker in adult mental health services.* London: The College of Social Work

All Party Parliamentary Group on Mental Health (2010) *Health and social care reform: making it work for mental health*, www.mind.org.uk/media/552972/

Andreasen, N.C. (1995) Posttraumatic stress disorder: Psychology, biology, and the Manichaean warfare between false dichotomies. *The American Journal of Psychiatry*, 152(7): 963–35

Appleby, L., Kapur, N., Shaw, J., Hunt, I.M., While, D., Flynn, S., Windfuhr, K. and Williams, A. (2013) *The National Confidential Inquiry into Suicide and Homicide by People with Mental Illness, Annual Report: July 2013*, http://documents.manchester.ac.uk/display.aspx?DocID=37595

Arendt, H. (1973) *The origins of totalitarianism.* New York: Houghton Mifflin Harcourt

Backwith, D. (2015) *Social work, poverty and social exclusion.* Maidenhead: Open University Press

Baker, S. (2000) *Environmentally friendly: Patients' views of conditions on psychiatric wards.* London: MIND, www.mind.org.uk

Barker, P. (2013) *The regeneration trilogy.* London: Penguin

Barton, W.R. (1959) *Institutional neurosis.* Bristol: Wright and Sons

Barr, B., Taylor-Robinson, D., Stuckler, D., Loopstra, R., Reeves, A. and Whitehead, M. (2015) 'First do no harm': Are disability assessments associated with adverse trends in mental health? A longitudinal study. *Journal of Epidemiology & Community Health,* 70: 339–45

Bauman, Z. (2007) *Liquid times: living in an age of uncertainty.* Cambridge: Polity Press

Beatty, C. and Fothergill, S. (2016) *The uneven impact of welfare reform: the financial losses to places and people.* Sheffield Hallam University: Centre for Regional Economic and Social Research, Oxfam and Joseph Rowntree Foundation, https://www4.shu.ac.uk/research/cresr/sites/shu.ac.uk/files/welfare-reform-2016.pdf

Beck, A.T. (1997) The past and future of cognitive therapy. *The Journal of Psychotherapy Practice and Research*, 6(4): 276

Beck, U. (1992) *Risk society: towards a new modernity*. Translated by Mark Ritter. London: Sage

Beck, U. (2008) *World at risk*. Cambridge: Polity Press

Bengtsson-Tops A. and Ehliasson, K. (2012) Victimization in individuals suffering from psychosis: a Swedish cross-sectional study. *Journal of Psychiatric and Mental Health Nursing*, 19(1): 23–30

Bennett, H.A., Einarson, A., Taddio, A., Koren, G. and Einarson, T.R. (2004) Prevalence of depression during pregnancy: systematic review. *Obstetrics & Gynecology*, 103(4): 698–709

Bentall, R.P. (2004) *Madness explained: Psychosis and human nature*. London: Penguin

Bentall, R.P., de Sousa, P., Varese, F., Wickham, S., Sitko, K., Haarmans, M. and Read, J. (2014) From adversity to psychosis: pathways and mechanisms from specific adversities to specific symptoms. *Social psychiatry and psychiatric epidemiology*, 49(7): 1011–22

Bentall, R. (2016) Mental illness is a result of misery, yet still we stigmatise it, *Guardian*, 26 February, www.theguardian.com/commentisfree/2016/feb/26/mental-illness-misery-childhood-traumas

Beresford, P (2013) *Mental health is in no fit state, whatever the politicians say*, https://theconversation.com/mental-health-is-in-no-fit-state-whatever-the-politicians-say-15743

Beresford, P. and Wallcraft, J. (1997) Psychiatric system survivors and emancipatory research: issues, overlaps and differences, in C. Barnes and G. Mercer (eds), *Doing disability research*. Leeds: The Disability Press, pp 66–87

Bhui, K., Stansfeld, S., Hull, S., Priebe, S., Mole, F. and Feder, G., 2003. Ethnic variations in pathways to and use of specialist mental health services in the UK: systematic review. *The British Journal of Psychiatry*, 182(2): 05–16

Bilson, A. and Martin, K.E.C. (2016) Referrals and child protection in England: One in five children referred to children's services and one in nineteen investigated before the age of five. *The British Journal of Social Work*, 47 (3): 793–811

Black, M.C., Basile, K.C., Breiding, M.J., Smith, S.G., Walters, M.L., Merrick, M.T. and Stevens, M.R. (2011) *The national intimate partner and sexual violence survey: 2010 summary report*. Atlanta, GA: National Center for Injury Prevention and Control, Centers for Disease Control and Prevention, 19, pp 39–40

Blofeld, J., Sallah, D., Sashidharan, S., Stone, R. and Struthers, J. (2003) *Independent inquiry into the death of David Bennett*. Washington, DC: NSCHA

Blom-Cooper, L., Hally, H. and Murphy, E. (1995) *The falling shadow: one patient's mental health care 1978–1993*. London: Duckworth

Bloom, S.L. and Farragher, B. (2010) *Destroying sanctuary: the crisis in human service delivery systems*. Oxford: Oxford University Press

Blyth, M. (2013) *Austerity: history of a dangerous idea*. Oxford: Oxford University Press

Boffey, D. (2015) Prescriptions for Ritalin and other ADHD drugs double in a decade, *Guardian*, 15 August, www.theguardian.com/society/2015/aug/15/ritalin-prescriptions-double-decade-adhd-mental-health

Borschmann, R.D., Gillard, S., Turner, K., Lovell, K., Goodrich-Purnell, N. and Chambers, M. (2010) Demographic and referral patterns of people detained under Section 136 of the Mental Health Act (1983) in a south London Mental Health Trust from 2005 to 2008. *Medicine, Science and the Law*, 50(1): 15–18

Bourdieu, P. (1986) The forms of capital, in J. Richardson (ed), *Handbook of Theory and Research for the Sociology of Education*. New York, Greenwood, pp 241–58

Bourdieu, P. (1989) Social space and symbolic power. *Sociological theory*, 7(1): 14–25

Bourdieu, P. (2001) *Acts of Resistance: Against the New Myths of Our Time*, 2nd reprint. Cambridge: Polity Press

Bourdieu, P. (2010) *Distinction*. London: Routledge Classics

Bourdieu, P. and Wacquant, L. (1992) *An invitation to reflexive sociology,* Chicago, IL: University of Chicago Press.

Bourdieu, P., Sayad, A., Christin, R., Champagne, P., Balazs, G., Wacquant, L.J.D., Lenoir, R., Pialoux, M., Beaud, S., Garcia, S., Pinto, L., Broccolichi, S., Œuvrard, F., Accardo, A., Soulié, C., Bourdieu, E., Podalydès, D., Faguar, J.-P. and Bonvin, F. (1999) *The weight of the world: Social suffering in contemporary society*. Cambridge: Polity Press

Bramley, G., Hirsch, D., Littlewood, M. and Watkins, D. (2016) *Counting the cost of UK poverty*, York: Joseph Rowntree Foundation, www.jrf.org.uk/report/counting-cost-uk-poverty

Braslow, J. (1997) *Mental ills and bodily cures: psychiatric treatment in the first half of the twentieth century*. Berkeley, CA: University of California Press

Britain, G. (2005). *Delivering race equality in mental health care: an action plan for reform inside and outside services* and *The government's response to the independent inquiry into the death of David Bennett*. London: Department of Health

Brown, J.M., Hamilton, C. and O'Neill, D. (2007) Characteristics associated with rape attrition and the role played by scepticism or legal rationality by investigators and prosecutors. *Psychology, Crime & Law*, 13(4): 355–70

Brown, G.W. and Harris, T. (1978) Social origins of depression: a reply. *Psychological Medicine*, 8(4): 577–88

Brown, W. (2015) *Undoing the demos*. Cambridge, MA: MIT Press

Browne, A. and Finkelhor, D. (1986) Impact of child sexual abuse: a review of the research. *Psychological Bulletin*, 99(1): 66

Browne, D. (2009) Black communities, mental health and the criminal justice system, in J. Reynolds, R. Muston, T. Heller, J. Leach, M. McCormick, J. Wallcraft and M. Walsh (eds), *Mental health still matters*. Basingstoke: Palgrave Macmillan, pp 169–73

Buckland, R. (2014) The decision by approved mental health professionals to use compulsory powers under the Mental Health Act 1983: A Foucauldian discourse analysis. *The British Journal of Social Work*, 46(1): 46–62

Burns, K., Novick, L. and War, V., 2017. *The Vietnam War*. Public Broadcasting Service.

Butler, A.C., Chapman, J.E., Forman, E.M. and Beck, A.T. (2006) The empirical status of cognitive-behavioral therapy: a review of meta-analyses. *Clinical Psychology Review*, 26(1): 17–31

Butler, I. and Drakeford, M. (2005) *Scandal, social policy and social welfare*. Bristol: Policy Press

Cameron, D. (2010) *Prime Minister's speech on the economy*, Milton Keynes, 7 June, https://www.gov.uk/government/speeches/prime-ministers-speech-on-the-economy

Campbell, P. (1996) Challenging loss of power, in J. Read and J. Reynolds (eds), *Speaking our minds*. Basingstoke: Palgrave Macmillan, pp 56–62

Carey, J. (2012) *The intellectuals and the masses: pride and prejudice among the literary intelligentsia 1880–1939*. London: Faber & Faber

Care Quality Commission (2011) *Count me in 2010*. London: NHS

Care Quality Commission (2015) *Monitoring the Mental Health Act in 2013/14*, www.cqc.org.uk/sites/default/files/monitoring_the_mha_2013-14_report_web_0303.pdf.pdf

Cavadino, M., Crow, I. and Dignan, J. (1999) *Criminal Justice 2000*. Winchester: Waterside Press

Centre for Welfare Reform (2015) *A fair society?* Sheffield: Centre for Welfare Reform, www.centreforwelfarereform.org

Chang, H. (2011) *23 things they don't tell you about capitalism.* London: Pelican

Chang, H. (2014) *Economics: The user's guide.* London: Pelican

Choe, J.Y., Teplin, L.A. and Abram, K.M. (2008) Perpetration of violence, violent victimization, and severe mental illness: balancing public health concerns. *Psychiatric Services*, 59(2): 153–64

Chopra, R. (2003) Neoliberalism as doxa: Bourdieu's theory of the state and the contemporary Indian discourse on globalization and liberalization. *Cultural studies,* 17(3–4): 419–44

CMH (Centre for Mental Health)/LSE (London School of Economics) (2014) *The costs of perinatal mental health problems.* London: CME

Cohen, S. (1972) *Folk devils and moral panics.* London: Macgibbon and Kee

Corston, J. (2008) *A report by Baroness Jean Corston of a review of women with particular vulnerabilities in the Criminal Justice system.* www.justice.gov.uk/publications/docs/corston-report-march-2007.pdf

Costa, L. (2014) Mad studies – What it is and why you should care. *The Bulletin*, 518: 4–5

Cox, C. and Marland, H. (2015) 'A burden on the county': madness, institutions of confinement and the Irish patient in Victorian Lancashire. *Social History of Medicine*, 28(2): 263–87

CQC (Care Quality Commission)(2018) *Mental Health Act: The rise in the use of the MHA to detain people in England,* www.cqc.org.uk/sites/default/files/20180123_mhadetentions_report.pdf

Cross, S. (2010) *Mediating madness mental distress and cultural representation.* Basingstoke: Palgrave Macmillan

Crossley, S. (2016) The Troubled Families Programme: in, for and against the state? *Social Policy Review: Analysis and Debate in Social Policy*, 28: 127

Crossley, N. (1999) Fish, field, habitus and madness: the first wave mental health users movement in Great Britain. *The British Journal of Sociology*, 50(4): 647–70

Crossley, N. (2004) Not being mentally ill: Social movements, system survivors and the oppositional habitus. *Anthropology & Medicine*, 11(2): 161–80

Crossley, N. (2006) *Contesting psychiatry: social movements in mental health.* Oxford: Psychology Press

Cummins, I.D. (2007) Boats against the current: vulnerable adults in police custody. *The Journal of Adult Protection*, 9(1): 15–24

Cummins, I.D. (2008) A place of safety? Self-harming behaviour in police custody. *The Journal of Adult Protection*, 10(1): 36–47

Cummins, I. (2012) Mental health and custody: a follow on study. *The Journal of Adult Protection*, 14(2): 73–81

Cummins, I. (2013a) Using Simon's 'Governing through crime' to explore the development of mental health policy in England and Wales since 1983. *Journal of Social Welfare and Family Law*, 34(3): 325–37

Cummins, I (2013b) Sun splash missed the point on 'mental patient murders', https://theconversation.com/the-sun-splash-missed-point-on-mental-patient-murders-18971

Cummins, I. (2015a) Discussing race, racism and mental health: two mental health inquiries reconsidered. *International Journal of Human Rights in Healthcare*, 8(3): 160–72, https://doi.org/10.1108/IJHRH-08-2014-0017

Cummins, I. (2015b) Reading Wacquant: social work and advanced marginality. *European Journal of Social Work*, 19(2): 263–74.

Cummins, I. (2016a) Putting diagnosis into brackets: Franco Basaglia, radical psychiatry, and contemporary mental health services. *Illness, Crisis & Loss*, 26(3): 187–99.

Cummins, I. (2016b) From hero of the counterculture to risk assessment: a consideration of two portrayals of the 'psychiatric patient'. *Illness, Crisis & Loss*, 26(2): 113–23.

Cummins, I. (2017a) Rereading Rosenhan. *Illness, Crisis & Loss*, https://doi.org/10.1177%2F1054137317690377

Cummins, I. (2017b) *Critical psychiatry: a biography*. Northwich: Critical Publishing

Cummins, I. (2018) *Poverty, inequality and social work*. Bristol: Policy Press

Cummins, I.D. and Jones, S. (2010) Blue remembered skills: mental health awareness training for police officers. *Journal of Adult Protection*, 12(3): 14–19

Cummins, I.D., Foley, M. and King, M. (2016) The strange case of Ian Stuart Brady and the mental health review tribunal. *Internet Journal of Criminology*, https://docs.wixstatic.com/ugd/b93dd4_b4774d607d3f48319adef5dfd1030e5b.pdf

Cummins, I Foley, M and King, M (2019) *Serial Killers and the Media: The Moors Murders Legacy*, Basingstoke: Palgrave Macmillan

DHSC (Department of Health and Social Care) (2018) *Modernising the Mental Health Act: Increasing choice, reducing compulsion. Final report of the Independent Review of the Mental Health Act 1983*, London: DHSC.

DH (Department of Health) (1998) *Modernising mental health services*. London: HMSO, https://webarchive.nationalarchives.gov.uk/+/www.dh.gov.uk/prod_consum_dh/groups/dh_digitalassets/@dh/@en/documents/digitalasset/dh_4046660.pdf

DH (2002) *No secrets*. London: HMSO

DH (2003) F*air Access to Care Services Guidance on Eligibility Criteria for Adult Social Care*, London: DH

DH (2012). P*ost-legislative assessment of the Mental Health Act 2007*. Cm [HC] 8408. London: TSO

DH (2014) *Closing the gap*. London: HMSO

DH (2015a) *Future in mind: promoting, protecting and improving our children and young people's mental health and wellbeing*. London: HMSO

DH (2015b) *Department of Health guidance: response to the Supreme Court Judgment/Deprivation of Liberty Safeguards*, 22 October, www.gov.uk/government/uploads/system/uploads/attachment_data/file/485122/DH_Consolidated_Guidance.pdf

DH (2015c). *Mental Health Act 1983: Code of Practice*. London: TSO

DH (2016) *Social work for better mental health* https://assets.publishing.service.gov.uk/government/uploads/system/uploads/attachment_data/file/495500/Strategic_statement_-_social_work_adult_mental_health_A.pdf

DHSS (Department for Health and Social Security) (1988) *Report of the Committee of Inquiry into the care and aftercare of Sharon Campbell,* [chair: John Spokes]. London: HMSO

Dickinson, T. (2014) *'Curing queers': mental nurses and their patients, 1935–74*. Oxford: Oxford University Press

Docking, M., Grace, K. and Bucke, B. (2008) *Police custody as a 'place of safety': Examining the use of Section 136 of the Mental Health Act 1983*. Independent Police Complaints Commission (IPCC) Research and Statistics Series. London: IPCC.

Dostoyevsky, F. (1862) *The House of the Dead*. London: Penguin Classics

Drake, C. and Cayton, H. (1993) *Black metropolis: a study of negro life in a northern city*. Chicago, IL: University of Chicago Press

Duggan, M., Cooper, C. and Foster, J. (2002) Modernising the social model in mental health: a discussion paper. London: Social Perspectives Network

Dunn, J. and Fahy, T.A. (1990) Police admissions to a psychiatric hospital: demographic and clinical differences between ethnic groups. *The British Journal of Psychiatry*, 156(3): 373–78

Durkheim, E. (1984/1893) *The division of labor in society*. New York: Free Press

Eastman, N. and Starling, B. (2006) Mental disorder ethics: theory and empirical investigation. *Journal of Medical Ethics*, 32: 94–9

Edge, D. (2007) Ethnicity, psychosocial risk, and perinatal depression—a comparative study among inner-city women in the United Kingdom. *Journal of psychosomatic research*, 63(3): 291–5

Edge, D. (2010) Falling through the net—Black and minority ethnic women and perinatal mental healthcare: health professionals' views. *General Hospital Psychiatry*, 32(1): 17–25

Estrich, S. (1987) *Real rape: how the legal system victimises women who say no*. Cambridge, MA: Harvard University Press

Evans, S., Huxley, P., Webber, M., Katona, C., Gately, C., Mears, A. and Kendall, T. (2005) The impact of 'statutory duties' on mental health social workers in the UK. *Health and Social Care in the Community*, 13(2): 145–54

Featherstone, B., White, S. and Morris, K. (2014) *Re-imagining child protection: towards humane social work with families*. Bristol: Policy Press

Fineman, M. (2004) *The autonomy myth a theory of dependency*. New York: The New Press

Fisher, H.L., Jones, P.B., Fearon, P., Craig, T.K., Dazzan, P., Morgan, K., Hutchinson, G., Doody, G.A., McGuffin, P., Leff, J. and Murray, R.M. (2010) The varying impact of type, timing and frequency of exposure to childhood adversity on its association with adult psychotic disorder. *Psychological Medicine*, 40(12): 1967–78

Filer, N. (2013) *The shock of the fall*. London: Harper Collins

Foley, M. and Cummins, I. (2015) Reading the death of Mrs A: a serious case review. *The Journal of Adult Protection*, 17(5): 321–30

Foley, M. and Cummins, I. (2018) Reporting sexual violence on mental health wards. *The Journal of Adult Protection*, 20(2): 93–100

Foot, J. (2015) *The man who closed the asylums: Franco Basaglia and the revolution in mental health care*. London: Verso Books

Foucault, M. (1982) Afterword: The subject and power, in Dreyfus, H.L. and Rabinow, P. *Michel Foucault: Beyond structuralism and hermeneutics* [interview]. Chicago: University of Chicago Press

Foucault, M. (1991 [1975]) *Discipline and punish*. Translated by A. Sheridan. London: Penguin

Foucault, M. (2001 [1960]) *Madness and civilisation*. Translated by R. Howard. New York: Vintage

Foucault, M. (2005) *The order of things*. Abingdon: Routledge

Foucault, M. (2006) *The history of madness*. Abingdon: Routledge

Foucault, M. (2008) *The birth of biopolitics: lectures at the Collège de France. 1978–1979*. Translated by Graham Burchell. Basingstoke: Palgrave

Franiuk, R., Seefelt, J.L. and Vandello, J.A. (2008) Prevalence of rape myths in headlines and their effects on attitudes toward rape. *Sex Roles,* 58(11–12): 790–801

Flynn, M. and Citarella, V. (2013) Winterbourne View Hospital: a glimpse of the legacy. *The Journal of Adult Protection,* 15(4): 173–81

Friedman, M. (2002 [1962]) *Capitalism and freedom,* 40th anniversary edition. London: University of Chicago Press

Garland, D. (2001): *The Culture of Control: Crime and Social Order in Contemporary Society.* Chicago. University of Chicago Press

Garland, D. (2014) *What is the welfare state? A sociological restatement,* London School of Economics and Political Science. www.lse. ac.uk/website-archive/newsAndMedia/videoAndAudio/channels/ publicLecturesAndEvents/player.aspx?id=2695

Garrett, P.M. (2007) Making social work more Bourdieusian: why the social work profession should engage with the work of Pierre Bourdieu. *European Journal of Social Work,* 10(2): 225–43

Garrett, P.M. (2015) Words matter: deconstructing 'welfare dependency' in the UK. *Critical and Radical Social Work,* 3(3): 389–406

Garthwaite, K. (2016a) Stigma, shame and 'people like us': An ethnographic study of food bank use in the UK. *Journal of Poverty and Social Justice,* 24(3): 277–89

Garthwaite, K. (2016b) *Hunger pains: life inside foodbank Britain.* Bristol: Policy Press.

Gentleman, A. and Gayle, D. (2016) Sarah Reed's mother: 'My daughter was failed by many and I was ignored', *Guardian,* 17 February, www.theguardian.com/society/2016/feb/17/sarah-reeds-mother-deaths-in-custody-holloway-prison-mental-health

Gill, O. and Jack, G. (2007) *The child and family in context: developing ecological practice in disadvantaged communities.* Lyme Regis: Russell House Publishing

Giroux, H. (2011) Neoliberalism and the death of the social state: remembering Walter Benjamin's Angel of History Social Identities. *Journal for the Study of Race, Nation and Culture,* 17(4): 587–6-1

Giroux, H.A. (2017) Trump's neo-Nazis and the rise of illiberal democracy, *Truthout,* 16 August, www.truth-out.org/news/ item/41617-neo-nazis-in-charlottesville-and-the-rise-of-illiberal-democracy

Gittins, D. (1998) *Madness in its place.* London: Routledge

Goffman, E. (1963) *Stigma: notes on the management of spoiled identities.* New York: Simon & Schuster

Goffman, E. (1961) *Asylums: essays on the social situation of mental patients and other inmates.* Harmondsworth: Penguin.

Gostin, L. (2007) From a civil libertarian to a sanitarian. *Journal of Law and Society*, 34(4): 594–616

Gould, N. (2010) *Mental health social work in context*. Abingdon: Routledge

Green, H., McGinnity, Á., Meltzer, H., Ford, T. and Goodman, R. (2005) *Mental health of children and young people in Great Britain, 2004*. London: HMSO

Gregor, C. (2010) Unconscious aspects of statutory mental health social work: emotional labour and the Approved Mental Health Professional. *Journal of Social Work Practice*, 24(4): 429–43

Gregory, M. (2007) Newly qualified probation officers talk about their training. *Social Work Education*, 26(1): 53–68

Gregory, M. (2010) Reflection and resistance: probation practice and the ethic of care. *British Journal of Social Work*, 40(7): 2274–90.

Gupta, A. (2017) Poverty and child neglect – the elephant in the room? *Families, Relationships and Societies*, 6(1): 21–36

Hall, S., Critcher, C., Jefferson, T., Clarke, J. and Roberts, B. (2013) P*olicing the crisis: Mugging, the state and law and order*, 2nd edition. Basingstoke: Palgrave Macmillan

Hall, S. (2017a) The great moving right show, in S. Hall (ed), *Selected political writings, the great moving right show and other essays*. Durham, NC: Duke University Press, pp 172–89

Hall, S. (2017b) The great moving nowhere show, in S. Hall (ed), *Selected political writings, the great moving right show and other essays*. Durham, NC: Duke University Press, pp 283–300.

Hammen, C. and Goodman-Brown, T. (1990) Self-schemas and vulnerability to specific life stress in children at risk for depression. *Cognitive Therapy and Research*, 14(2): 215–27

Hampson, M. (2011) Raising standards in relation to Section 136 of the Mental Health Act 1983. *Advances in Psychiatric Treatment*, 17(5): 365–71

Hanley, L. (2012) *Estates: an intimate history*. London: Granta

Hanley, L. (2016) *Respectable: the experience of class*. London: Penguin

Harris, M.E. and Fallot, R.D. (2001) Using trauma theory to design service systems. *New Directions for Mental Health Services*, No. 89, San Francisco: Jossey-Bass

Harvey, D. (2005) *A brief history of neoliberalism*. Oxford: Oxford University Press

Hawthorne, N. (1850) *The scarlet letter*. Boston: Ticknor, Reed and Fields

Heron, J., O'Connor, T.G., Evans, J., Golding, J., Glover, V. and ALSPAC Study Team (2004) The course of anxiety and depression through pregnancy and the postpartum in a community sample. *Journal of Affective Disorders*, 80(1): 65–73

Hester M (2013). *From Report to Court: Rape Cases and the Criminal Justice System in the North East*. Bristol: University of Bristol in association with Northern Rock Foundation

Higgs, R. (1987) *Crisis and leviathan*. Oxford: Oxford University Press

Hills, J. (2015) *Good times, bad times: The welfare myth of them and us*. Bristol: Policy Press

Hillier, J. and Rooksby, E. (2002) *Habitus: a sense of place*. Ashgate: Routledge

HMCPS Inspectorate (2016) *Thematic Review of the CPS Rape and Serious Sexual Offences Units,* https://www.justiceinspectorates.gov.uk/hmcpsi/wp-content/uploads/sites/3/2016/02/RASSO_thm_Feb16_rpt.pdf

HMIC (Her Majesty's Inspectorate of Constabulary), HMIP (Her Majesty's Inspectorate of Prisons), CQC (Care Quality Commission) and HIW (Healthcare Inspectorate Wales) (2013) *A Criminal Use of Police Cells? The use of police custody as a place of safety for people with mental health needs,* www.justiceinspectorates.gov.uk/hmicfrs/media/a-criminal-use-of-police-cells-20130620.pdf

HMICFRS (Her Majesty's Inspectorate of Constabulary and Fire & Rescue Services) (2018) *Policing and mental health: Picking up the pieces,* www.justiceinspectorates.gov.uk/hmicfrs/wp-content/uploads/policing-and-mental-health-picking-up-the-pieces.pdf

Hogg, S. (2013) *Prevention in mind. All babies count: spotlight on perinatal mental illness*. London: NSPCC

Houston, S. (2002) Re-thinking a systemic approach to child welfare: A critical response to the framework for the assessment of children in need and their families. *European Journal of Social Work*, 5(3): 301–12

Howard, L.M., Trevillion, K. and Agnew-Davies, R. (2010) Domestic violence and mental health. *International Review of Psychiatry*, 22(5): 525–34

Howard, L.M., Oram, S., Galley, H., Trevillion, K. and Feder, G. (2013) Domestic violence and perinatal mental disorders: a systematic review and meta-analysis. *PLoS medicine*, 10(5): p.e1001452

Howe, D. (2014) *The complete social worker*. Basingstoke: Palgrave Macmillan

Howe, G. (1969) *Report of the Committee of Inquiry into Allegations of Ill-Treatment of Patients and other irregularities at the Ely Hospital,* Cardiff: Cm 3975

Hughes, E.C. (1971) *The sociological eye: selected papers.* Chicago, IL: Aldine-Atherton

Ignatieff, M. (1985) State, civil society and total institutions, in S. Cohen and A. Scull (eds), *Social control and the state: historical and comparative essays.* Oxford: Blackwell

Independent Mental Health Taskforce (2016) *The five year forward view for mental health*, A report to the NHS in England, www.england.nhs.uk/wp-content/uploads/2016/02/Mental-Health-Taskforce-FYFV-final.pdf

Ingleby, D. (1980) *Critical psychiatry: the politics of mental health.* New York: Pantheon Books

Innes, D. and Tetlow, G. (2015) Delivering fiscal squeeze by cutting local government spending. *Fiscal Studies*, 36(3): 303–25

Institute for Fiscal Studies (IFS) (2012) *Reforming council tax benefit*, IFS commentary 123, www.ifs.org.uk/comms/comm123.pdf

James, O. (2008) *The selfish capitalist: origins of affluenza.* London: Random House.

Jones, J., Nolan, P., Bowers, L., Simpson, A., Whittington, R., Hackney, D. and Bhui, K. (2010) Psychiatric wards: places of safety? *Journal of Psychiatric and Mental Health Nursing*, 17(2): 124–30

Jones, S.L. and Mason, T. (2002) Quality of treatment following police detention of mentally disordered offenders. *Journal of Psychiatric and Mental Health Nursing*, 9(1): 73–80

James, O. (2008) *The selfish capitalist: Origins of affluenza.* London: Vermilion

Karban, K. (2016) Developing a health inequalities approach for mental health social work. *British Journal of Social Work*, 47(3): 885–92

Keating, F., Robertson, D., McCulloch, A. and Francis, E. (2002) *Breaking the circles of fear: a review of the relationship between mental health services and African and Caribbean communities.* London: Sainsbury Centre for Mental Health

Kelly, L., Lovett, J. and Regan, L. (2005) *A gap or a chasm? Attrition in reported rape cases.* Home Office Research Study 293. London: Home Office Research Development and Statistics Division

Kesey, K. (2005) *One flew over the cuckoo's nest.* London: Penguin

Kessler, R.C., Davis, C.G. and Kendler, K.S. (1997) Childhood adversity and adult psychiatric disorder in the US National Comorbidity Survey. *Psychological Medicine*, 27(5): 1101–19.

Khalifeh, H., Moran, P., Borschmann, R., Dean, K., Hart, C., Hogg, J., Howard, L.M. (2015). Domestic and sexual violence against patients with severe mental illness. *Psychological Medicine*, 45(4): 875–86

Knowles, C. (2000) *Bedlam on the streets.* London: Routledge

Krugman, P. (2015) The case for cuts was a lie. Why does Britain still believe it?, *Guardian*, 29 April, www.theguardian.com/business/ ng-interactive/2015/apr/29/the-austerity-delusion

Krumer-Nevo, M. (2015) Poverty-aware social work: A paradigm for social work practice with people in poverty. *British Journal of Social Work*, 46(6): 1783–808

Laing, R. (1967) *The politics of experience and the bird of paradise.* Harmondsworth: Penguin

Larson, G. (2008) Anti-oppressive practice in mental health. *Journal of Progressive Human Services*, 19(1): 39–54

Latham, A. (1997) The Cinderella Section: room for improvement in the documentation and implementation of Section 136 of the Mental Health Act 1983. *Journal of clinical forensic medicine,* 4(4): 173–75

Law Commission (2017) *Mental capacity and deprivation of liberty*, www.lawcom.gov.uk/app/uploads/2017/03/lc372_mental_capacity.pdf

LeFrançois, B.A., Menzies, R. and Reaume, G. (eds) (2013) *Mad matters: a critical reader in Canadian mad studies.* Toronto: Canadian Scholars' Press

Limb, M. (2014) More children are being treated on adult psychiatric wards, investigation shows, *BMJ*, 2014; 348: g1725

Littler, J. (2016) *Mayritocracy: neoliberalism with new borders*, Lawrence & Wishart blog, 22 November, www.lwbooks.co.uk/blog/ mayritocracy-neoliberalism-with-new-borders

Lipsky, M. (1980) *Street level bureaucracy: Dilemmas of the individual public services.* New York: Russell Sage Foundation

Lombroso, C. (2006 [1876]) *Criminal man [L'uomo delinquent].* Durham, NC: Duke University Press

Loury, G.C. (1977) A dynamic theory of racial income differences, in P.A. Wallace and A.M. La Mond (eds), *Women, minorities, and employment discrimination.* Lexington, MA: Heath, pp 153–86

LSE (2012) *How mental illness loses out in the NHS*, a report by the Centre for Economic Performance's Mental Health Policy Group, http://cep.lse.ac.uk/pubs/download/special/cepsp26.pdf

Luhrmann, T.M. (2000) *Of two minds: The growing disorder in American psychiatry.* New York: Alfred A. Knopf

Macey, D. (2001) *Frantz Fanon: a life.* London: Granta Books

Malthus, T.R. (1798) *An Essay on the Principle of Population, as it Affects the Future Improvement of Society, with Remarks on the Speculations of Mr. Godwin, M. Condorcet, and Other Writers.* The Lawbook Exchange, Ltd

Manthorpe, J., Rapaport, J., Harris, J. and Samsi, K. (2009) Realising the safeguarding potential of the Mental Capacity Act 2005: early reports from adult safeguarding staff. *The Journal of Adult Protection*, 11(2): 13–24

Mantle, G. and Backwith, D. (2010) Poverty and social work. *British Journal of Social Work*, 40: 2380–97

Marcuse, H. (2013 [1964]) *One-dimensional man: studies in the ideology of advanced industrial society.* Abingdon: Routledge

Marmot, M. (2010) *Fair society, healthy lives, The Marmot Review.* London: DH, www.parliament.uk/documents/fair-society-healthy-lives-full-report.pdf

Martin, J.P. (1985) *Hospitals in Trouble.* Oxford: Blackwell

Marx, K. (1894) *Capital*, Vol. 3. New York: International

McMillan, L. and Thomas, M. (2009) Police interviews of rape victims: tensions and contradictions, in H. Horvath and J. Brown (eds), *Rape: Challenging contemporary thinking.* Cullompton, UK: Willan, pp 255–80

Meikle, J. (2016) Antidepressant prescriptions in England double in a decade, *Guardian*, 5 July, www.theguardian.com/society/2016/jul/05/antidepressant-prescriptions-in-england-double-in-a-decade

Merquior, J. (1991) *Foucault.* London: Fontana

Milanovic, B. (2016) *Global inequality: a new approach for the age of Globalization.* Cambridge, MA: Harvard University Press

Ministry of Justice (2009) *Guidance for social supervisors,* https://assets.publishing.service.gov.uk/government/uploads/system/uploads/attachment_data/file/631276/guidance-for-social-supervisors-0909_2.pdf

Mind (2007) *Another assault: Mind's campaign for equal access to justice for people with mental health problems.* London: Mind, www.mind.org.uk

Moncrieff, J. (2004) *Is psychiatry for sale? An examination of the influence of the pharmaceutical industry on academic and practical psychiatry,* www.critpsynet.freeuk.com/pharmaceuticalindustry.htm

Moon, G. (2000) Risk and protection: the discourse of confinement in contemporary mental health policy. *Health & Place*, 6(3): 239–50

Moore, C. (2014) *Margaret Thatcher: the authorized biography, Volume One: Not for turning.* London: Penguin

Morriss, L. (2014) Accomplishing social work identity in interprofessional mental health teams following the implementation of the Mental Health Act 2007. Doctoral thesis, University of Salford

Morriss, L. (2016a) Being seconded to a Mental Health Trust: the (in)visibility of mental health social work. *The British Journal of Social Work*, 47(5): 1344–60

Morriss, L. (2016b) AMHP work: dirty or prestigious? Dirty work designations and the approved mental health professional. *The British Journal of Social Work,* 46(3): 703–18

Munro, E. (2011) *The Munro review of child protection: final report, a child-centred system.* London: Stationery Office

Murray, C. (1990) *The emerging British underclass.* Choice in Welfare Series No. 2. London: IEA Health and Welfare Unit

Murray, R. (2017) Mistakes I have made in my research career. *Schizophrenia Bulletin,* 43(2): 253–56

National Collaborating Centre for Mental Health (2007) *NICE clinical guideline 45: Antenatal and postnatal mental health, Clinical management and service guidance.* London: NICE

NICE (National Institute for Health and Clinical Excellence)(2010) *Looked-after children and young people,* www.nice.org.uk/guidance/ph28

Nolan, P. (2000) *A history of mental health nursing.* Cheltenham: Nelson Thornes

Nozick, R. (1974) *Anarchy, state and utopia.* New York: Basic Books

Nyame S., Howard L., Feder G. and Trevillion, K. (2013) A survey of mental health professionals' knowledge, attitudes and preparedness to respond to domestic violence. *Journal of Mental Health,* 22(6): 536–43

Oates, M. and Cantwell, R. (2011) Deaths from psychiatric causes. *The confidential enquiry into maternal and child health (CEMACH). Saving mothers' lives—2006–2008,* pp 132–42. London: CEMACH

O'Hara, M. (2015) *Austerity bites: A journey to the sharp end of cuts in the UK.* Bristol: Policy Press

Omonira-Oyekanmi, R. (2014) Black and dangerous? Listening to patients' experiences of mental health services in London. Open Democracy, www. opendemocracy.net

ODPM (Office of the Deputy Prime Minister) (2004) *Mental health and social exclusion.* London: ODPM

Office for National Statistics (ONS) (2015) *Crime Statistics: Focus on Violent Crime and Sexual Offences 2013/14.*

Oxfam (2013) *Truth and lies about poverty: ending comfortable myths about poverty.* https://policy-practice.oxfam.org.uk/publications/truth-and-lies-about-poverty-ending-comfortable-myths-about-poverty-306526

Papeschi, R. (1985) The denial of the institution: A critical review of Franco Basaglia's writings. *The British Journal of Psychiatry,* 146(3): 247–254

Parsons, T. (1951) Illness and the role of the physician: A sociological perspective. *American Journal of Orthopsychiatry,* 21(3): 452–460

Paterson, B. (2014) *Mainstreaming Trauma*. Paper presented at the Psychological Trauma-Informed Care Conference, University of Stirling, 4 June, www.stir.ac.uk/media/schools/nursing/ documents/ Trauma14-Paterson-mainstreaming-trauma-workshop.pdf

Peck, J. and Theodore, N. (2010) Recombinant workfare, across the Americas: Transnationalizing 'fast' social policy. *Geoforum*, 41(2): 195–208

Peck, J. and Tickell, A. (2002) 'Neoliberalizing space', *Antipode*, 34(3): 380–404

Penhale, B., Brammer, A., Morgan, P., Kingston, P., and Preston-Shoot, M. (2017) The Care Act 2014: a new legal framework for safeguarding adults in civil society. *The Journal of Adult Protection*, 19(4): 169–74

Pettitt, B., Greenhead, S., Khalifeh, H., Drennan, V., Hart, T., Hogg, J., Borschmann, R., Mamo, E. and Moran, P. (2013) *At risk, yet dismissed*. London: Mind, www.mind.org.uk

Philo, C. (1987) 'Fit localities for an asylum': the historical geography of the nineteenth-century 'mad-business' in England as viewed through the pages of the Asylum Journal. *Journal of Historical Geography*, 13(4): 398–415

Pilgrim, D. and Rogers, A. (2013) *Sociology of mental health and illness*. Buckingham: Open University Press

Plath, S. (2005) *The bell jar*. London: Bloomsbury

Pollitt, C. and Bouckaert, G. (2003) *Public management reform: a comparative analysis*. Oxford: Oxford University Press

Porter, R. (1987) *Mind-forg'd manacles: A history of madness in England from the Restoration to the Regency*. Cambridge, MA: Harvard University Press

Portes, A. (1998) Social capital: its origins and applications in modern sociology. *Annual Review of Sociology*, 24(1): 1–24

Powell, E. (1961) Summary of Powell's 'Water Tower' speech. www.canehill.org/history/enoch-powells-1961-speech

Prospero, M. and Kim, M. (2009) Ethnic difference in the effects of coercion on mental health and the use of therapy. *Journal of Social Work Practice*, 23(1): 77–91

Public Accounts Committee (2016) *Transforming Rehabilitation inquiry*. www.parliament.uk/business/committees/committees-a-z/commons-select/public-accounts-committee/inquiries/parliament-2015/transforming-rehabilitation-16-17/

Putkowski, J. and Sykes, J. (1990) *Shot at dawn*. Barnsley: Pen and Sword.

Putnam, R. (1993) *Making democracy work: civic traditions in modern Italy*. Princeton, NJ: Princeton University Press

Quirk, A. and Lelliott, P. (2001) What do we know about life on acute psychiatric wards in the UK? A review of the research evidence. *Social Science & Medicine*, 53(12): 1565–74

Rawlinson, K., Bowcott, O. and Campbell, D. (2017) Judge warns of 'blood on our hands' if suicidal girl is forced out of secure care, *Guardian*, 3 August, www.theguardian.com/society/2017/aug/03/judge-warns-of-blood-on-our-hands-if-suicidal-girl-is-forced-out-of-secure-care

Rechtman, R. (2004) The rebirth of PTSD: the rise of a new paradigm in psychiatry. *Social Psychiatry and Psychiatric Epidemiology*, 39(11): 913–915

Reid, J. and Poole, J. (2013) Mad students in the social work classroom? Notes from the beginnings of an inquiry. *Journal of Progressive Human Services*, 24(3): 209–22

Riley, G., Freeman, E., Laidlaw, J. and Pugh, D. (2011) 'A frightening experience': detainees' and carers' experiences of being detained under Section 136 of the Mental Health Act. *Medicine, Science and the Law*, 51(3): 164–69

Ritchie, J. (1994) *The report of the inquiry into the care and treatment of Christopher Clunis.* London: HMSO

Rogers, A. and Faulkner, A. (1987) *A place of safety. MIND's research into police referrals to the psychiatric services.* London: MIND, www.mind.org.uk

Rosenhan, D.L. (1975) On being sane in insane places. *Science*, 179(4070): 250–8

RCP (Royal College of Psychiatrists) (2011) *Do the right thing: How to judge a good ward.* Occasional Paper series, 79. London: RCP.

Russo, J. (2012) Survivor-controlled research: A new foundation for thinking about psychiatry and mental health. *Forum: Qualitative Social Research,* 13(1): Art. 8

Sandbrook, D. (2013) *Seasons in the sun: the battle for Britain, 1974–1979.* London: Penguin

Savage, M. (2016) End class wars. *Nature*, 537(7621): 475–8

Savage, M. (2017) Theresa May pledges mental health revolution will reduce detentions, *Guardian*, 7 May, www.theguardian.com/politics/2017/may/07/theresa-may-pledges-mental-health-revolution-will-reduce-detentions

Sayce, L. (2016) *From psychiatric patient to citizen: revisited.* Basingstoke: Palgrave Macmillan

Scott, R.D. (1973) The treatment barrier, part 1. *British Journal of Medical Psychology*, 46(57): 45–53

Scull, A. (1977) *Decarceration: community treatment and the deviant – a radical view*. Englewood Cliffs, NJ: Prentice-Hall

Scull, A. (1986) Mental patients and the community: a critical note. *International Journal of Law and Psychiatry*, 9(3): 383–92

Scull, A. (1989) *Social order/mental disorder: Anglo-American psychiatry in historical perspective*. Berkeley: University of California Press

Scull, A. (2011) The peculiarities of the Scots? Scottish influences on the development of English psychiatry, 1700–1980. *History of Psychiatry*, 22(4): 403–15

Scull, A. (2015) *Madness in civilization*. London: Thames and Hudson

Said, E. (1978) *Orientalism: Western representations of the Orient*. New York: Pantheon

Seddon, T. (2007) *Punishment and madness*. Abingdon: Routledge-Cavendish

Sedgwick, P. (1982) *Psychopolitics*. London: Pluto Press

Seltzer, M. (1997) Wound culture: trauma in the pathological public sphere. *October*, 80: 3–26.

Sheehan, N. (1990) *A bright shining lie: John Paul Vann and America in Vietnam*. New York: Vintage.

Simmel, G. (1964 [1903]) The metropolis and mental life, in *The Sociology of Georg Simmel*, edited and translated by K.H. Wolff. New York: Free Press, pp 409–24

Simpson, A., Miller, C. and Bowers, L. (2003) The history of the care programme approach in England: where did it go wrong? *Journal of Mental Health*, 12(5): 489–504

Singh, S.P. and Burns, T. (2006) Controversy: race and mental health: there is more to race than racism. *British Medical Journal*, 333(7569): 648

Singleton, N., Meltzer, H. and Gatward, R. (1998) *Psychiatric morbidity among prisoners in England and Wales*. London: HMSO

Skelcher, C. (2000) Changing images of the state: Overloaded, hollowed-out, congested. *Public Policy and Administration*, 15(3): 3–19

Skinner, B.F. (1971) *Freedom and dignity*. New York: Alfred A. Knopf

Skinner, B.F. (1976) *About behavourism* New York: Vintage Books

Slater, T. (2009) 'Ghettos' and 'Anti-urbanism' [entries], in R. Kitchin and N. Thrift (eds) *The International Encyclopaedia of Human Geography*, London: Elsevier

Slasberg, C. and Beresford, P. (2014) Government guidance for the Care Act: undermining ambitions for change? *Disability & Society*, 29(10): 1677–82

Somers, M. (2008) *Genealogies of citizenship: Markets, statelessness and the right to have rights*. Cambridge: Cambridge University Press

Sontag, S. (1978) *Illness as metaphor.* New York: Strauss & Giroux

Spandler, H. (2001) *Who's hurting who? Young people, self-harm and suicide.* Gloucester: Handsell Publishing

Spandler, H. and Warner, S. (2007) *Beyond fear and control: working with young people who self harm.* Monmouth: PCCS Books

Spitzer, R.L. (1975) On pseudoscience in science, logic in remission, and psychiatric diagnosis: A critique of Rosenhan's 'On being sane in insane places'. *Journal of Abnormal Psychology*, 84(5): 442–52

Spitzer, R.L. and Wilson, P.T. (1975) Nosology and the official psychiatric nomenclature. *Comprehensive Textbook of Psychiatry*, 2: 826–45

Stedman-Jones, D. (2012) *Masters of the universe: Hayek, Friedman, and the birth of neoliberal politics.* Oxford: Princeton University Press

Stedman-Jones, G. (2014) *Outcast London: a study in the relationship between classes in Victorian society.* New York: Verso Books

Stenhouse, R.C. (2013) 'Safe enough in here?' Patients' expectations and experiences of feeling safe in an acute psychiatric inpatient ward. *Journal of Clinical Nursing*, 22(21–22): 3109–19

Stone, L. (1984) *An exchange with Michel Foucault.* New York: New York Review of Books

Summerfield, D. (2001) The invention of post-traumatic stress disorder and the social usefulness of a psychiatric category. *BMJ*, 322(7278): 95

Sweeney, A., Clement, S., Filson, B., and Kennedy, A. (2016) Trauma-informed mental healthcare in the UK: what is it and how can we further its development? *Mental Health Review Journal*, 21(3): 174–92

Szasz, T. (1963) *Law, liberty and psychiatry.* New York: Macmillan

Szasz, T. (1971) *The manufacture of madness.* London: Routledge and Kegan Paul

Taggart, H., Lee, S. and McDonald, L. (2014): *Perceptions of wellbeing and mental health in English secondary schools: a cross sectional study.* CentreForum Commission

Taylor-Gooby, P. (2012) Overview: resisting welfare state restructuring in the UK. *Journal of Poverty and Social Justice*, 20(2): 119–32

Tobis, D. (2013) *From pariahs to partners: how parents and their allies changed New York City's child welfare system.* Oxford: Oxford University Press

Toolis, K. (2009) The great trauma gold rush: How 'post-traumatic stress disorder' has become the compensation culture's new money-spinner, *Daily Mail*, 28 July, www.dailymail.co.uk/news/article-1202347/The-great-trauma-gold-rush-How-post-traumatic-stress-disorder-compensation-cultures-new-money-spinner.html

Tudor Hart, J. (1971) The inverse care law. *The Lancet*, 297(7696): 405–12

Turner, T. and Colombo, A. (2008) Risk, in R. Tummey and T. Turner (eds), *Critical issues in mental health*. Basingstoke: Macmillan, pp 161–175

Tyler, I. (2014) *Revolting subjects: social abjection and resistance in neoliberal Britain*. London: Zed Books

Varese, F., Smeets, F., Drukker, M., Lieverse, R., Lataster, T., Viechtbauer, W., Read, J., van Os, J. and Bentall, R.P. (2012) Childhood adversities increase the risk of psychosis: a meta-analysis of patient-control, prospective-and cross-sectional cohort studies. *Schizophrenia Bulletin*, 38(4): 661–71

Wacquant, L. (1998) Pierre Bourdieu, in R. Stones (ed), *Key sociological thinkers*. Palgrave, London, pp 215–29

Wacquant, L. (2008) *Urban outcasts: a comparative sociology of advanced marginality*. Cambridge: Polity Press

Wacquant, L. (2009a) *Punishing the poor: the neoliberal government of social insecurity*. Durham, NC: Duke University Press

Wacquant, L. (2009b) *Prisons of poverty*. Minneapolis: University of Minnesota Press

Wacquant, L. and Wilson, W.J. (1989) The cost of racial and class exclusion in the inner city. *ANNALS of the American Academy of Political and Social Science*, 501(1): 8–25

Wagner, E.H., Austin, B.T. and Von Korff, M. (1996) Organizing care for patients with chronic illness. *The Milbank Quarterly*, 74(4): 511–44

Warden, J. (1998) England abandons care in the community for the mentally ill. *BMJ*, 317: 1611

Warner, J. (2015) *The emotional politics of social work and child protection*. Bristol: Policy Press

Warner, J. and Gabe, J. (2006). Risk, mental disorder and social work practice: A gendered landscape. *British Journal of Social Work*, 38(1): 117–134

Watson, D. (2016) Becoming an approved mental health professional: an analysis of the factors that influence individuals to become approved mental health professionals. *Journal of Mental Health*, 25(4): 310–14

Webb, S.A. (2006) *Social work in a risk society: social and political perspectives*. Basingstoke: Palgrave Macmillan

Webb, S.A., 2008. Modelling service user participation in social care. *Journal of Social Work*, 8(3): 269–90

Webber, M., Reidy, H., Ansari, D., Stevens, M. and Morris, D. (2014) Enhancing social networks: a qualitative study of health and social care practice in UK mental health services. *Health & Social Care in the Community*, 23(2): 180–9.

Weissman, G. (1982) Foucault and the bag lady. *Hospital Practice*, 17(8): 26–39

Welshman, J. (2013) *Underclass: a history of the excluded since 1880.* London: Bloomsbury

Wilkinson, R. and Pickett, K. (2009) *The spirit level: why equality is better for everyone.* London: Penguin

Wing, J. (1962) Institutionalism in mental hospitals. *British Journal of Social and Clinical Psychology*, 1(1): 38–51

WHO (2012) Social determinants of health. www.who.int/social_determinants/sdh_definition/en/

Wolff, N. (2005) Community reintegration of prisoners with mental illness: a social investment perspective. *International Journal of Law and Psychiatry*, 28(1): 43–58

Wright, E.O. (2015) *Understanding class.* London: Verso Books.

Wurtzel, E. (1994) *Prozac nation: young and depressed in America.* London: Penguin

Zubin, J., Steinhauer, S.R. and Condray, R. (1992) Vulnerability to relapse in schizophrenia. *British Journal of Psychiatry,* 161(Suppl 18): 13–18

Index

A

activism, mental health 80–3
advance choice documents (ACDs) 151
African Americans 59, 60, 70–1
aftercare, MHA and right to 48, 127, 133, 145
Allen, R. 111, 117, 118
AMCPs (approved mental capacity professionals) 106
AMHPs
   see approved mental health professionals (AMHPs)
anti-depressant prescriptions 8, 68
anti-psychiatry movement 30–1, 80–3
Appleby, L. 132, 152
approved mental capacity professionals (AMCPs) 106
approved mental health professionals (AMHPs) 118–23
   gendered work 122
   motivating factors 122–3
   responsibilities 119
   risk 122
   skills and knowledge 119–20
   status 121
   tensions within role 121, 123
Arendt, H. 60
asylum seekers 22, 60, 144
asylums 4–5
   Basaglia and reform of 37–8
      critical perspectives 38–9
   in crisis 28–9
   critical psychiatry and challenge to 30–5
   declining admissions 28
   denying patients their rights 39, 62
   failings of 27, 28–9, 34–5
   Foucault on 6–7, 33–4
      criticism of 7–8
   Law 180 and abolition of Italian 38
   link between leprosaria and 6, 7
   as a means of social control 3, 6–7, 30
   mental health funding concentrated in 36–7
   scandals 29, 35
   Severalls Hospital study 35

as total institutions 29–30
underinvestment in 33
Whig interpretation of history of 34
audit culture 43, 45, 48, 49
austerity 57
   impact on mental health services 141–2
   'literature of' 74
   pincer effect 122
   poverty, mental health and 57, 64–6, 74–5, 141–2
autism, experiences of people with 155, 156
autonomy
   myth of 61
   principle of choice and 151–2

B

Backwith, D. 22, 74, 75, 144, 147
BAME (black, Asian and minority ethnic) groups
   experiences of mental health services 41, 141, 156
   over-representation in mental health services 41, 128, 149–50, 156
   racist stereotypes of black young men 44
   women and perinatal mental health care 98–9
Barker, P. 17
Barr, B. 68
Basaglia, F. 36, 37–9, 81, 143
   critical perspectives on 38–9
Bauman, Z. 48, 59
Beck, A.T. 19, 20
Beck, U. 48, 56, 69
behavioural models of mental illness 15–16
The bell jar 31
Bengtsson-Tops, A. 92
Bentall, R.P. 12, 13–14
Beresford, P. 87, 107, 141
Bhugra, D. 139
big pharma 8–10
Big Society 61
bio-psychiatry 9, 13

biomedical models 8–9, 13–14
  challenges to 66, 87, 143
bipolar disorder 12, 20
black people
  see African Americans; BAME (black,
    Asian and minority ethnic) groups
Black Skin, White Masks 40
Bloom, S.L. 22, 23
Borschmann, R.D. 128, 131
Bourdieu, P. 66, 83, 112–16
  doxa 53, 112, 114
  field 81, 112–13, 113–14
  habitus 113, 114, 115–16
  social capital 69–71, 73–4
  symbolic violence 81
Brady, I. 132
brain research 12
Brown, G.W. 24
Brown, J.M. 90
Brown, W. 52, 53, 57, 58
bureaucracy 115–16
  street level 116–18
Burns, T. 41

C

Cameron, D. 61, 65
CAMHS (child and adolescent mental
  health services), transition from
  102–3
Campbell, P. 84
capacity 103–6
  decisions about 104–5
Care Act 2014 106–7
care and treatment plans (CTPs) 153
care programme approach (CPA) 43, 45
Care Quality Commission (CQC) 41,
  96, 127, 155, 156
Cavadino, M. 135
Cayton, H. 71
CBT (cognitive behavioural therapy)
  19–20
Centre for Mental Health (CMH) 97
Cheshire West 105, 106
children and young people
  medications prescribed to 10
  see also young people
choice
  and autonomy principle 151–2
  neoliberalism and 54, 55, 58, 61
chronic care model 80
citizenship 58, 59–61, 76, 82
  mental health and 62–3
  social 14, 42, 62, 76
civil rights 31, 74, 82
Closing the Gap 97, 98
Clunis, C. 44
CMHTs (community medical health
  teams) 77, 118, 120, 143–4

co-production 111–12
cognitive behavioural therapy (CBT)
  19–20
Cohen, S. 43, 44
community care
  Basaglia and Italian model for 37–9
  campaigns against failures in 82–3
  case for 27–8
  challenge to asylums and development
    of 31–5
  deinstitutionalisation and drive
    towards 36–7
  failures of 27, 36, 42–3, 82–3, 122,
    137–8
  focus on risk management 28, 43,
    48, 147
  Foucault blamed for failings in 7–8
  inquiries into failures of 43, 46
  media reporting 43–5, 48–9, 131–2
  policy responses to crisis in 45–7, 48
  a rupture with institutional approach
    2, 4, 63
community medical health teams
  (CMHTs) 77, 118, 120, 143–4
Community Organisation for
  Psychiatric Emergencies (COPE) 81
community rehabilitation companies
  (CRCs) 134
community treatment orders (CTOs)
  45, 46–7, 83, 126
  over-representation of black people
    subject to 149–50
  review of 141, 145, 154
  trends in use of 127
conditional discharge supervision 133–5
conjuncture 142–3
consumerism 59, 61, 83, 143
Corston Inquiry 90
Court of Protection 104, 105
CPA (care programme approach) 43, 45
CQC (Care Quality Commission) 41,
  96, 127, 155, 156
crime, experiences of 92–3
criminal archetype 17
Criminal Justice and Courts Services
  Act 2000 134
criminal justice system (CJS)
  mental health care in 135
  MHA review and issues in 156–7
  women in 90, 91
criminally insane, attributes of 16–17
critical psychiatry 11, 30–5
*Critical psychiatry: The politics of mental
  health* 37
Crossley, N. 80, 81, 82, 83
Crossley, S. 65, 66
Crown Prosecution Service (CPS) 92–3
CTOs

see community treatment orders (CTOs)

CTPs (care and treatment plans) 153

D

degeneration 16, 17

deinstitutionalisation of mental care 2, 8, 42, 76, 147
  perspectives on 36–7
  removal of funding 62–3
  see also community care

Delivering race equality 41

dementia 105

depression
  perinatal 97, 98–9
  services for treatment of 19, 20, 21
  vulnerability factors for 24, 142

Deprivation of Liberty Safeguards (DOLs) 105–6, 152

detention under Mental Health Act 124
  AMHP role in 119, 120, 121
  capacity for consent to 151, 153
  deaths in 152
  impact on individuals 22–4
  increase in numbers 144–5, 149
  MHA review recommendations 153–4
  over-representation of black people in 41, 128, 149
  pressure on beds 140
  Section 2 125
  Section 3 125

deviance, management of 2, 3, 5–7, 34

diagnosis
  as a destiny 12, 84
  as a form of symbolic violence 81
  resistance to 12–13, 80
  stigma of 9
  testing reliability of psychiatric 3

dignity, fundamental issues of 139, 150

'dirty work' 120, 121

disease model of mental illness 7, 12–14

Do the right thing: How to judge a good ward 95–6

DOLs (Deprivation of Liberty Safeguards) 105–6, 152

domestic violence 92, 98

Dorrell, S. 140–1

Dostoyevsky, F. 135

doxa 53, 112, 114

Drake, C. 71

Durkheim, E. 69

E

Edge, D. 98

Ehliasson, K. 92

electroconvulsive therapy (ECT) 38, 82, 87

employment 63, 65, 71

epistemes 6

Epstein, M. *14*

Estrich, S. 89

F

Fanon, F. 39, 40, 41–2

Farragher, B. 22, 23

field 81, 112–13
  'mental health' 113–14

Filer, N. 23, 28

Fineman, M. 58, 61, 62

The five year forward view for mental health 20

Foley, M. 89, 90, 91

folk devils, modern 43–4

Foot, J. 36, 37, 39, 51, 81, 86

forensic mental health services 131–5
  social supervision 133–5
  social work in 133

Foucault, M. 1, 5–8, 31, 33–4, 53
  criticism of 7–8

Future in mind 99–101

G

Gabe, J. 122

gender issues in working with 'high risk' service users 122

ghettoes 71

Giroux, H. 58, 59, 62

Gittins, D. 35

Goffman, E. 10, 11, 13, 29–30, 36, 37

Goodman-Brown, T. 24

Gorizia, asylum at 37–8, 143

Gramsci, A. 37, 142–3

Grenfell Tower 60

Guidance on the Introduction of Supervision Registers 45–6

H

habitus 113, 114
  mental health social worker 115–16

Hall, S. 44, 114, 142–3

Hammen, C. 24

havoc, management of 29

Hawthorne, N. 10

Hayek, F. 53, 55

health inequalities approach to mental health 66, 98, 141–2

historical perspectives on mental illness 1–5

homicides committed by mentally ill people 43, 83, 131, 132

House of Commons Health Committee 140–1

Hughes, E. 29, 120

human rights
  asylums as an issue of 39

poverty a violation of 74, 144
Human Rights Act 1998 46, 105, 137
Hurricane Katrina 59, 60

I

Ignatieff, M. 12, 34
Improving Access to Psychological
    Therapies (IAPT) 20–1, 101
independent mental capacity advocates
    (IMCAs) 105
independent mental health advocates
    (IMHAs) 125, 152, 154
Independent Mental Health Taskforce
    20
individualism 53, 54, 58, 61–2, 70
Ingleby, D. 37
inpatient services
    see mental health units
inquiries into failures of community
    care 43, 46
institutional racism 150, 156
issues in mental health services,
    contemporary 88–110
    Care Act 2014 106–7
    improving mental health units 95–6
    life on wards 89, 90–1
    Mental Capacity Act 2005 103–6
    patient safety 93–5
    perinatal mental health 96–9
    safeguarding 107–8
    Safeguarding Adults Boards (SABs)
        109
    sexual violence 89–93
    young people 99–103
Italy
    Basaglia and mental health reform 36,
        37–9, 143
    civic participation in 72
    Law 180 38
    Psichiatra Democratia 81

J

Janner, M. 96

K

Keating, F. 40, 99, 150
Kesey, K. 31, 38
Krugman, P. 57, 64
Krumer-Nevo, M. 74, 75, 77, 144

L

labels 80
Laing, R. 23, 31, 36, 81, 143
Larson, G. 87
Lasting Power of Attorney 104
Law 180 38
Law Commission 106

learning disabilities, people with 35,
    125, 149, 156
least restriction principle 152–4
Lee, N. 80
LeFrançois, B.A. 86
leprosaria 6, 7
Levi, P. 37
The Liberty Protection Safeguards 106
Lipsky, M. 76, 116
Lombroso, C. 16
London School of Economics (LSE)
    97, 141
Loury, G.C. 70, 71
Lunatics Asylums Act 1845 4–5

M

Mad Studies 86–8
madhouses, private 4
Mantle, G. 75, 147
MAPPA (multi agency public
    protection arrangements) 134
market fundamentalism 59, 60
Marmot Review 64, 68, 76, 141
Martin, J.P. 34–5
Marx, K. 69
Maternal Mental Health Alliance
    (MMHA) 96–7
May, T. 41, 137, 145, 149, 156
MCA (Mental Capacity Act) 2005
    103–6
media 19, 43–5, 48–9, 131–2
medicalisation of social or behavioural
    issues 9, 10, 19, 24
Mental Capacity Act (MCA) 2005
    103–6
Mental Capacity and Deprivation of Liberty
    106
Mental Health Act (MHA) 1983 83,
    123–7
    assessment under 124
    campaigns for reform 83
    definition of mental disorder 125
    impact of being detained under 22–4
    independent mental health advocates
        125
    May and case for reform 41, 144–5
    mental health review tribunals 126
    nearest relative 125
    New Labour review of 46
    role of AMHP under 119
    Section 2 125
    Section 3 125
    Section 5(2) 126
    Section 37 132
    Section 41 132
    Section 117 48, 127
    Section 136 128–31
        MS V. UK 130

outcomes 130–1
police cells as a place of safety 129
service user perspectives 129–30
use of 127, 128–9
supervised CTOs 126, 127
trends in use of 127
Mental Health Act (MHA) 1983
Review 149–57
concerns over 157
drivers for 149–50
patients in criminal justice system 157
policing and mental health 156–7
reform principles 150–5
choice and autonomy 151–2
least restriction 152–4
person as an individual 155–6
therapeutic benefit 154–5
Mental Health Crisis Care Concordat
145
'mental health field' 113–14
mental health review tribunals
(MHRTs) 125, 126, 132, 154, 155
mental health units
CQC inspections 155
feeling unsafe in 91
improving 95–6
life on wards 89, 90–1, 139–40
MHA review recommendations
154–5
out of area placements 102, 140, 155
patient safety 93–5
pressure on beds 140
sexual violence 89, 90–1
single sex wards 94
mental state examination (MSE) 14–15
Mental Treatment Act 1930 17
Merquior, J. 6
MHA
see Mental Health Act (MHA) 1983
MHRTs (mental health review
tribunals) 125, 126, 132, 154, 155
migrant groups, mental illness in 41, 98
Mind 82, 92, 140
'minimum eligibility threshold' 107
MMHA (Maternal Mental Health
Alliance) 96–7
models of mental health and illness
11–24
behavioural models 15–16
cognitive models 19–20
disease model 12–14
Improving Access to Psychological
Therapies programmes 20–1
mental state examination 14–15
social models 24
social workers' views on 25
trauma-informed approaches 21–4
war and psychiatry 16–19

modern folk devils 43–4
Modernising Mental Health Services 42–3,
46, 47, 137–9
Moncrieff, J. 8, 9, 10
moral panics 43, 44–5
Morriss, L. 115, 118, 120, 123, 143,
147
mother and baby units 97
MS V. UK 130
multi agency public protection
arrangements (MAPPA) 134
Munby, Sir J. 99
Murray, C. 56, 75
Murray, R. 64, 143

N
National Confidential Inquiry into
Homicide and Suicide 132, 152–3
National Patient Safety Agency (NPSA)
93–4
National Reporting and Learning
System (NRLS) 94–5
National Schizophrenia Fellowship
(NSF) 81, 82
nearest relative (NR) 119, 125, 151
neoliberalism 52–7
choice 54, 55, 58, 61
Giroux on impact of 58
and impact on mental health services
141–2
individualism 53, 54, 58, 61–2
key themes 52–5
as 'market fundamentalism' 59, 60
responses to challenges of 58–62
and the state 55–7
see also austerity
Network Rail 145
NHS and Community Care Act 1990
36
No secrets 107–8
Nozick, R. 54, 55, 56
NPSA (National Patient Safety Agency)
93–4
NRLS (National Reporting and
Learning System) 94–5
NSF (National Schizophrenia
Fellowship) 81, 82

O
One flew over the cuckoo's nest 31
Othering 39, 40, 75
out of area placements 102, 140, 155

P
panopticon 34
Papeschi, R. 39
parenting and mental ill health 11
Parsons, T. 79

"passing" 11
paternalism 47, 82, 117, 123
Paterson, B. 23
patient safety 93–5
penal policy 134–5
perinatal mental health 96–9
person as an individual, principle of
    155–6
Pettitt, B. 91, 93
pharmaceutical industry 8–10
Platt, Sylvia 31
police
    cells 127, 129, 156, 157
    concerns over involvement in mental
        health issues 127, 156–7
    powers and Section 136 of MHA
        128–31
*Policing and mental health: Picking up the
    pieces* 156
Poole, J. 87
Poor Law 1601 2
Poor Law Amendment Act 1834 4
poor relief 3–4
Porter, R. 4, 80
post-natal depression 97
post-traumatic stress disorder (PTSD)
    17–19
postpartum psychosis 97
poverty
    and citizenship 59–60
    mental health, austerity and 57, 64–6,
        74–5, 141–2
    as a moral issue 3–4
    Othering of those living in 75
    a risk factor for mental illness 13
    and social work 74–6, 76–7
    as a structural issue 4, 75
'poverty aware paradigm' 74, 76, 77,
    144
'poverty blindness' 76
'poverty paradox' 74, 76
Powell, E. 36
power, exercise of 33
Pringle, J. 82
prisons
    Foucault on design of asylums and 34
    linking of asylums and 6
    review of mental health patients in
        157
    shifts in penal policy 134–5
    as a social control mechanism 31, 32
    as 'total institutions,' 29
    women in 90
    see also forensic mental health services
private sector 67, 127, 132, 134–5
Probation Service 134
Professional Capabilities Framework
    147–8

progress, assumptions of 1, 51
Prozac 10
pseudopatient experiment 3
psychiatry
    anti- 30–1, 80–3
    challenging power of institutionalised
        83–4, 143
    critical 11, 30–5
    a form of social control 27, 31, 34,
        82, 86
    introduction of drug treatments in
        9–10
    pseudopatient experiment 3
    race and 39–42
    surviving 79–83
    war and 16–19
psychopolitics 82
PTSD (post-traumatic stress disorder)
    17–19
public guardian 104
'punitive managerialism' 135
Putnam, R. 72–3, 74

R

racism and mental health services
    39–42, 44, 150, 156
railways, suicide prevention on 145–6
rape
    incidence in mental health units 95
    'real' 89–90
Rawlinson, K. 99
Reagan, R. 52
'real rape' 89–90
recall to hospital
    power of 46–7, 126, 133, 145
    review of 154
    statistics 127
Rechtman, R. 18
Recovery in the Bin (RITB) 81, 84–6,
    88
recovery model 83–6, 110
reform, narratives of 137–41
Regeneration 17
Regional Forensic Secure Units (RSUs)
    132
Reid, J. 87
retraumatisation 22
'right to rights' 60
rights of mentally ill 43, 44, 47, 48, 82
risk and risk management
    audit culture and 43, 48
    focus in social work on 28, 117, 118,
        120
    need for challenge to paradigm of
        144, 152–3
    in work of AMHPs 122
At risk, yet dismissed 93
Ritalin 10

RITB (Recovery in the Bin) 81, 84–6, 88
Ritchie Inquiry 44, 46, 47
Road to Serfdom 52
Rosenhan, D. 3, 9, 35
Royal College of Psychiatrists (RCP) 95–6

S

safeguarding 107–8
Safeguarding Adults Boards (SABs) 109
safety, patient 93–5
Said, E. 40
Samaritans 145
'sanctuary harm' 91
SANE 81, 82, 83
scandals 5, 29, 35
The scarlet letter 10
schizophrenia 12, 28, 41, 44, 143
schools, promotion of emotional wellbeing in 101–2
SCPs (statutory care plans) 155
Scull, A. 1, 2–3, 4, 7, 31, 32, 33, 42, 51, 63, 73
Sedgwick, P. 7, 82
self-harm 16, 23
Seltzer, M. 132–3
service users/survivors movement 80–3, 88, 110
  research to challenge biomedical approach 87
  social work's relationship with 88
Severalls Hospital, Essex 35
sexual violence 89–93
  barriers to reporting 92, 93
  in mental health units 89, 90–1
  NRLS study of reports of 94–5
  'real rape' 89–90
shell shock 17
The Shock of the Fall 23, 28
sick role 79–83
Simmel, G. 72
Simpson, A. 45
Singh, S.P. 41
Skelcher, C. 56
Skinner, B.F. 15, 16
Slasberg, C. 107
social anxiety disorders 9
social capital 68–74
  Bourdieu 69–71
  a comparative approach 73–4
  Putnam 72–3
social citizenship 14, 42, 62, 76
social control
  AMHP role of 123
  asylums a a means of 3, 6–7, 30
  prisons as a mechanism of 31, 32

psychiatry a form of 27, 31, 34, 82, 86
social exclusion of people with mental health problems 39, 63
social factors impacting mental health 13–14, 24, 98, 122, 147
social models of mental illness 24
social movements challenging power of psychiatry 80–3
social state
  neoliberalism and 55–6, 58, 59, 60
  rebuilding 58–62
  vulnerability 61–2
social work, contemporary mental health ix–x, 111–35
  attitudes to models of mental health and illness 25
  Bourdieusian analysis 112–16
  in context 111–12
  difficulties in sustaining positive working relationships 118
  focus on risk and risk management 28, 117, 118, 120
  in forensic settings 133
  importance of co-production 111–12
  key areas for practice 117
  Mad Studies' critique of 87
  MHA Section 136 128–31
  MHA, trends in use of 123–7
  new approaches to suicide prevention 145–7
  outside statutory settings 117–18
  poverty, mental health and 74–6, 76–7
  relationship with user/survivor movement 88
  role of AMHPs 118–23
  street level bureaucracy 116–18
  therapeutic pessimism 23, 28
  towards a mental health social worker *habitus* 115–16
  ways forward 142–5
social work education 74, 75, 76, 87, 144
society, 'triadic' model of 59, 60–1
Somers, M. 58, 59, 60, 74, 76, 82
Sontag, S. 9
Spandler, H. 23
Spitzer, R.L. 9
Star Wards 96
state
  models of 56
  neoliberalism and the 55–7
  see also social state; welfare state
State of Mind programme 146–7
statutory care plans (SCPs) 155
Stenhouse, R.C. 91
stigma 9, 10–11, 29
  well/ill binary increasing 13

suicide prevention
  on railways 145–6
  State of Mind programme 146–7
Summerfield, D. 18–19
supervision registers 43, 45
survivors
  terminology 81–2, 83
  see also service users/survivors
    movement
Survivors Speak Out 81
Sweeney, A. 21, 22, 23, 24
symbolic violence 31, 74, 81, 88
Szasz, T. 25, 31

T

tabloid press 19, 43–5, 48–9, 131–2
taxation 56
terminology, mental health x, 1–2
Thatcher, Margaret 52, 56, 62
therapeutic benefit principle 154–5
therapeutic pessimism 23, 28
TIA
  see trauma-informed approaches (TIA)
'token economy' 16
'total institutions' 29
traffic light systems 118
transitions from CAMHS to adult
  services 102–3
trauma industry 19
trauma-informed approaches (TIA)
  21–2
  on being detained 22–4
  retraumatisation 22
'triadic' model of society 59, 60–1
tribunals, mental health review 125,
  126, 132, 154, 155

U

underclass 56, 60, 75
United Nations 142

V

victimisation of people with mental
  health problems 92, 94, 95
Vietnam War 18
voluntary admissions under MHA 151,
  153
vulnerability 61–2
  factors for mental health problems 13,
    24, 25
  of inpatients 93–4
'vulnerable adults' 108

W

Wacquant, L. 52, 53, 59, 71, 73–4, 112,
  113, 114
Wagner, E.H. 80
Wallace, M. 44, 82

war and psychiatry 16–19
  post-traumatic stress disorder 17–19
  shell shock 17
Warner, J. 48, 122
Warner, S. 23
WCAs (work capability assessments) 63,
  67–8, 75
Weight of the world 112
welfare state
  austerity and reductions to 57, 58,
    64–6, 67
  impact of reforms 66–8, 142
  neoliberal attitudes to 53, 54, 56
Wessely Review
  see Mental Health Act (MHA) 1983
    Review
Wessely, Sir S. 137, 139, 149
Wilson, P.T. 9
Wilson, W.J. 71
work capability assessments (WCAs) 63,
  67–8, 75
World War I, trauma of 16, 17
'wound culture' 132–3
Wurtzel, E. 10

Y

York Retreat 4, 5, 7
young people 99–103
  in crisis 99, 102
  Future in mind report 99–101
  investment programme 101
  MHA review recommendations 156
  transitions from CAMHS to adult
    services 102–3
  whole school approach 101–2

Z

Zito Trust 44, 83